THE LITERATURE OF CONTROVERSY

Polemical Strategy from Milton to Junius

Edited by
THOMAS N. CORNS
University College of North Wales,
Bangor

FRANK CASS

First published 1987 in Great Britain by
FRANK CASS AND COMPANY LIMITED
Gainsborough House, Gainsborough Road,
London, E11 1RS, England

and in the United States of America by
FRANK CASS AND COMPANY LIMITED
c/o Biblio Distribution Centre
81 Adams Drive, P.O. Box 327, Totowa, N.J. 07511

British Library Cataloguing in Publication Data

Corns, Thomas N.
The Literature of controversy : polemical
strategy from Milton to Junius.
1. English literature — Early modern,
1500–1700 — History and criticism
2. English literature — 18th century —
History and criticism
I. Title
820.9   PR431
ISBN 0-7146-3292-9

Library of Congress Cataloging-in-Publication Data

The Literature of controversy.
    "This group of studies first appeared in a special
issue on 'The literature of controversy' of Prose
studies, vol. 9, no. 2, published by Frank Cass & Co.,
Ltd." — T.p. verso.
    Includes bibliographies.
    1. English prose literature — 17th century — History
and criticism. 2. Polemics. 3. English prose literature
— 18th century — History and criticism. I. Corns,
Thomas N.
PR756.P64L5   1987   828'.408'09   86-17523
ISBN 0-7146-3292-9

This group of studies first appeared in a Special Issue on "The
Literature of Controversy" of *Prose Studies*, Vol. 9, No. 2,
published by Frank Cass & Co. Ltd.

Typeset by Williams Graphics, Abergele, North Wales, U.K.
Printed in Great Britain by
Adlard & Son Ltd, Dorking, Surrey

Contents

Notes on Contributors

Charles Cantalupo   is an assistant professor of English at the Pennsylvania State University. He has published articles on Hobbes in *Language and Style, Mid-Hudson Language Studies*, and *Seventeenth Century News*, and has published on Kipling and Synge in the *Dictionary of Literary Biography*. He has recently completed a book-length study of *Leviathan*. In 1983 he published *The Art of Hope*, a book of poems, and has just finished another.

Jennifer Chibnall   was formerly a lecturer in English at the University of South Africa. She has contributed to *The Court Masque* (1984), edited by David Lindley, and is engaged on a major study of Marvell's life and work.

Thomas N. Corns   is a lecturer in the Department of English, University College of North Wales, Bangor. He is reviews editor of *Prose Studies* and honorary secretary of the Association for Literary and Linguistic Computing. He has written several articles, mainly on Milton, and his *Development of Milton's Prose Style* was published in 1982. His *Computers and Literature: A Practical Guide* (written in collaboration with B. H. Rudall) is shortly forthcoming.

J. A. Downie,   a principal lecturer in English at Goldsmiths' College, London, is author of *Robert Harley and the Press* (1979), *Jonathan Swift: Political Writer* (1984), and numerous articles and notes, mainly in eighteenth-century studies. He is co-editor of *The Scriblerian*.

N. H. Keeble   is a lecturer in English at the University of Stirling. He has edited Baxter's *Autobiography* for Everyman's Library (1974; corrected rpt. 1985) and Bunyan's *Pilgrim's Progress* for the World's Classics (1984), and has published *Richard Baxter: Puritan Man of Letters* (1982). His *Literary Culture of Nonconformity in later seventeenth-century England* is forthcoming.

David W. Lindsay   is a senior lecturer in the Department of English, University College of North Wales, Bangor. His publications include articles on Blake and anthologies of eighteenth-century poetry and drama.

Margarette Smith   was formerly a lecturer in English at the University College of North Wales, Bangor, and now works as a consultant to the Further Education Unit. She has published a number of articles and notes, mainly on eighteenth-century writers.

Nigel Smith   is a tutorial fellow of Keble College, Oxford. He has published an edition of Ranter tracts, and his study of radical religious literature, 1640–1660, is forthcoming.

Michael Wilding   is a reader in English at the University of Sydney. His critical works include *Milton's "Paradise Lost"* (1969), *Political Fictions* (1980), and the shortly forthcoming *Dragon's Teeth: Literature in the English Revolution*. His fiction includes *Living Together* (1974), *Pacific Highway* (1982), *The Paraguayan Experiment* (1985), and *The Man of Slow Feeling: Selected Short Stories* (1985).

Introduction

It is not my purpose to offer a manifesto for the essays which make up this collection: they are the work of individuals, not a group, and it would be presumptuous to present too precise a preface to the plurality of practices which they constitute. Yet a number of characteristics are to be found in several of the essays, and to these I draw attention.

Appreciation of polemical strategy involves much more than simply contextualising texts. The emphasis is not on illuminating obscurities through the explanation of historical or biographical allusion. Rather, it is the exploration of the complex ways in which the text engages other texts, addresses the reader, and participates in the political struggles which it is intended to shape and influence. *Intended* — at once, perhaps unfortunately, the familiar battlelines of a long-disputed field of critical conflict suggest themselves, and the reader locates the contributors among the ranks of friends or foes. Probably most of the essays in the collection do attempt to define the polemical objectives of the text concerned in terms of political intention, and with "intention" comes the author, the active agent who actually "intends."

No one, however, argues that the issues are simple. Jennifer Chibnall, for example, spends some of her essay responding to Antony Easthope's objection to the "unnecessary and impossible search for the 'real man' behind the text,"[1] but, as she situates *The Rehearsal Transpros'd* in the "complex of circumstances" for which Marvell designed it, she explains that such situations are not, ultimately, recoverable: rather, to read the text, "we must imaginatively reconstruct the possibilities and probabilities."

J. A. Downie, in a cognate but different argument, concerns himself with the problems posed when the author of a text — in this case, Defoe's *Shortest Way with Dissenters* — offers alternative explanations of the purpose of his work, and questions are raised about the status of such glosses and the ways appropriate for their evaluation.

Less explicitly, examination of intention and situation almost pervasively informs the essays, as contributors attempt reconstruction — albeit, perhaps, tentatively, partially, imaginatively — of the polemical framework, the crisis, the ideological configuration, and the historical author's insertion within them. Biography and the critique of polemical strategy are interwoven.

For biographers and historians texts offer a kind of evidence which demands considerable tact in interpretation: as it has been argued elsewhere,

"It is vital to establish the nature of the relationship between polemic and reality if literary sources are to be used as historical documents."[2] The sorts of strategy for the presentation of the self which are persistently noted in the following essays, the strategies, too, for the suppression and distortion of views and beliefs which can reasonably be ascribed to authors, all have implications for biographers and historians who would draw on such texts. That same historical scholarship upon which much of this work is premissed in part requires redefinition, refinement, and reinterpretation in the light of the sorts of insights disclosed by the critique of polemical strategy.

The anonymity or pseudonymity of several of the works selected here obviously complicates discussion of authorial intention and offers interesting opportunities for exploring the relationship between the person realised in the text and the historical author, insofar as that figure is recoverable. Questions arise about the polemical usefulness of the voice produced in the text, an aspect considered most fully here in Margarette Smith's assessment of Swift's "Drapier" persona. But even when the text is signed, even when it is explicitly autobiographical, the "author" produced within it relates in no straightforward way to the "real man," to adopt the term Easthope sets up. Of course, every work is, in Valéry's fine phrase, "the work of many things besides an author."[3] Many factors, the necessity of satisfying genre expectations not least among them, mediate. Yet the polemical dimension can rewardingly explain some of the transformations which occur as life becomes autobiography. Thus, N. H. Keeble's essay on the *Reliquiae Baxterianae* appraises Richard Baxter's "moderate persona, the generalising of personal experience, the marshalling of evidence, all deployed in the service of an interpretation of events."

The notion of intertextuality also has a place. Barthes writes:

> Any text is a new tissue of past citations. Bits of codes, formulae, rhythmic models, fragments of social languages, etc. pass into the text and are redistributed within it, for there is always language before and around the text. Intertextuality, the condition of any text whatsoever, cannot, of course, be reduced to a problem of sources and influences. ...[4]

This classic formulation suggests a blizzard of contingency, of random elements producing the meaning of each text. But, for the most part, these essays regard the relationship of text to other texts and, indeed, to "bits of code" and "fragments of social language" as somewhat more purposeful. Several of the works considered are explicitly refutations of other texts. Milton in *Areopagitica*, describing, perhaps, the controversialist's ideal, speaks of an active virtue "that sallies out and sees her adversary":[5] there is much sallying out in controversial prose. Previous texts are not so much alluded to as hunted and destroyed, not so much played off as tormented to extinction. Thus, the First Book of *The Rehearsal Transpros'd* nominates its primary target on the titlepage. Thus, too, Junius falls upon the minor apologists for the Grafton administration, producing, from his contemptuous dismissals of them, an image of assurance and of both ethical and cultural superiority which is central to the persona which is being constructed.

But not only other texts are attacked and destroyed: in some works, rumour, reports of behaviour and personality, the common stuff of political innuendo, are absorbed into the polemic. Again, the text may be designed to negotiate a passage away from received positions and from hostile stereotyping which the author seeks to escape. I have argued that Milton's writing in the 1640s was often concerned with distancing him from the reactionaries' stereotype of the radical as propertiless, dissolute, and blasphemous.[6] In an analogous way, Richard Baxter, on Dr Keeble's account, "excludes extremists from his estimate of the godly and distances himself from those radicals with whom royalists and episcopalians identified all nonconformists." The climate of anti-puritan sentiment and the familiar tendency of episcopalian propaganda constitute an intertext with which the *Reliquiae Baxterianae* must be related if its strategy is to be properly appreciated. Again, Michael Wilding demonstrates how Milton's imagery in *Areopagitica* gains in polemical power by its oblique invocations of current debates about monopolies and the recent gruesome spate of judicial mutilations.

Thus, author and intertext: the third category I shall consider is the reader. Charles Cantalupo's title, "How to be a Literary Reader of Hobbes's Most Famous Chapter," indicates sharply enough the aspect on which he has focussed. But some essays raise questions not about "*the* reader" but about reade*rs*. Thus, Margarette Smith considers how Swift's choice of the Drapier persona "has obvious advantages" in addresses to "petty traders and the common people," but she also appraises the difficulties it poses when he speaks more technically or authoritatively to rather different audiences. Much of Dr Downie's essay on *The Shortest Way with Dissenters* is concerned with the identification of Defoe's target readership, which he sees as an essential element in producing valid conclusions about Defoe's polemical technique, and the answers he develops postulate a diverse audience, some of whom Defoe intends to recognise his irony, others he intends to fool.

Finally, a note on the scope of this collection. It is possible to conceive a project for writing a continuous and exhaustive narrative of the changing, developing elements over the period from Milton to Junius, though such an undertaking, I suspect, would require such an investment of time that the critical moment which gave it birth would have long passed by its completion. This collection does not purport to present such a narrative. Certainly, something like a tradition of radical strategy emerges from some of the essays, a core of manoeuvres shared, in different forms, by Overton, Milton, Marvell, Baxter, and, perhaps, Defoe. Nigel Smith has much to say about the influence on Overton of the Martin Marprelate tracts, and it is a presence noted elsewhere by other contributors. As more research is directed at polemical writing, other points of continuity will emerge, no doubt. But readers should not expect a formal dovetailing of the individual essays, which constitute, rather, discrete readings of major texts within the shared problematic of the critique of ideology.

I decided to invite essays within the period extending from the early 1640s through to roughly 1770 because that seemed, arguably, a period in which the work of the political press could be distinguished from that of earlier and later eras. There is, of course, a great deal of polemic before the 1640s. Peter Milward's admirable bibliographies catalogue over 600 items of religious controversy alone from the Elizabethan period and over 750 from the Jacobean.[7] Many of the issues and some of the strategies which inform the outpouring of controversy in the 1640s have their origins in these debates. Yet, apart from the Marprelate controversy, there seems little to interest the critic. Much of the debate is technical discussion of points of doctrine and discipline. Moreover, before the early 1640s, the apparatus of state control, managed for the most part through Star Chamber and the licensing mechanism, works very efficiently at largely suppressing the open expression of dissent. Control of the press remains an ambition of each group that achieves power, and we must not underestimate the difficulties and constraints under which later oppositional writers operated. Overton was gaoled, Milton's printer did not dare to put his name to *Areopagitica*, Baxter and Marvell had considerable problems, the publisher of Junius' letters was prosecuted, and Defoe was pilloried. Yet the nature of the press – and of English political life – had changed. The genie of dissent was out of the bottle, and the available means of repression could not make it return.

The *terminus ad quem* is even more tentatively fixed. Yet the late eighteenth century witnesses changes in the nature of English politics which mark it off from what has gone before. The French Revolution together with what E. P. Thompson has felicitously termed the making of the English working class alter the political agenda, as the pressure for electoral reform and the later progressive extension of the franchise redefine the boundaries of the political nation. All of this transforms the role of politically motivated writing as new issues and a new audience produce a new, perhaps more demotic idiom. The boundaries of my "period" are not to be perceived too rigidly: no doubt there are many continuities of polemical strategy which link the twentieth century to the seventeenth. Yet the sorts of rhetorical power and literary achievement realized in Milton and in Junius would seem somewhat incongruous in the political writing of our own age.

THOMAS N. CORNS

NOTES

1. See note 5 to Jennifer Chibnall's essay, below.
2. T. N. Corns, W. A. Speck, and J. A. Downie, "Archetypal Mystification: Polemic and Reality in English Political Literature, 1640–1750," *Eighteenth Century Life*, 7 (1982), 24.
3. Quoted by Terry Eagleton, *Criticism and Ideology* (1976; London: Verso, 1978), p. 44.
4. Roland Barthes, "Theory of the Text," in Robert Young, ed., *Untying the Text: A Post-Structuralist Reader* (London: Routledge and Kegan Paul, 1981), p. 39.

5. John Milton, *Areopagitica*, in *Complete Prose Works of John Milton*, II, edited by Ernest Sirluck (New Haven: Yale U. P., 1959), 515.
6. Thomas N. Corns, "Milton's Quest for Respectability," *Modern Language Review*, 77 (1982), 769–79.
7. Peter Milward, *Religious Controversies of the Elizabethan Age: A Survey of Printed Sources* (London: Scolar, 1978), and *Religious Controversies of the Jacobean Age: A Survey of Printed Sources* (London: Scolar, 1978).

Milton's Areopagitica:
Liberty for the Sects

The immediate occasion of Milton's *Areopagitica* (November, 1644) was *An Order of the Lords and Commons Assembled in Parliament* of 14 June 1643. It was an attempt yet again to impose a control over the press that previous orders had failed to achieve, since the effective collapse of censorship that ensued upon the abolition of the Court of Star Chamber on 5 July 1641. The controls parliament attempted to impose were far-reaching.

> It is therefore Ordered by the Lords and Commons in *Parliament*, That no Order or Declaration of both, or either House of *Parliament* shall be printed by any, but by order of one or both the said Houses: Nor other Book, Pamphlet, paper, nor part of any such Book, Pamphlet, or paper, shall from henceforth be printed, bound, stitched or put to sale by any person or persons whatsoever, unlesse the same be first approved of and licensed under the hands of such person or persons as both, or either of the said Houses shall appoint for the licensing of the same, and entred in the Register Book of the Company of *Stationers*, according to Ancient custom, and the Printer therof to put his name thereto. And that no person or persons shall hereafter print, or cause to be reprinted any Book or Books, or part of Book, or Books heretofore allowed of and granted to the said Company of *Stationers* for their relief and maintenance of their poore, without the licence or consent of the Master, Wardens and Assistants of the said Company; Nor any Book or Books lawfully licensed and entred in the Register of the said Company for any particular member thereof, without the license and consent of the Owner or Owners therof. Nor yet import any such Book or Books, or part of Book or Books formerly Printed here, from beyond the Seas, upon paine of forfeiting the same to the Owner, or Owners of the Copies of the said Books, and such further punishment as shall be thought fit.[1]

Two issues were involved in the order, as Milton makes clear: the preservation of copyright and the control of free expression. This devious political strategy of entangling commercial self-interest with political and religious censorship he confronts early on:

> For that part which preserves justly every mans Copy to himselfe, or provides for the poor, I touch not, only wish they be not made

pretenses to abuse and persecute honest and painfull Men, who offend
not in either of these particulars. But that other clause of Licencing
Books, which we thought had dy'd with his brother *quadragesimal*
and *matrimonial* when the Prelats expir'd, I shall now attend... .[2]

This new order is in effect a reassertion of those earlier Star Chamber decrees
that had from 1586 to 1637 attempted a massive repression. The prelates had
not in strict truth yet "expir'd" in 1644: Milton is polemically proleptical
here, as if by asserting their expiration it might be hastened. Episcopacy was
not formally abolished until 9 October 1646. But they had been excluded
from the House of Lords, 13 February 1642, and the abolition of Star
Chamber had removed their authority for licensing publications. Milton
refers to these defunct powers in his reference later to Lambeth House and
the West end of Pauls, the residences of the Archbishop of Canterbury and
the Bishop of London respectively, who had been appointed licensers of all
books by the Star Chamber Decree of 1586,[3] and of "all other Books,
whether of Divinitie, Phisicke, Philosophie, Poetry, or whatsoever" that
were not specifically the concern of authorities from the law, universities,
secretaries of state or the Earl Marshal, by the 1637 *Decree of Starre-
Chamber, Concerning Printing*.[4]

> These are the prety responsories, these are the deare Antiphonies that
> so bewitcht of late our Prelats, and their Chaplaines with the goodly
> Eccho they made; and besotted us to the gay imitation of a lordly
> *Imprimatur*, one from Lambeth house, another from the West end
> of *Pauls*; so apishly Romanizing, that the word of command still was
> set downe in Latine; as if the learned Grammaticall pen that wrote
> it, would cast no ink without Latine: or perhaps, as they thought,
> because no vulgar tongue was worthy to expresse the pure conceit of
> an *Imprimatur*; but rather, as I hope, for that our English, the
> language of men ever famous, and formost in the atchievements of
> liberty, will not easily finde servile letters anow to spell such a
> dictatorie presumption English. (504−5)

The bishops are very much Milton's target. *Areopagitica* in this regard can
be seen as continuing that anti-episcopalism that was the subject of his first
polemical tracts. But insofar as the bishops were clearly on the way out,
if not quite "expir'd," Milton is now tactically conscripting that substantial
body of anti-episcopal feeling in the community into the resistance to
licensing. Licensing, his strategy reminds the reader, is to be identified with
the Laudian repression of the 1630s. It was one of Laud's major weapons
in his persecution of puritanism.

It is part of Milton's strategy to present the licensing and control of
printing as an unEnglish activity imported from the Roman church. It is
with great delight that he focusses on the imported term *imprimatur*. Insofar
as licensing has been enforced in England, this has been done by those quasi-
Roman Catholics, the bishops. "And this was the rare morsell so officiously
snatcht up, and so ilfavourdly imitated by our inquisiturient Bishops,

and the attendant minorites their Chaplains'' (506–7). Thomas Corns cites Milton's ''coining 'inquisiturient''' and ''clever extension of the word 'minorites''' as part of Milton's showing ''how alien the activity of censorial investigation is to the English political tradition.''[5] Drawing on Pietro Sarpi's *Historie of the Councel of Trent* and amplifying it from his own further researches,[6] Milton is able to present a convincing picture of Roman Catholic oppressions of true liberty, at the end of which he addresses parliament:

> That ye like not now these most certain Authors of this licencing order, and that all sinister intention was farre distant from your thoughts, when ye were importun'd the passing it, all men who know the integrity of your actions, and how ye honour Truth, will clear yee readily. (507)

It is unlikely that Milton was under any delusions about how parliament honoured truth; and the introduction of such a concept may have allowed him to feel uninhibited in his own honouring of truth, which is perhaps more political than strictly historical here. For printing had never been without controls in England. ''Printing was introduced into England by Caxton in 1476, and one of the first acts of Henry VII was to take over the control of the Press,'' writes William M. Clyde.[7] Fredrick S. Siebert writes ''From Henry VII's warning against 'forged tydings and tales' in 1486 to Elizabeth's announcement of 1601 submitting the question of patents to the common-law courts, the royal proclamation was the chief implement employed in the control of printing.''[8] The first act for the regulation of printing was passed in 1534, the first licensing restrictions came into force in 1549.[9] The charter establishing the Stationers Company in 1557 opened with an explicit concern to restrict the

> several seditious and heretical books, both in verse and prose, (that) are daily published, stamped and printed by divers scandalous, schismatical, and heretical persons, not only exciting our subjects and liegemen to sedition and disobedience against us, our crown and dignity, but also to the renewal and propagating very great and detestable heresies... .[10]

Elizabeth's *Injunctions given by her Majestie* (1559) declared ''that no manner of person shall print any manner of boke or paper, of what sort, nature, or in what language soever it be, excepte the same be first licenced.'' In 1556 Elizabeth issued a Star Chamber decree on licensing which empowered searchers to enforce the controls, and twenty years later the Star Chamber decree of 1586 was issued, ''the most important act of its kind till the Star Chamber decree of 1637.''[12] When Milton claims of licensing that ''We have it not, that can be heard of, from any ancient State, or politie, or Church, nor by any Statute left us by our Ancestors elder or later'' (505) he is, as Sirluck notes, ''distinguishing between 'statute' and 'decree''' (505n.). And since Star Chamber along with other prerogative courts had been abolished, its decrees were in 1644 irrelevant. But this legalistic quibbling, appropriate enough on a legalistic issue, should not be taken to mean that there had not been an enormous set of precedents for licensing and controlling printing and free expression. After all, it is that very weight of historical precedent that necessitated the writing of *Areopagitica*. We should not let the effortless rhetorical strategies blind us to the all too oppressive historical and contemporary realities.

While eliding the indubitable English tradition of licensing, censorship and repression, Milton nonetheless has the punishments meted out to those who fell foul of that tradition firmly in mind. Milton at this date clearly prefers to maintain the fiction that evil came from evil counsellors rather than the monarch, and he offers no attacks on monarchical preoccupations with licensing and censorship. But the Laudian persecution of the puritans is not something that is allowed to be forgotten. In 1630 Alexander Leighton was arrested for writing an *An Appeal to the Parliament, or Sion's Plea against the Prelacie* which, published in Holland in 1628, had circulated in England. "He was severely whipt before he was put in the pillory; being set in the pillory, he had one of his ears cut off; then one side of his nose slit; then he was branded on the cheek with a red-hot iron, with the letters S.S., signifying a stirrer up of sedition."[13] He was also fined £10,000, degraded from holy orders, and imprisoned for life. He was released by order of the Long Parliament in 1640. The persecution of Prynne for writing *Histriomastix* (1632) was another of the great injustices of those pre-revolutionary years. Fined £5,000, deprived of his university degrees, condemned to lose his ears in the pillory and gaoled for life, Prynne was another living embodiment of prelatical oppression, something which his second conviction four years later for "writing and publishing against the hierarchy" only confirmed.[14] One of the prosecutors at this second trial "complained that Prynne's ears were not as closely cropped as the law had a right to expect"; found guilty, Prynne was "sentenced to have his ears more closely shaved," fined another five thousand pounds and sentenced to perpetual imprisonment.[15] John Bastwick, prosecuted at the same time for his *Letanie*, and Henry Burton, for the publication of his sermons, were similarly fined, condemned to perpetual imprisonment, and had their ears cropped. Burton's ears were pared so close that the temporal artery was cut.[16] When Burton and Prynne were released by order of the Long Parliament in 1640, ten thousand people turned out to escort them from Charing Cross to the city. It was the first of the mass demonstrations marking the early course of the revolution.[17] The mutilation of Leighton, Prynne, Burton and Bastwick provided unforgettable images of political and prelatical oppression. At their every appearance, the image was reinforced. "It was not in the power of malice to desire, or of ingenuity to suggest, a weekly spectacle so hurtful to the royal cause" as that of Burton preaching without his ears.[18] The horror informs the subtext of one of the best known passages of *Areopagitica*, introduced and precisely evoked in the verbal suggestions of "cropping" and "sharpest justice." Licensing, writes Milton,

> will be primely to the discouragement of all learning, and the stop
> of Truth, not only by disexercising and blunting our abilities in what
> we know already, but by hindring and cropping the discovery that
> might bee yet further made both in religious and civill Wisdome.
>
> I deny not, but that it is of greatest concernment in the Church
> and Commonwealth, to have a vigilant eye how Bookes demeane
> themselves, as well as men; and thereafter to confine, imprison, and
> do sharpest justice on them as malefactors: For Books are not
> absolutely dead things, but doe contain a potencie of life in them to
> be as active as that soule was whose progeny they are; nay they do
> preserve as in a violl the purest efficacie and extraction of that living
> intellect that bred them. I know they are as lively, and as vigorously
> productive, as those fabulous Dragons teeth; and being sown up and
> down, may chance to spring up armed men. And yet on the other hand
> unlesse warinesse be us'd, as good almost kill a Man as kill a good
> Book; who kills a Man kills a reasonable creature, Gods Image; but
> hee who destroyes a good Booke, kills reason it selfe, kills the Image
> of God, as it were in the eye. Many a man lives a burden to the Earth;
> but a good Booke is the pretious life-blood of a master spirit,
> imbalm'd and treasur'd up on purpose to a life beyond life. (491–3)

At one level Milton seems to be idealizing books, privileging them even
above human life; but the stress on physicality, on killing, on precious life-
blood refuses any such final conclusion. The dialectical tension between
the value of men and books – "as good almost kill a Man as kill a good
Book" – sustains the issue in disturbing suspension with that so simple
and so irremovable "almost." For the horror evoked at mutilating or
murdering books depends on the horror evoked at the murder and mutilation of men. It is the unacceptability of spilling precious life-blood that
is the base on which the unacceptability of destroying books is established.
We might remember the punishment meted out to John Lilburne in 1638,
accused of involvement in the importation of some 10–12,000 seditious
books. Refusing to take the oath he was fined £500 and whipped through
the streets of London, some five hundred blows from a three-thonged
corded whip, stood in the pillory, and imprisoned till he should conform
himself. Continuing to denounce the bishops from the pillory, he "was
gagged so roughly that the blood spurted from his mouth." But even
gagging failed to subdue him. "He thrust his hands into his pockets and
drew out pamphlets, which he threw among the crowds."[19] It was a telling
contemporary example of Ovid's story of armed men springing up from
the teeth of the slaughtered dragon, the books that could not be suppressed
for all the spilling of precious life-blood.

Contemporary readers of *Areopagitica* could not but have recalled such
mutilations when Milton later introduces the story of Osiris. Sirluck writes
that "the appropriateness of the Egyptian myth was probably suggested
to Milton by Plutarch's 'On Isis and Osiris,' which, reporting the narrative
legend much as Milton summarizes it, repeatedly insists that it must be

understood as an allegory'' (549n.). But the prefatory allusion to Christ's ascension, with its consequent inevitable reminder of the all too physical crucifixion and sword in the side, should prevent us from forgetting the quite unallegorical, very literal torn and mangled body and hewn off members observed and recorded in the punishments meted out to those who paid the penalty for illegal printing, publication and distribution in the decade before the revolution.

> Truth indeed came once into the world with her divine Master, and was a perfect shape most glorious to look on: but when he ascended, and his Apostles after him were laid asleep, then strait arose a wicked race of deceivers, who as that story goes of the *AEgyptian Typhon* with his conspirators, how they dealt with the good *Osiris*, took the virgin Truth, hewd her lovely form into a thousand peeces, and scatter'd them to the four winds. From that time ever since, the sad friends of Truth, such as durst appear, imitating the carefull search that *Isis* made for the mangl'd body of *Osiris*, went up and down gathering up limb by limb still as they could find them. We have not yet found them all, Lord and Commons, nor ever shall doe, till her Masters second comming; he shall bring together every joynt and member, and shall mould them into an immortall feature of lovelines and perfection. Suffer not these licencing prohibitions to stand at every place of opportunity forbidding and disturbing them that continue seeking, that continue to do our obsequies to the torn body of our martyr'd Saint. (549–50).

It was Lilburne while in the pillory who publicly referred to Bastwick, Burton and Prynne as "those three renowned living martyrs of the lord."[20]

The remarkable concreteness and vividness of the passage have been well described by Thomas Corns:

> Note how Milton makes concrete the elements of the story. He emphasizes the physical appearance of Truth–Osiris – the 'lovely form,' 'mangl'd body,' and 'immortal feature' – and the violence of the assault – the body 'hewd ... to a thousand peeces' so that it must be reconstructed 'limb by limb' and 'joynt and member'. 'Truth' is an abstract term for 'truths', things that are in themselves intellectual abstractions. Yet Milton describes its abuse in a savage anecdote of considerable visual vividness.[21]

This powerful specificity establishes the historical particularity of the subtextual reference. But to reinsert the historical horrors is not to deny that the other mythic, mysterious and allegoric meanings are also an important part of Milton's rhetoric. His skill lay in uniting such apparent extremes, in demonstrating an acquaintance with both the most elegant and esoteric literary productions of the past, and the immediate consequences of unacceptable contemporary literary activity. What is remote to us now was all too vivid to Milton's contemporaries. There was no need to cite Leighton, Prynne, Burton, Bastwick or Lilburne by name. Moreover by

1644 the released martyr Prynne had come forward as one of the leaders of the anti-sectarian reaction. In September 1644 he urged Parliament to suppress such dangerous "Anabaptisticall, Antinomian, Hereticall, Atheisticall opinions, as of the soules mortality, divorce at pleasure, &c."[22] To offer specific victims by name would only complicate the general case. The details of punishment are left to the subtext; but along with the recurrent vocabulary and imagery of restraint and gaoling[23] – "enthrall'd" (541), "fetters" (542) "shuts us up" (541), "jayler" (536) – they provide an effective reminder of the tools of repression licensing would be likely to require. To read of the Spanish Inquisition's "Indexes that rake through the entralls of many an old good Author" (503) is to be reminded of horrors that happened not only to books but also to people. The sardonic wit is only possible because the tortures projected onto books had indeed been applied to humankind.

The immediate controversial context of *Areopagitica*, the 1643 Licensing order, widens out to include the infamous 1637 Star Chamber decree, and beyond that to the preceding decrees of which 1637 was but the culmination. But to see *Areopagitica* only in the context of the arguments of the freedom of the press is to limit it. Simply to situate it amidst Milton's other polemical writings is to see its fuller significance. The issue is not the abstract liberal one of freedom of expression, but the functional one of allowing the expression of what has hitherto been suppressed. Milton is arguing for the freedom to print radical political and spiritual ideas; and the purpose of printing such radical ideas is to effect social change. That early comparison of books to "Dragons teeth" that "may chance to spring up armed men" (492) expresses it all. Books are like soldiers. They are part of the battle for change, part of the revolutionary armoury. It has been remarked that Milton makes no specific reference to the Army in his pamphlet:[24] but the "Dragons teeth" image makes it clear that a body of armed men is presupposed. It is there in the "warfaring" emendation.[25] And the recurrent imagery of battle, seige and other such military reference is unmistakable.[26] Books are part of the revolutionary war, the fuel, the armoury, the fighters for change. The liberal reputation of *Areopagitica* as "the first work devoted primarily to freedom of the press"[27] has been at the expense of its historical context. It was a work that appeared in the midst of a revolution. It confronted the attempt to control the press at a time when the press was pouring out increasingly radical materials, when the traditional controls had at last broken down.

Clarendon expresses the conservative horror at the situation that had developed by the mid-1640s.

> THIS temper in the Houses raised another Spirit in the Army; which did neither like the Presbyterian Government that they saw ready to be settled in the Church, nor that the Parliament should so absolutely dispose of them, by whom they had gotten power to do all they had done; and *Cromwell*, who had the sole influence upon the Army, under hand, made them Petition the Houses against any thing that

was done contrary to his opinion. He himself, and his Officers, took upon them to Preach and Pray publickly to their Troops; and admitted few or no Chaplains in the Army, but such as bitterly inveighed against the Presbyterian Government, as more Tyrannical than Episcopacy; and the Common Soldiers, as well as the Officers, did not only Pray, and Preach among themselves, but went up into the Pulpits in all Churches, and Preached to the People; who quickly became inspired with the same Spirit; Women as well as Men taking upon them to Pray and Preach; which made as great a noise and confusion in all opinions concerning Religion, as there was in the Civil Government of the State; scarce any Man being suffer'd to be called in question for delivering any opinion in Religion, by speaking or writing, how Prophane, Heretical, or Blasphemous soever it was; "which", they said, "was to restrain the Spirit."

LIBERTY of Conscience was now the Common Argument and Quarrel, whilst the Presbyterian Party proceeded with equal bitterness against the several Sects as Enemies to all Godliness, as they had done, and still continued to do, against the Prelatical Party.[28]

This was the wider situation in which the licensing controversy was situated. Restraint of printing is only part of an ideological battle involving democratization of access to and expression of ideas. The lower orders and women were now giving voice, and more than giving voice, seeking expression in print. As David Petergorsky writes,

The Printing Ordinance of June 1643 is designed not merely to curb Royalist propaganda, but to suppress the sects through which the discontented are beginning to utter their inchoate but unmistakable protests in an effort to silence the aggressive and irrepressible spokesmen of the poor.[29]

Milton's commitment to this democratization is quite explicit. Of the proposed licensing he writes:

Nor is it to the common people lesse then a reproach; for if we be so jealous over them, as that we dare not trust them with an English pamphlet, what doe we but censure them for a giddy, vitious, and ungrounded people; in such a sick and weak estate of faith and discretion, as to be able to take nothing down but through the pipe of a licencer. That this is care or love of them, we cannot pretend, whenas in those Popish places where the Laity are most hated and dispis'd the same strictnes is us'd over them. Wisdom we cannot call it, because it stops but one breach of licence, nor that neither; whenas those corruptions which it seeks to prevent, break in faster at other dores which cannot be shut.

And in conclusion it reflects to the disrepute of our Ministers also, of whose labours we should hope better, and of the proficiencie which thir flock reaps by them, then that after all this light of the Gospel which is, and is to be, and all this continuall preaching, they should be still frequented with such an unprincipl'd, unedify'd, and laick rabble, as that the whiffe of every new pamphlet should stagger them out of thir catechism, and Christian walking. This may have much reason to discourage the Ministers when such a low conceit is had of all their exhortations, and the benefiting of their hearers, as that they are not thought fit to be turn'd loose to three sheets of paper without a licencer, that all the Sermons, all the Lectures preacht, printed, vented in such numbers, and such volumes, as have now wellnigh made all other books unsalable, should not be armor anough against one single *enchiridion*, without the castle St. *Angelo* of an *Imprimatur*. (536–7)

Reading the passage we might remember Dryden's information to John Aubrey of Milton: "He pronounced the letter R (littera canina) very hard – a certaine signe of a satyricall witt."[30] The satirical wit at the dubious labours of the clergy and their overproduction of volumes of sermons should not distract us from the firm populism of Milton's commitment to the "common people" here. Of course, as Milton well knew, from the standpoint of parliament the common people were a giddy, vicious, and ungrounded people. It was just that giddy, vicious ungroundedness that was the fertile seedbed of revolutionary change. But that commitment to revolutionary change is a subtext not intended to be read by the parliament to whom the pamphlet is addressed. The clergy are brought in as a ready target for the contempt of the political and business classes; their incompetence is introduced as a distraction to be seized upon. If the people are troublesome, then it is the fault of the clergy. Though from the point of view of the law and order authorities, it is immaterial whose fault it is; if the people are giddy, vicious and ungrounded, then to allow the spread of seditious pamphlets would be akin to fuelling the flames of revolution.

Against that frequently alleged élitism of Milton, the evidence of such commitment to the common people needs to be firmly pointed out. And his rhetoric takes on the radical polemics of emergent activism, "the people's birthright":[31] "while Bishops were to be baited down, then all Presses might be open; it was the peoples birthright and priviledge in time of Parlament, it was the breaking forth of light" (541). Eleven months later appeared *Englands Birth-right justified*, usually ascribed to Lilburne. "From such an embryo was to grow the first *Agreement of the People*," writes Don M. Wolfe.[32] Pauline Gregg writes that it "covered all that the sects, the small farmers and tradesmen, the artisans, the poor, the imprisoned, and those with any feeling of injustice in city or country could demand."[33]

It is towards the end of the *Areopagitica* that Milton delivers his unforgettable defence of the sects. Having mounted his various rhetorical and historical arguments against licensing, he has prepared the ground for the argument that he is ultimately making. Earlier he threw in a small, provocative grenade parenthetically: "The Christian faith, for that was once a schism ..." (529). Now he launches the full offensive:

> Behold now this vast City; a City of refuge, the mansion house
> of liberty, encompast and surrounded with his protection; the
> shop of warre hath not there more anvils and hammers waking,
> to fashion out the plates and instruments of armed Justice in defence
> of beleaguer'd Truth, then there be pens and heads there, sitting by
> their studious lamps, musing, searching, revolving new notions and
> idea's wherewith to present, as with their homage and their fealty the
> approaching Reformation: others as fast reading, trying all things,
> assenting to the force of reason and convincement. (553–54)

From this image of harmony in variety, productive, progressive activity
from the multiplicity of individual, differentiated concerns, he moves to
stress the clashes, the confrontations so inevitable and necessary and no
less productive:

> Where there is much desire to learn, there of necessity will be much
> arguing, much writing, many opinions; for opinion in good men is
> but knowledge in the making. Under these fantastic terrors of sect
> and schism, we wrong the earnest and zealous thirst after knowledge
> and understanding which God hath stirr'd up in this City. What some
> lament of, we rather should rejoyce at, should rather praise this pious
> forwardness among men, to reassume the ill deputed care of their
> Religion into their own hands again. (554)

And from this stress on the necessities of argument and opinion he moves
on to the positive values of separation and division with images of cutting,
quarrying, dissection:

> Yet these are the men cry'd out against for schismaticks and sectaries;
> as if, while the Temple of the Lord was building, some cutting,
> some squaring the marble, others hewing the cedars, there should
> be a sort of irrationall men who could not consider there must be
> many schisms and many dissections made in the quarry and in the
> timber, ere the house of God can be built. And when every stone
> is laid artfully together, it cannot be united into a continuity, it
> can but be contiguous in this world; neither can every peece of the
> building be of one form; nay rather the perfection consists in this,
> that out of many moderat varieties and brotherly dissimilitudes
> that are not vastly disproportionall arises the goodly and the gracefull
> symmetry that commends the whole pile and structure. (555)

What had been harsh and ugly terms of abuse and contempt – schismatics,
sectaries – are now resituated in this beautiful account of the building of
the Temple of the Lord. The class implications are unmistakable. A clue
was given in "we rather should rejoyce at" men reassuming the "care of
their Religion into their own hands again" (554); it is not aristocrats or
bishops or business men who take things "into their own hands": there
is a powerful respect here for manual labourers. This is made quite explicit
in the unambiguously mechanical trades that are specified in the building

of the temple; people are shown cutting, squaring, hewing. These are all manual activities; there is "spirituall architecture" (555) but no architect, only "builders" (555). The physical labours of the common people are here properly presented as dignified, noble, beautiful.

The appropriateness of such analogies from physical labour, from working with one's hands, to defend the sects, composed in large part from the working classes, is yet another denial of that asserted Miltonic élitism. That the manual labour of the lower class sects is presented as beautiful makes clear Milton's sympathies. It is not only the radical ideas of the sects that he defends, but the social composition of the sects that he glorifies. His recurrent identification of mental labour with physical labour is one that consistently respects the labour of the manual workers. To write "when a man hath bin labouring the hardest labour in the deep mines of knowledge" (562) is, as its reiteration of "labour" underlines, to respect the hard lot of the miners, the workers. Knowledge, mental labour, is ennobled by this analogy from the life of the workers. In pointed contrast is his recurrent portrayal of the laziness and ineffectiveness of the clergy. He offers a fine satirical evocation of the life of intellectual sloth consequent upon a society closed off by licensing:

> there be delights, there be recreations and jolly pastimes that will fetch the day about from sun to sun, and rock the tedious year as in a delightfull dream. What need they torture their heads with that which others have tak'n so strictly, and so unalterably into their own pourveying. These are the fruits which a dull ease and cessation of our knowledge will bring forth among the people. (545)

And he continues with that telling portrait of the cosy, privileged laziness of the clergy:

> Nor much better will be the consequence ev'n among the Clergy themselvs; it is no new thing never heard of before, for a *parochiall* Minister, who has his reward, and is at his *Hercules* pillars in a warm benefice, to be easily inclinable, if he have nothing else that may rouse up his studies, to finish his circuit in an English concordance and a *topic folio*, the gatherings and savings of a sober graduatship, a *Harmony* and a *Catena*, treading the constant round of certain common doctrinall heads, attended with their uses, motives, marks and means, out of which as out of an alphabet or sol fa by forming and transforming, joyning and dis-joyning variously a little book-craft, and two hours meditation might furnish him unspeakably to the performance of more then a weekly charge of sermoning: not to reck'n up the infinit helps of interlinearies, breviaries, *synopses*, and other loitering gear. (546)

Running throughout the *Areopagitica* is this structural contrast between the dignity of labour, manual and intellectual, and its opposite, the lazy, loitering easy life readily imaged in the beneficed clergy or Roman church. "Doe not make us affect the laziness of a licencing Church," Milton implores God (547). That Puritan commitment to productive labour, allied with a contempt for the clergy, is basic to Milton's thought.

> If any Carpenter, Smith, or Weaver, were such a bungler in his trade, as the greater number of them are in their profession, he would starve for any custome. And should he exercise his manifacture as little as they do their talents, he would forget his art: and should he mistake his tools as they do theirs, he would marre all the worke he took in hand,

Milton writes of the Laudian clergy in *An Apology Against a Pamphlet*.[34]

Milton's hostility to the privileged learned and his support for the unlettered poor expresses itself more generally than in relation to manual labour. Ready to take any opportunity to discredit the clergy he ingeniously suggests,

> It will be hard to instance where any ignorant man hath bin ever seduc't by Papisticall book in English, unlesse it were commended and expounded to him by some of that Clergy: and indeed all such tractats whether false or true are as the Prophesie of *Isaiah* was to the *Eunuch*, not to be *understood without a guide*. But of our Priests and Doctors how many have bin corrupted by studying the comments of Jesuits and *Sorbonists*, and how fast they could transfuse that corruption into the people, our experience is both late and sad. (519)

This contempt for the easily suborned and potentially treacherous clergy is of a piece with the radical sectarians' contempt for the establishment intelligentsia: "I never found cause to think that the tenth part of learning stood or fell with the Clergy" (531). Against university acquired learning he covertly insinuates the subversive alternative of divine inspiration. Discussing the injustices liable to be perpetrated on the work of an author now dead by posthumous licensing and censorship Milton remarks "if there be found in his book one sentence of a ventrous edge, utter'd in the height of zeal, and who knows whether it might not be the dictat of a divine Spirit" (534). "Zeal" and "the dictat of a divine Spirit" are part of the rhetoric of the radical sects; it is just such things that licensing was concerned to suppress, as Milton well knew. The concepts are introduced again later: "Under these fantastic terrors of sect and schism, we wrong the earnest and zealous thirst after knowledge which God hath stirr'd up in this City" (554). To write of a "zealous thirst ... God ... stirr'd up" is to write from the ideology of the radical sects and schisms. As Petergorsky put it,

> Puritanism had insisted that knowledge of God could come only through study and understanding of the Bible. By substituting the written word of the scriptures for the hierarchy as the final authority in religious life, it took the effective direction of religious affairs from the hands of the prelates only to make it the monopoly of a literate class. The reply of the poor − and hence, the illiterate and uneducated − was that not formal learning but an inner spiritual experience and

inspiration were the true source of religious knowledge, that contact with God was not the exclusive privilege of a superior class, but could be attained by any man however humble his station. On the contrary, that inner spiritual experience by which alone men could be saved was far more likely to occur in those whom suffering had rendered meek and humble than in those whose wealth had made them haughty and proud.[35]

One of the ingenious structural strategies of *Paradise Lost* was to present Satan, the rebel against God, in terms of a tyrannical monarch. The powerful implicit argument is that monarchs are the actual rebels, while those concerned to resist tyranny and monarchy, falsely called rebels, are the true godly people concerned with the true restoration ("till one greater man / Restore us," I. 4–5), not that false "restoration" of 1660.[36] That same strategy exists in brief in *Areopagitica*:

> There be who perpetually complain of schisms and sects, and make it such a calamity that any man dissents from their maxims. 'Tis their own pride and ignorance which causes the disturbing, who neither will hear with meekness, nor can convince, yet all must be supprest which is not found in their *Syntagma*. They are the troublers, they are the dividers of unity, who neglect and permit not others to unite those dissever'd peeces which are yet wanting to the body of Truth. (550–1)

As Thomas Kranidas remarks, Milton has "commandeered the adversaries' image for Puritan controversy and used it against them."[37]

It is in this context that the strategic employment of patriotic feeling and nationalistic fervour in *Areopagitica* is most profitably understood. The unargued but ever present case that socialism, communism, radicalism are somehow unEnglish, are somehow against the spirit of the nation, is a powerful instrument of reactionary propaganda. Milton's strategy is simply to assert a huge and resonant patriotism, a powerful emotional nationalism, which he intertwines with his radical polemics. We have already noted the way in which he rejects censorship and licensing as concepts to be identified with the foreign tyranny of Rome and the Spanish Inquisition. He simply appropriates the arguments of patriotism and nationalism and applies them to confront the establishment law and order position. It is the reactionaries who are unEnglish. The very spirit of the English language is against licensing, and has no word for *"imprimatur."* As Corns remarks, "In the context of linguistic borrowing, Milton, ironically so often regarded as the arch-classicist, is avowedly a populist and nationalist."[38] The proud identification of a tolerance of conflicting belief, of a commitment to the value of free expression, as something almost uniquely English, produces one of the most memorable passages of *Areopagitica*:

> And lest som should perswade ye, Lords and Commons, that these arguments of lerned mens discouragement at this your order, are meer flourishes, and not reall, I could recount what I have seen and heard

in other Countries, where this kind of inquisition tyrannizes; when I have sat among their lerned men, for that honor I had, and bin counted happy to be born in such a place of *Philosophic* freedom, as they suppos'd England was, while themselvs did nothing but bemoan the servil condition into which lerning amongst them was brought; that this was it which had dampt the glory of Italian wits; that nothing had bin there writt'n now these many years but flattery and fustian. There it was that I found and visited the famous *Galileo* grown old, a prisner to the Inquisition, for thinking in Astronomy otherwise then the Franciscan and Dominican licencers thought. And though I knew that England then was groaning loudest under the Prelaticall yoak, neverthelesse I took it as a pledge of future happines, that other Nations were so perswaded of her liberty. (537–8)

The note of personal experience comes in powerfully here. The visit to Galileo is a moving reminiscence, as well as a telling example. And this assertion of that splendid reputation for philosophic freedom that England had in the eyes of the world, lays the ground for Milton's defence of the sects. A powerful patriotic fervour is expressed in resonant apocalyptic terms – a millenarianism in itself characteristic of and identified with the radical sects. That vision of London as "the mansion house of liberty" (554) is part of a paragraph that opened:

Lords and Commons of England, consider what Nation it is wherof ye are, and wherof ye are the governours: a Nation not slow and dull, but of a quick, ingenious, and piercing spirit, acute to invent, suttle and sinewy to discours, not beneath the reach of any point the highest that human capacity can soar to. Therefore the studies of learning in her deepest Sciences have bin so ancient, and so eminent among us, that Writers of good antiquity, and ablest judgement have bin perswaded that ev'n the school of *Pythagoras*, and the *Persian* wisdom took beginning from the old Philosophy of this Iland. (551–2)

It is an extraordinary claim that would attribute the classical Greek theories of metempsychosis and the Zoroastrian wisdom of the Persian magi to an English original source. It is one that would put Britain as the fountainhead of that inspired wisdom that seventeenth-century neoplatonism, hermeticism, and alchemy were concerned to regain, and that gives a nationalistic context to those references to Ovidian metamorphoses and alchemical transmutations with which *Areopagitica* is studded. And Milton moves easily on to England's contemporary spiritual leadership: "Why else was this Nation chos'n before any other, that out of her as out of *Sion* should be proclam'd and sounded forth the first tidings and trumpet of Reformation to all *Europ*" (552). That powerful concept of the English as God's chosen people, the concept that so motivated the parliamentary army and that permeates the revolutionary thought and Cromwellian propaganda of the period, is here proclaimed:

> Now once again by all concurrence of signs, and by the generall
> instinct of holy and devout men, as they daily and solemnly expresse
> their thoughts, God is decreeing to begin some new and great period
> in his Church, ev'n to the reforming of Reformation it self: what does
> he then but reveal Himself to his servants, and as his manner is, first
> to his English-men. (553)

That reading the "concurrence of signs" of the last days, in the flood
of learned commentaries on *Daniel* and *Revelation* that poured forth
at last after the breakdown of press controls, fuelled the activist millenarianism of the radical sects.[39] Millenarianism became the mark of radical
activism; nationalism its organizing ideology; the pressing forward of
the uncompleted revolution – "the reforming of Reformation it self" –
its inexorable aim.

This concatenation of a proclaimed nationalism, an apocalyptic
millenarianism, an assertion of visionary furor and a commitment to the
sects is found again in that memorable and justly famous expression of
Milton in his prophetic role:

> Methinks I see in my mind a noble and puissant Nation rousing herself
> like a strong man after sleep, and shaking her invincible locks:
> Methinks I see her as an Eagle muing her mighty youth, and kindling
> her undazl'd eyes at the full midday beam; purging and unscaling her
> long abused sight at the fountain it self of heav'nly radiance; while
> the whole noise of timorous and flocking birds, with those also that
> love the twilight, flutter about, amaz'd at what she means, and in their
> envious gabble would prognosticat a year of sects and schisms.
> (557–8)

This wider political commitment to a support of the radicalism of the
sects makes better sense of explaining Milton's writing *Areopagitica* than
that other more reductively personal view often enough expressed. Hilaire
Belloc wrote,

> the "Areopagitica" has no relation to the angry feelings of those days,
> when men on the rebel side were divided into two hostile forces full of
> mutual recrimination. ... It is one of the divorce tracts in that it was an
> off-shoot from them, provoked by his irritation with the censorship
> which *might have* interfered with his divorce propaganda.[40]

It is a view repeated by Arthur Barker: "The *Areopagitica*, though
expressing convictions long held, was an answer to the Presbyterian
condemnation which, to Milton's evident surprise, greeted the publication
of his first pamphlet on divorce."[41] And Barker went on to assert,

> his defence of the sects arose from common opposition to Presby-
> terianism, not from an identity of fundamental principles. The first
> divorce pamphlet was offered to 'the choicest and learnedest'; the
> *Areopagitica* is less a defence of the sects than of learning and learned
> men.[42]

The Bellocian case is unpersuasive. As Arnold Williams wrote,

> Belloc has certainly overstated the purely personal motive behind
> *Areopagitica*. No one who reads it without previous bias can really
> feel that Milton is concerned principally about the fate of his divorce
> tracts. A narrowly individual cause simply cannot draw forth such
> high-principled and universalized treatment as Milton gives us.[43]

The degree of Milton's kinship with the sects, however, perhaps remains a
matter for further exploration and argument. Christopher Hill's formulation is one that at least allows the thinking of the sects to have a significant presence along with that of Barker's "learning and learned men";
with *Areopagitica*, writes Hill, Milton's "dialogue with the radicals had
begun."[44] And he goes on to note, "There is much similarity between the
arguments of Walwyn's *The Compassionate Samaritane* and *Areopagitica*.
In their turn Lilburne and Overton seem to have been influenced by Milton's
tract."[45]

The 1643 Licensing Order confirmed the Stationers Company in its long
established role as the instrument of licensing and the enforcer of the
regulations. Prelatical reaction was one component of licensing, monopolistic greed the other. Siebert records:

> The crown had traded valuable monopolistic grants in return for the
> assistance of the officers of the Company in suppressing obnoxious
> printing. These grants had been protected by the king through the
> Star Chamber and the High Commission. With the fall of the king
> and the abolition of the two judicial agencies, the privileged position
> of the officers of the Company and of the wealthy printers became
> exceedingly vulnerable. ...
>
> By 1640 the internal affairs of the Stationers Company had been
> concentrated in the hands of a group of wealthy stationers. The master
> and wardens, instead of being elected by the membership at large as
> provided in the charter, were chosen annually by the Court of
> Assistants. This court, or 'Table' as it was called, consisted of a self-
> perpetuating group of monopolists in the printing trade. They
> controlled the funds of the Company; they participated in the
> publication of the various stocks to the exclusion of other printers;
> and by the system of patents and monopolies managed to get control
> of most of the valuable printing properties. The journeymen and
> apprentices after securing their freedom found themselves unable to
> make an honest living. Either they must work for the monopolists
> at a starving wage or they must engage in surreptitious printing of
> forbidden or patented works.[46]

Opposition to the monopolists had been expressed in a tract of 1641 ascribed
to George Wither, *Scintilla, or A Light broken into darke Warehouses. With
Observations upon the Monopolists of Seaven severall Patents, and Two
Charters Practised and performed, By a Mistery of some Printers, Sleeping
Stationers, and combining Book-sellers. Anatomised and layd open in a*

Breviat, in which is only a touch of their forestalling and ingrossing of Books in Pattents, and Raysing them to excessive prises.[47] And the attacks flared up again in 1645 with the result that Parliament's "Committee on Examinations was forced to call in the master and wardens who were ordered to call a meeting ('common hall') of the entire membership of the Company."[48]

Areopagitica appeared amidst these disputes and Milton's opposition to the monopolistic greed of the Stationers Company is clearly expressed:

> Truth and understanding are not such wares as to be monopoliz'd and traded in by tickets and statutes, and standards. We must not think to make a staple commodity of all the knowledge in the Land, to mark and licence it like our broad cloath, and our wooll packs. (535–6)

To consider this as a species of rhetorical imagery divorced from its immediate historical reality is to miss the urgency and relevance of Milton's polemic.[49] There were indeed strong pressures to monopolize truth. "The proposal by the committee of the House of Commons to grant to eleven stationers an exclusive right to print Bibles brought the matter to a head. The excluded stationers and printers immediately petitioned the Commons to withdraw the grant and to issue it in favor of the entire Company."[50] The financial greed of the master printers was a crucial factor in press control. Economic power no less than governmental order was one of the primary factors in effective censorship and repression. By the 1643 Licensing Order the Stationers Company was

> Authorized and required, from time to time, to make diligent search in all places, where they shall think meete, for all unlicensed Printing Presses, and all Presses any way imployed in the printing of scandalous or unlicensed Papers, Pamphlets, Books, or any Copies of Books belonging to the said Company, or any member thereof, without their approbation and consents, and to seize and carry away such printing Presses Letters, together with the Nut, Spindle, and other materialls of every such irregular Printer, which they find so misimployed, unto the Common Hall of the said Company, there to be defaced and made unserviceable according to Ancient Custom; And likewise to make diligent search in all suspected Printing-houses, Ware-houses, Shops and other places for such scandalous and unlicensed Books, papers, Pamphlets and all other Books, not entred, nor signed with the Printers name as aforesaid, being printed, or reprinted by such as have no lawfull interest in them, or any way contrary to this Order, and the same to seize and carry away to the said common hall, there to remain till both or either House of *Parliament* shall dispose thereof, And likewise to apprehend all Authors, Printers, and other persons whatsoever imployed in compiling, printing, stitching, binding, publishing and dispersing of the said scandalous, unlicensed, and unwarrantable papers, books and pamphlets as aforesaid, and all those who shall resist the said Parties in searching after them . . . .[51]

The motivation and incentive for the Stationers Company to undertake these policing activities was the protection of their economic interests. In such a context of the privileging of monopolistic economic power before the free diffusion of truth and knowledge, it should come as no surprise that, in *Areopagitica*, "images based on money, exchange, commerce, even custom house, constitute the most important group of images."[52] In that sustained portrait of the "wealthy man" with his hired divine, it is not illegitimate to suppose that Milton had wealthy printers, amongst other monopolists, in mind. The terms of trade in which the man is portrayed as conceptualizing his religion, that splendid capturing of the way in which the economic mode of thinking Midas-like destroys everything it touches, are terms readily applicable to printing – one of the "mysteries" with its "piddling accounts," "stock," "trade" and "ware-house."

> A wealthy man addicted to his pleasure and to his profits, finds Religion to be a traffick so entangl'd, and of so many piddling accounts, that of all mysteries he cannot skill to keep a stock going upon that trade. What should he doe? fain he would have the name to be religious, fain he would bear up with his neighbours in that. What does he therefore, but resolvs to give over toyling, and to find himself out som factor, to whose care and credit he may commit the whole managing of his religous affairs; som Divine of note and estimation that must be. To him he adheres, resigns the whole ware-house of his religion, with all the locks and keyes into his custody; and indeed makes the very person of that man his religion; esteems his associating with him a sufficient evidence and commendatory of his own piety. So that a man may say his religion is now no more within himself, but is becom a dividuall movable, and goes and comes neer him, according as that good man frequents the house. He entertains him, gives him gifts, feasts him, lodges him; his religion comes home at night, praies, is liberally supt, and sumptuously laid to sleep, rises, is saluted, and after the malmsey, or some well spic't bruage, and better breakfasted then he whose morning appetite would have gladly fed on green figs between *Bethany* and *Jerusalem*, his Religion walks abroad at eight, and leavs his kind entertainer in the shop trading all day without his religion. (544–5)

As a portrayal of that alienation consequent upon capitalism, the passage has not been bettered in three and a half centuries. The wealthy man is divided within himself, alienated from his own religious impulse which is objectified, reified and becomes this autonomous quality, "his Religion," "a dividuall movable" which, revivified by a cash payment, "walks abroad" in the person of a hireling "Divine." Amongst the most enduringly amusing of Milton's satirical passages, it succinctly targets both the wealthy businessman and the hireling clergy. And who were more involved in marketing religion than the printers, booksellers and the clergy?

In admiring the wit, we should not forget the moral indictment of the hypocrisy portrayed. The businessman is left "in the shop trading all day without his religion" the better to practise fraud or some other unrestrained immoral money-making activity. Fraud was certainly in Milton's mind in the context of the book trade. The final paragraph of *Areopagitica* carries his explicit denunciation of that business:

> Whereby ye may guesse what kinde of State prudence, what love of the people, what care of Religion, or good manners there was at the contriving, although with singular hypocrisie it pretended to bind books to their good behaviour. And how it got the upper hand of your precedent Order so well constituted before, if we may beleeve those men whose profession gives them cause to enquire most, it may be doubted there was in it the fraud of some old *patentees* and *monopolizers* in the trade of book-selling; who under pretence of the poor in their Company not to be defrauded, and the just retaining of each man his severall copy, which God forbid should be gainsaid, brought divers glosing colours to the House, which were indeed but colours, and serving to no end except it be to exercise a superiority over their neighbours, men who doe not therefore labour in an honest profession to which learning is indetted, that they should be made other mens vassalls. Another end is thought was aym'd at by some of them in procuring by petition this Order, that having power in their hands, malignant books might the easier scape abroad, as the event shews. But of these *Sophisms* and *Elenchs* of marchandize I skill not: This I know, that errors in a good government and in a bad are equally almost incident; for what Magistrate may not be mis-inform'd, and much the sooner, if liberty of Printing be reduc't into the power of a few.... (570)

The indictment of the Stationers Company could not be more absolute or more specific. Milton alleges a conspiracy by "some old patentees and monopolizers," beneficiaries from the old court granted restrictive rights, to protect their own financial advantage, and to control the press under the guise of licensing so that Roman Catholic propaganda can be slipped through. That the pamphlet should end on this note demonstrates how seriously Milton took the threat to a free press from the monopolists within the Stationers Company. For all his attacks on prelates and clergy and the relics of the old ecclesiastical repression, the bishops have effectively "expir'd." The immediate enemies to a free press are those who have powerful financial interests in the existing system of the press, who have most to lose from the breaking down of their old monopolies.

Milton's attitude to commerce is more complex, perhaps more strategically ambiguous, than those commentators who have noted the recurrent imagery have allowed. Alan Price wrote, "This satiric juxtaposition of commerce and religion clearly implies a loathing of commercialized religion and a disdain of traders,"[53] and J.-F. Camé remarked,

> Milton uses his contempt of commerce several times to show what real religion should be. The connection with the main theme is fairly

clear. If the two main themes of *Areopagitica* are the freedom of the press and religious liberty, we see that money and commerce restrict both sorts of liberty.[54]

The contempt is certainly there in the portrayal of "a wealthy man." But it was the monopolist Milton particularly opposed. He was happy to use the arguments of free trade against monopolists; and that dispute was of course central to the economic issues of the book trade, as indeed of all trades in the course of this bourgeois revolution. The journeyman printers, the small booksellers and importers, wanted a share of the lucrative, protected, closed market. Milton is happy enough to support the small businessman against the monopolist if this will break the stranglehold on truth.

> There is yet behind of what I purpos'd to lay open, the incredible losse and detriment that this plot of licencing puts us to. More then if som enemy at sea should stop up all our hav'ns and ports, and creeks, it hinders and retards the importation of our richest Marchandize, Truth. (548)

It is a metaphor that in its literal sense is intimately related to the issue of a free press. Lilburne had been arrested because of involvement with the illegal importation of banned books from Holland. Truth had been literally imported into "our hav'ns and ports, and creeks," especially when it could not be published in England.[55] But the prohibitions had been grotesquely not the work of an enemy at sea imposing a blockade, but of the enemy within, the Laudian church and the Stationers Company acting as its policing agent. Characteristically of the imagery of *Areopagitica*, the metaphor evokes, like the mutilation of Osiris, like the spilling of precious life-blood, the all too literal strategies employed in the immediate past to prevent the free circulation of books: strategies now all too likely to be reimposed. To write of "the importation of our richest Marchandize, Truth" is not in any way to degrade Truth to merchandise, but to recognize the economic realities, then as now. Books are a money-making business; but to impose controls on the book trade is to keep that potential for wealth generation in the hands of a monopolistic few. The presentation of truth as "merchandize" demonstrates clearly that Milton's hostility was not to commerce, but to the monopolistic merchant oligarchies. As Andrew Milner writes,

> This opposition between the policies of the absolutist state and the needs of the developing capitalist mode of production informs the whole of early seventeenth-century English history. Thus, for example, the Crown supported both internal monopolies and monopolistic trading companies, such as the Merchant Adventurers, so much so that in 1621 some 700 of them were in existence. Parliament, on the other hand, generally opposed these restrictions on both internal and external free trade. In 1601 it declared free trade with France, Spain and Portugal; in 1624 its Statute of Monopolies declared all

monopolies not granted to corporations illegal; and in the same year it specifically abolished the Merchant Adventurers' monopoly on the cloth trade. Significantly, this monopoly was restored by Charles I during the period of personal government.[56]

It is just that explosive monopoly on the cloth trade that Milton introduces in the passage cited earlier:

> Truth and understanding are not such wares as to be monopoliz'd and traded in by tickets and statutes, and standards. We must not think to make a staple commodity of all the knowledge in the Land, to mark and licence it like our broad cloath, and our wooll packs. (535–6)

It is not treating Truth as a merchandize that is degrading, for books are products that are, when allowed, bought and sold; the degradation is in treating truth as a monopolizable commodity, whose circulation and exchange is restricted, licensed and limited to the inflated profit of the few and the disadvantage of the many.

Until 1644 none of Milton's prose works was registered or licensed. The first of his works to appear after the June 1643 order, *The Doctrine and Discipline of Divorce* (August, 1643) was neither registered nor licensed, nor did it carry the author's name; the printers were identified only by initials. The second edition, however, carried the initials J.M. on the title page and the name John Milton at the end of the prefatory address "To the Parlament of England, with the Assembly." *Of Education* was the first of his works to be licensed and registered, 4 June 1644, followed by his translation *The Judgment of Martin Bucer Touching Divorce* on 15 July 1644. But conformity with these two titles did not prevent an attempt at harassment.

> On August 24 the Stationers' Company delivered to the House of Commons a petition whose substance is not known but which that House referred, on the 26th, to its Committee for Printing with instructions to prepare an ordinance and 'diligently to inquire out the Authors, Printers, and Publishers of the Pamphlet against the Immortality of the Soul, and concerning Divorce.'[57]

When *Areopagitica* appeared it had been neither registered nor licensed, nor did it carry a printer's name; the printer remains unknown to this day. Its authorship, however, was proclaimed in italic capitals on the title page. *Tetrachordon* and *Colasterion* of the following year, 1645, were similarly neither registered nor licensed, nor were the printers' names given, nor were there any identifying printers' devices. Both displayed the author's initials on the title page, and *Tetrachordon* contained the author's name at the end of "The Address to the Parliament." But Humphrey Moseley registered and submitted for licence Milton's *Poems*, 6 October 1645. Plainly, various strategies were being tried by various printers and booksellers, involving speculations about the likelihood or otherwise of a book's being licensed, and the gains and risks involved in flouting the order.

Areopagitica is clearly a deliberate challenge. The refusal to supply
a printer's name had the practical advantage of evading detection, but
the provision of the information "LONDON / Printed in the Year,
1644" merely assured the Stationers Company that printing was going
on in the capital without their control. The author's name is defiantly
provided; though not without ambiguity. For the pamphlet purports
to be a "SPEECH." If the pamphlet were designed as a provocative
test case, Milton could always have claimed that no licence was required
to prepare a speech; and what evidence could be adduced that he the
author was involved in the printing? The paradox that what might freely
be delivered as a speech could not be printed offered a telling point
against the restrictions on printing. It is a speech addressed "To the
PARLAMENT OF *ENGLAND*," the place of parley, of speech. There
is perhaps a residual sense that parliament is a place of free speech, with
the privilege of uttering things that outside its assembly would not be
allowable. But since someone who is not a member of parliament –
"wanting such accesse in a private condition" (486) – cannot readily deliver
a speech to parliament, how else can the speech be delivered except by
printing? The address to parliament is very much a strategy, as parliament
could not but be aware; a way, as Wittreich points out, "of openly
addressing Parliament and then marking off a much wider audience," a
"technique, initiated in *The Doctrine and Discipline of Divorce*."[58] The
very title *Areopagitica*, from the seventh oration of Isocrates, usually called
the *Areopagitic Discourse* or *Areopagiticus*, hints at the ambiguous nature
of this speech that is perhaps not a speech at all: as Sirluck notes, "Isocrates
(436–338 B.C.) conducted a famous school of rhetoric at Athens. Physical
and nervous weakness prevented him from speaking in public; hence he
composed his 'orations' to be read" (486 n.). If a speech is designed to be
read, how else in this modern age is it to be circulated except by printing?
The absurdity of having to make "A / SPEECH ... For the Liberty of
UNLICENC'D / PRINTING" is a purely conceptual absurdity; the speech
is not spoken but printed, and printed unlicensed, enacting that very liberty
it demands.

The argument that if printing is to be licensed, so should speeches and
much else be, is one made at length a third of the way into the tract. The
case is that such ultra-repressive logic is absurd; but that since printing is
so small a part of our communicative arts, to single it out for licensing while
these other communications go free, is in itself illogical and absurd:

> If we think to regulat Printing, thereby to rectifie manners, we must
> regulat all recreations and pastimes, all that is delightfull to man. No
> musick must be heard, no song be set or sung, but what is grave and
> *Dorick*. There must be licencing dancers, that no gesture, motion,
> or deportment be taught our youth but what by their allowance shall
> be thought honest; for such *Plato* was provided of; It will ask more
> then the work of twenty licencers to examin all the lutes, the violins,
> and the ghittarrs in every house; they must not be suffer'd to prattle

as they doe, but must be licenc'd what they may say. And who shall
silence all the airs and madrigalls, that whisper softnes in chambers?
The Windows also, and the *Balcone's* must be thought on, there are
shrewd books, with dangerous Frontispices set to sale; who shall
prohibit them, shall twenty licencers? The villages also must have their
visitors to enquire what lectures the bagpipe and the rebbeck reads
ev'n to the ballatry, and the gammuth of every *municipal* fidler, for
these are the Countrymans *Arcadia's* and his *Monte Mayors.* Next,
what more Nationall corruption, for which England hears ill abroad,
then houshold gluttony; who shall be the rectors of our daily rioting?
and what shall be done to inhibit the multitudes that frequent those
houses where drunk'nes is sold and harbour'd? Our garments also
should be referr'd to the licencing of some more sober work-masters
to see them cut into a lesse wanton garb. Who shall regulat all the
mixt conversation of our youth, male and female together, as is
the fashion of this Country, who shall still appoint what shall be
discours'd, what presum'd, and no furder? Lastly, who shall forbid
and separat all idle resort, all evil company? (523—6)

It is a powerful, beautiful, amusing and plangent passage. But the extension
of logic to absurdity is not its only mode. For much of what Milton raises
to mock had been at times seriously proposed, and was to be proposed
again. These were absurdities that all too readily could be implemented.
The comedy is fragile; our expected freedoms are very vulnerable. Sirluck
notes how Plato (*Laws* VII) discussed the kinds of music to be allowed and
prohibited; Wither in 1641 suggested "Scurrilous and obscaene *Songs*"
should be censored; Laud required every bishop to send "visitors" to report
on the state of each parish (1634) and the universities (1636) and put
restrictions on lecturers (1629, 1633); while between 1363 and 1597 there
had been laws regulating dress.[60] This dialectical confrontation of fantasy
and history is a characteristic of political polemic. Having thought up an
extreme expression of what might be the logical extension of the opponent's
position, all too readily it appears that the supposed absurdity has been
true all along. The joke returns in full, educative horror.

Of course it is no logic to say, if we suppress this we ought to suppress
that, and since we cannot suppress everything we must suppress nothing.
Far more socially subversive ideas were emerging from the press than from
village dances. And Milton's intention is to allow the emergence of these
dangerous ideas, to educate the village dancers away from those village
sports and form them into a revolutionary vanguard. The argument, in this
context, is mere subterfuge. It is making a case as he had learned to make
a case in those academic exercises at Cambridge. The true case — let us
open the floodgates to subversion — was not one that could be put; yet
that quite clearly is the implication and consequence of the sort of arguments
he makes, and to prevent which the repressive licensing was proposed.
Looked at in this way, the whole argument is in bad faith. It is strategic,
decorative, rhetorical. Obviously the more controls over free expression

and the media, the more static and controlled will be, at least in the short view, the society.

But Milton does not depend only on these logical extensions and dialectical surprises for his effects. Simultaneously he offers an insinuating sensuality. There is a sardonic, erotic, suggestive lilt in "who shall silence all the airs and madrigalls, that whisper softnes in chambers." A sexual double entendre runs through "who shall regulat all the mixt conversation of our youth, male and female together, as is the fashion of this Country" where the play on conversation/intercourse and the punning associations of country (country matters) bring in a suggestive subtext. And as so often in these metaphors and resonances, there is an all too literal reminder of repressive realities. The voyeuristic snooping that led to prosecutions for fornication and adultery in the church courts and the Court of the Marches had helped, as much as the search for heresy and subversion, to lead to the discrediting of church and prerogative courts in the years leading up to the revolution.

But more than those academic issues of logicality and illogicality, Milton is concerned to demonstrate the impracticality of the licensing proposals. In suggesting sardonically the extension of licensing to dance, music and conversation, he repeatedly asks whether twenty licensers will be enough.[61] His stress on practicality, that we see in his support for the mechanics and working-men of the sects against the untested, cloistered, inexperienced clergy, appears with the full force of personal experience in his arguments from authorial practice.

> And what if the author shall be one so copious of fancie, as to have many things well worth the adding, coming into his mind after licencing, while the book is yet under the Presse, which not seldom happ'ns to the best and diligentest writers; and that perhaps a dozen times in one book. The Printer dares not go beyond his licenc't copy; so often then must the author trudge to his leav-giver, that those his new insertions may be viewd; and many a jaunt will be made, ere that licencer, for it must be the same man, can either be found, or found at leisure; mean while either the Presse must stand still, which is no small damage, or the author loose his accuratest thoughts, & send the book forth wors then he had made it, which to a diligent writer is the greatest melancholy and vexation that can befall. (532)

The evidence from normal creative practice – revision – and of the commercial pressures of a press lying idle – "no small damage" – is succinctly conveyed; while a wealth of resented useless toil is summed up in that "trudge." Against this detail of active experience is put the question of what sort of person would want to be a licenser. Again the specific realistic detail of the job is adduced, making its own irresistible argument:

> It cannot be deny'd but that he who is made judge to sit upon the birth, or death of books whether they may be wafted into this world, or not, had need to be a man above the common measure, both

studious, learned, and judicious; there may be else no mean mistakes
in the censure of what is passable or not; which is also no mean injury.
If he be of such worth as behoovs him, there cannot be a more tedious
and unpleasing journey-work, a greater losse of time levied upon his
head, then to be made the perpetuall reader of unchosen books and
pamphlets, oftimes huge volumes. There is no book that is acceptable
unlesse at certain seasons; but to be enjoyn'd the reading of that at
all times, and in a hand scars legible, whereof three pages would not
down at any time in the fairest Print, is an imposition which I cannot
beleeve how he that values time, and his own studies, or is but of a
sensible nostrill should be able to endure. (530)

That Puritan commitment to the proper use of time, that experienced
awareness that books are only acceptable "at certain seasones" and cannot
intelligibly be force read, and that specific, telling detail of "in a hand scars
legible" combine to demonstrate the obstacles against a valid licensing
practice. Those properly qualified to perform such a task would be most
unlikely to undertake it: "we may easily foresee what kind of licencers we
are to expect hereafter, either ignorant, imperious, and remisse, or basely
pecuniary" (530).

   To situate *Areopagitica* in its immediate context of the English revolution
is in no way to reduce its significance. Its place as a lasting document in
the ongoing struggle for freedom of expression is assured. But in its
immediate context the argument was for freedom of expression for the
radicalism of the sects, not absolute freedom in an abstract sense. The
immediate revolutionary situation was Milton's concern. And just as
that encapsulation of authoritarian repression, the Roman church, was
presented as the originator of licensing and censorship, likewise its advocates
were excluded from any of the claims for toleration put forward:

> Yet if all cannot be of one mind, as who looks they should be? this
> doubtles is more wholsome, more prudent, and more Christian that
> many be tolerated, rather then all compell'd. I mean not tolerated
> Popery, and open superstition, which as it extirpats all religions and
> civill supremacies, so it self should be extirpat, provided first that all
> charitable and compassionat means be us'd to win and regain the weak
> and the misled: that also which is impious or evil absolutely either
> against faith or maners no law can possibly permit, that intends not
> to unlaw it self: but those neighboring differences, or rather indiffer-
> ences, are what I speak of, whether in some point of doctrine or of
> discipline, which though they may be many, yet need not interrupt
> *the unity of Spirit*, if we could but find among us *the bond of peace*.
> (565)

This exemption of "Popery" from toleration occurs in the third paragraph
from the end. It comes in almost as an afterthought; as if having read
through what he had already written, Milton realized that his position on
this point had to be made clear. But do we interpret this late explicitness

as a consequence of the point's being so obvious and uncontentious that there had been no perceived need to make it before? Almost no one on the left was arguing for toleration for catholic writings. But for legalistic precision Milton decided to spell out his position unambiguously. Or does this seeming explicitness in fact only create a doubt and suggest an ambiguity? Do we interpret Milton's exemption of Popery from toleration as concessional, as "politically expedient," as Wittreich has suggested,[62] so that he would not lose the support of hard-line puritans, anglicans and radicals, but not as a position he felt much commitment to? His earlier claim that "all such tractats whether false or true are as the Prophesie of *Isaiah* was to the *Eunuch*, not to be *understood without a guide*" (519) might suggest that he would happily have tolerated catholic publications: they caused trouble with "any ignorant man" only when "expounded to him by some of that Clergy." The problem was not in the books but in the clergy, catholic and otherwise.

Milton's position on the extent of the freedoms he advocates has always been problematical, and this has not been the consequence simply of liberal "misreadings" of *Areopagitica*,[63] but of ambiguities embedded in the pamphlet. He was certainly not making an absolute case for absolute freedom: to have attempted that would have been to have advocated something that had never been the case; the extremity of such a case at such an historical moment would have invalidated the tract altogether. His argument is for the removal of prepublication censorship: he concedes the inevitable:

> I deny not, but that it is of greatest concernment in the Church and Commonwealth, to have a vigilant eye how Bookes demeane themselves, as well as men; and thereafter to confine, imprison, and do sharpest justice on them as malefactors: For Books are not absolutely dead things, but doe contain a potencie of life in them . . . .(492)

Yet this seeming stress on the punishment of books as malefactors reverses itself into an argument that books should not be summarily destroyed but should receive the respect due to human life. What begins as an apparently authoritarian law-and-order obsession turns into a case for toleration. This internal shift within the images and arguments is an ambiguity characteristic of Milton's writing in *Areopagitica*. Looked at again, we see that Milton is not advocating police measures but conceding them. He recognizes their existence; this is not the same as recommending them. The double negative formulation indicates his concessional strategy: "I deny not, but that. . . ." These discriminations may seem legalistic; with a father, brother and brother-in-law in the legal and related professions, they would come readily to Milton. He is significantly not writing "we must have a vigilant eye how Bookes demeane themselves. . . ." Rather, he is conceding the status quo situation that there are those "in the church and commonwealth" who find it "of greatest concernment" to regulate books; this is something "I deny not." The phrasing distances Milton himself from such concerns.

He scrupulously avoids positive endorsement. In effect he can be seen as taking a modified ranter position: not exactly lying strategically, as the ranters were happy to do: but giving the impression of agreeing, conforming, while satisfying his own verbal conscience. After all, to say "I deny not, but that" is only to say, I am not at this moment arguing against this, while reserving the right to deny the case at the earliest effective moment. He significantly offers no arguments for such "concernment," no historical evidence. And to move on in the next sentence to "as good almost kill a Man as kill a good Book; who kills a Man kills a reasonable creature, Gods image" undercuts all that concession about "do sharpest justice on them as malefactors." Theoretical, abstract, concessional punishment is one thing: killing "God's image," "the image of God, as it were in the eye," spilling "the pretious life-blood of a master spirit" is something else.

The tortured, negative formulation is found again in the passage arguing against the suppression of books before publication. Till the Council of Trent, Milton writes,

> Books were ever as freely admitted into the World as any other birth; the issue of the brain was no more stifl'd then the issue of the womb: no envious *Juno* sate cros-leg'd over the nativity of any mans intellectual off spring; but if it prov'd a Monster, who denies, but that it was justly burnt, or sunk into the Sea. (505)

Again the image runs through a complex of positions. The powerful right to life argument is confronted by the peremptory savagery of "justly burnt, or sunk into the Sea." After all, who has decided that this *was* a monster necessary to be so summarily destroyed? Milton certainly avoids endorsing any such decision: "who denies, but that it was justly burnt." His own attitude is undeclared, but the negative expression, the raised question, allow the ready possibility that there might well be those who would deny the justice of the suppression.

A closely legalistic reading directs us to ask how real are Milton's seeming acceptances of punishments for offending books, expressed within such complex negatives. Are these in essence tactical, distanced concessions, Milton knowing full well that once the principle of non-licensing is accepted, the remaining censorship structures will ultimately be unsustainable? The final paragraph of *Areopagitica* opens with a reiteration of the existing punishments available to parliament:

> And as for regulating the Presse, let no man think to have the honour of advising ye better then your selves have done in that Order publisht next before this, that no book be Printed, unlesse the Printers and the Authors name, or at least the Printers be register'd. Those which otherwise come forth, if they be found mischievous and libellous, the fire and the executioner will be the timeliest and the most effectual remedy, that mans prevention can use. (569)

Once again the seeming hard line is not as clear cut as it might at first glance appear. Sirluck points out,

> There is an ambiguity here. It was a legal offence for books to be published anonymously or without the publisher's imprint, even though they were neither 'mischievous' nor libellous; it was another offence to publish 'mischief' or libel, even though the publication carried the name of author and publisher. (569n)

We might add the reminder that *Areopagitica* itself was not registered; and though it carried the author's name, it did not carry the printer's − which from Milton's "at least the Printers" might have been thought to have been the basic requirement he put forward, more important than carrying the author's name. The cited methods of "regulating the Presse" are, in the very work asserting them, deliberately not observed. As for "the fire," we might recall, as the Parliament to whom the pamphlet was addressed would surely have recalled, that Herbert Palmer had suggested in a sermon preached before Parliament and the Westminster Assembly on 13 August 1644, that Milton's *Doctrine and Discipline of Divorce* was "deserving to be burnt."[64] We are justified in wondering how committed Milton was to such a "remedy."

We might notice, too, that though the earlier negative formulations are not repeated, a no less cumbersome and tortuous phraseology is used: "And as for regulating the Presse, let no man think to have the honour of advising ye better then your selves have done." Does this allow us to consider that some man may have advised parliament better, but don't let him think to have any honour from it; how could parliament allow that anyone could think better than itself? Is this a sardonic way of saying that there is no honour to be had by thinking up schemes of regulating the press, anyway, that it is something best unregulated? To say that "the fire and the executioner will be the timeliest and the most effectual remedy, that mans prevention can use" is to say no more than they will be a quick and effective destructive solution, if destruction, prevention, is what is required. It is scrupulously not endorsing the remedy. Milton employed the same sort of circularity, significantly free of moral endorsement, when he had Manoah blandly declare in *Samson Agonistes*, "Samson hath quit himself / Like Samson, and heroicly hath finished / A life heroic" (lines 1709−11), leaving hanging there the question of whether that sort of violent destructive heroism is morally good, in any way recommendable. And to continue from "the fire and the executioner" to, in the next sentence, "For this *authentic* Spanish policy of licencing books" (569) simply, or cunningly, reminds the reader that fire and executioners were the hideous instruments of the Inquisition, no more endorsable than the licensing explicitly opposed.

These minute subtleties of argumentative sleight of hand, which might be overlooked by the cursory reader, are paralleled by devious tricks that can be overlooked because of the much larger scale on which they work. The historical evidence that Milton adduces from classical, biblical and medieval times is supremely irrelevant; before the invention of printing the labour involved in transcribing manuscripts was its own system of control. It is only with the widespread dissemination of books that the written word becomes a wide-scale threat to social and religious order. The arguments from authority also turn out to be other than they seem, as Sirluck noted:

> The second argument, which proposes to show that the promiscuous reading of bad along with good books is beneficial, seems at first glance, with its citations from prophets, apostles, and fathers, to be an argument from authority. The reverse, however, is true: the primary function of these citations is to free the issue from the influence of miscellaneous Christian authorities (an arbitration not much to Milton's taste, nor, perhaps, to the advantage of his present position). The 'authority' of one primitive father is opposed to that of another in such a way as to prevent either from being decisive, and hence the way is cleared for submitting the issue to the test of reason alone. (If, in this matching of opinions, Milton's selection makes the preponderance seem to be in favor of unrestricted reading, that is only a secondary – although certainly not accidental – result of the method.) (164–5)

His radical contempt for argument from authority is shown in that deadpan way in which a comic anecdote is introduced in the same manner as if it were a revered authority along with all the Biblical and classical citation: "that gallant man who thought to pound up the crows by shutting his Parkgate" (520). Authorities can be found for any position. This, of course, is Milton's argument. In the end the individual has to make up his or her own mind: we cannot let authorities do it for us, hand over our morality to a hired divine and leave it at that. This is the meaning of that most frequently quoted passage:

> I cannot praise a fugitive and cloister'd vertue, unexercis'd and unbreath'd, that never sallies out and sees her adversary, but slinks out of the race, where that immortal garland is to be run for, not without dust and heat. Assuredly we bring not innocence into the world, we bring impurity much rather: that which purifies us is triall, and triall is by what is contrary. (515)

Although Milton is arguing for a single specific aim – the abolition of licensing – this commitment to "triall is by what is contrary" informs the whole pamphlet. His method is truly dialectical. Image after image embodies its own necessary rethinking, its own resituation. His citations from authority serve to challenge the very concept of argument from authority. His hypothetical logical exaggerations redefine themselves as the literal recording of appalling reality. These are dynamic devices. The paradoxes – a speech for the liberty of printing – do not remain as static wit; they generate an immense charge of redefining intellectual energy. Books are presented as alive: never as reified, alienated commodities. Books embody ideas, truth, and truth is dynamic: hence the imagery of life-blood, bodies, fountains. And these material images are ennobling; there are no concepts of transcending the body, the image of God, here. Life is a value; books are valuable because their ideas are alive. It is such life that still speaks to us through *Areopagitica* three centuries and more after its first publication.

MICHAEL WILDING

NOTES

1. *Complete Prose Works of John Milton*, Vol. II, ed. Ernest Sirluck (New Haven: Yale U. P., 1959) (hereafter *CPW*), 797–98.
2. *CPW*, II, 491. All quotations from *Areopagitica* are from this edition.
3. William M. Clyde, *The Struggle for the Freedom of the Press from Caxton to Cromwell* (London: O. U. P., 1934), p. 20.
4. *CPW*, II, 794.
5. Thomas N. Corns, *The Development of Milton's Prose Style* (Oxford: Clarendon P., 1982), p. 72.
6. Ernest Sirluck, "Milton's Critical Use of Historical Sources: An Illustration," *Modern Philology*, 50 (1953), 226–31.
7. Clyde, p. 1.
8. Fredrick Seaton Siebert, *Freedom of the Press in England 1476–1776* (Urbana: U. of Illinois P., 1952), p. 30.
9. Clyde, p. 11.
10. Clyde, p. 12.
11. Clyde, p. 13.
12. Clyde, p. 20.
13. David Masson, *The Life of John Milton* (London: Macmillan, revised edition, 1881), I, 405.
14. Clyde, p. 39.
15. Clyde, p. 40.
16. The details are recorded in *The Dictionary of National Biography*, II, 1309–10, III, 457–9.
17. Brian Manning, *The English People and the English Revolution* (Harmondsworth, Penguin, 1978), p. 15.
18. *DNB*, III, 459.
19. Pauline Gregg, *Free-born John* (London: Harrap, 1961), p. 66.
20. Clyde, p. 47.
21. Corns, *Milton's Prose Style*, pp. 91–2.
22. *CPW*, II, 142.
23. Discussed in J.-F. Camé, 'Images in Milton's *Areopagitica*,' *Cahiers Elisabethains*, 6 (1974), 30. The literary consequences of the censorship are discussed in Christopher Hill, 'Censorship and English Literature,' in *Collected Essays of Christopher Hill: Volume One, Writing and Revolution in Seventeenth Century England* (Brighton: Harvester, 1985), pp. 32–71, and in David Norbrook, *Poetry and Politics in The English Renaissance* (London: Routledge and Kegan Paul, 1984) pp. 217–21, 227–34, 276–7 and passim.
24. *CPW*, II, 175.
25. *CPW*, II, 515.
26. See Camé, 32–3; Alan F. Price, "Incidental Imagery in *Areopagitica*," *Modern Philology*, 49 (1952), 218, 221–2; John X. Evans, "Imagery as Argument in Milton's *Areopagitica*," *Texas Studies in Literature and Language*, 8 (1966), 200–2.
27. *CPW*, II, 163.
28. Edward, Earl of Clarendon, *The History of the Rebellion and Civil Wars in England*, III (Oxford: at the Theater, 1704), 32.
29. David W. Petergorsky, *Left-Wing Democracy in the English Revolution* (London: Gollancz, 1940), p. 55.
30. John Aubrey, *Brief Lives*, ed. Andrew Clark (Oxford: Clarendon P., 1898), II, 67.

31. On the "birthright" and enclosures in radical rhetoric, see Jack Lindsay, *John Bunyan* (London: Methuen, 1937), pp. 253–4.
32. Don M. Wolfe, *Milton in the Puritan Revolution* (London: Cohen and West, 1963), *Renascence*, p. 144.
33. Gregg, p. 131.
34. *Complete Prose Works of John Milton*, Vol. I, ed. Don M. Wolfe (New Haven: Yale U.P., 1953), 934. Thomas Corns cites a number of examples of Milton's contempt for "serving-men" as evidence of "Milton's distancing himself from the archetype of the radical enragé and expressing his solidarity with the mainstream of respectable Puritanism." ("Milton's Quest for Respectability," *Modern Language Review*, 77 (1982), 775–6). However Corns' identification of "serving-man" with "working man" is not one that the radical sectaries would necessarily have accepted. The Levellers notoriously proposed to exclude servants from the extended franchise. Serving-men and women were seen as sharing in the middle or ruling-class attitudes of their employers, or at least hopelessly vulnerable to political pressure from them: hence they were unlikely to have solidarity with radical or proletarian aims. For Milton to be contemptuous of a "serving-man" may at one level have seemed to show how "he appeals to his educated and propertied readers": but at the same time would not show any rejection of true, radical working-class solidarity.
35. Petergorsky, p. 65.
36. Fredric Jameson, "Religion and Ideology," in Francis Barker et al., ed., *1642: Literature and Power in the Seventeenth Century* (Colchester: Essex U.P., 1981), p. 329. Quotations from Milton's poems are from *The Poems of John Milton*, ed. John Carey and Alastair Fowler (London: Longmans, 1968).
37. Thomas Kranidas, "Polarity and Structure in Milton's *Areopagitica*," *English Literary Renaissance*, 14 (1984), 188.
38. Corns, *Milton's Prose Style*, p. 70. Cf. also Elbert N.S. Thompson's remark, "In his use of homely English expressions and metaphors drawn from common experience Milton showed himself of the new age," "Milton's Prose Style," *Philological Quarterly*, 14 (1935), 10.
39. Christopher Hill, *Antichrist in Seventeenth Century England* (London: O.U.P., 1971), pp. 11, 68, 111.
40. Hilaire Belloc, *Milton* (1935) (London: Cassell, 1970), p. 167.
41. Arthur E. Barker, *Milton and the Puritan Dilemma 1641–1660* (Toronto: U. of Toronto P., 1942), p. 63. The view is reiterated in Keith W. Stavely, *The Politics of Milton's Prose Style* (New Haven: Yale U.P., 1975), p. 66 where *Areopagitica* is described as "a direct result of Milton's advocacy of reformed divorce laws."
42. Barker, p. 80.
43. Arnold Williams, "*Areopagitica* Revisited," *University of Toronto Quarterly*, 14 (1944), 70.
44. Christopher Hill, *Milton and the English Revolution* (London: Faber, 1977), p. 92.
45. Hill, *Milton*, pp. 81–2.
46. Siebert, p. 167.
47. Siebert, pp. 167–8.
48. Siebert, p. 169.
49. Cf. Christopher Kendrick, "Ethics and the Orator in *Areopagitica*," *ELH*, 50 (1983), 677–9.
50. Siebert, p. 169.
51. *CPW*, II, 798. A graphic attack on these search parties in *England's Birthright* (1645) is quoted in Clyde, pp. 105–8.
52. Camé, p. 23.
53. Price, p. 219n.
54. Camé, p. 24.
55. Clyde, pp. 23–4, 42–7.
56. Andrew Milner, *John Milton and the English Revolution* (London: Macmillan, 1981), p. 70.
57. *CPW*, II, 142.

58. Joseph Anthony Wittreich, Jr., " 'The Crown of Eloquence': The Figure of the Orator in Milton's Prose Works," in *Achievements of the Left Hand: Essays on the Prose of John Milton*, ed. Michael Lieb and John T. Shawcross (Amherst: U. of Massachusetts P., 1974), p. 18.

59. *CPW*, II, 486n.

60. *CPW*, II, 523–6nn.

61. There were in fact more than twenty appointed by the 1643 order. See Hilary Gatti, "The 'Twenty Ingrossers' of Milton's *Areopagitica*," *Notes and Queries*, NS 29 (1982), 498–9.

62. Joseph Anthony Wittreich, Jr., "Milton's *Areopagitica*: its Isocratic and Ironic Contexts," *Milton Studies*, IV (1972), 110.

63. John Illo's widely disseminated claim that "no one, Marxist or liberal ... had read it (*Areopagitica*) and understood it" in relation to its exclusion of press freedoms to catholics and in its acceptance of post-publication penalties is untrue: "The Misreading of Milton," in *Radical Perspectives in the Arts*, ed. Lee Baxandall (Baltimore: Penguin, 1972), p. 179, reprinted from *Columbia University Forum*, 8 (1965), 38–42. The limitations on press freedom were remarked by Masson, III, 288; Barker, pp. 88, 96; Williams, p. 72; and Ivor Montague and Kingsley Martin in *Freedom of Expression*, ed. Herman Ould (London: Hutchinson International, 1944), pp. 37, 140, the symposium marking the tercentenary of Milton's tract. The point is stressed in Warner G. Rice, "A Note on *Areopagitica*," *Journal of English and Germanic Philology*, 40 (1941), 474–81.

64. William Riley Parker, *Milton* (Oxford: Clarendon P., 1968), I, 263.

Richard Overton's Marpriest Tracts: Towards a History of Leveller Style

The history of the origins and development of the Leveller movement in the 1640s is a much-explored topic in recent historical writing. Standing for the most extreme version of personal and political liberty in that decade, the Levellers braved persecution in order to criticise Parliament and the New Model Army leaders. At various points between 1646 and 1649, they had considerable influence among the radical Puritan churches and in the Army itself. Their ideas for franchise reform have been seen in this century as the foundations of modern political democracy. Now, however, there is a need for an equally complex account of the genesis and development of the writings by individual Levellers, and the joint compositions which accompanied the main Leveller campaigns. Each individual brought a particular style or styles of writing from different religious or secular roots, and made that writing part of the very fabric of the movement. Especially in the work of the three most famous Levellers, John Lilburne, Richard Overton and William Walwyn, style changed in accordance with the changing conditions of freedom to which the writers were subject.

While we know increasingly more about the conditions of production of these writings as published pamphlets, and about the relationship between publication and the physical organisation of the movement, the persuasive and imaginative content of the pamphlets has taken second place. In the argument which follows, a series of pamphlets by Richard Overton, the Marpriest tracts, published in the year prior to the emergence of the Leveller party proper, are shown to reveal just such a persuasive attempt to inculcate toleration in the minds of the public by means of popular forms of symbolism and jest. At the same time, the pamphlets may be said to reveal a response to the violence of ecclesiastical persecution and religious difference, while articulating an early and unextended version of the Leveller theory of natural rights.

Richard Overton's role as one of the most outspoken leaders of the Leveller movement in the 1640s and the early 1650s is a familiar one to historians of the Civil War. More recently, Overton's reputation as a writer of satire and polemic has been mooted, though we are still far from a full appreciation of his worth. There have been several statements concerning the quality of Overton's writing, as well as a full-length biography, which deals with the delicate problem of attribution.[1] Despite

Margot Heinemann's crisp insights on the dramatic element in Overton's pamphlets, we are still in need of an assessment of the various polemical techniques employed in those pamphlets, in terms of the political, religious and publishing context within which Overton wrote.[2] There is insufficient space here to do full justice to the variety and complexity of Overton's writing, to compare Overton's arguments in detail with those of the participants in the same debates, or to substantiate the recent attempts to extend radically the Overton canon.[3] Rather, this article will consider the seven pamphlets (and three of these seven in particular) which Overton wrote and published in 1645 and 1646, the "Marpriest" pamphlets, in order to show how Overton saw his role as a polemicist, what materials he chose to use, and what his achievement amounted to in these tracts.

The Marpriest tracts, so-called because they are centred on the persona of Martin Marpriest, are important as examples of extremely fine polemical writing. In many ways highly-wrought and patterned, they make hilarious reading in a popular festive mode, which had been taken into the realms of ecclesiastical discourse. They also mark a transition in radical religious writing in which the tradition of Puritan anti-prelatical satire established in the late 1580s by "Martin Marprelate" merged with secular, perhaps drama-based, forms of representation, to express both religious satire and the potent, emergent theories of natural or fundamental rights. These theories were the ideological fuel of the Leveller movement at its height. The Marpriest tracts were produced just at that juncture where the individuals who were later to lead the Levellers, were beginning to join their hitherto individual protesting voices together in a single movement. The Marpriest pamphlets reveal that nexus between tradition, readerships and persuasion, at that very point where religious sectarianism came forward to assess its relationship with the state and with the public at large.

The key for making a reassessment of Overton's satires lies in an exploration of Overton's understanding of Marprelate's writings and the related "Martinist" tracts. Quite recently, Overton has been compared unfavourably with Marprelate in the following terms: "This sense of character [in Marprelate], which represents an emerging and markedly modern consciousness, sets the satires apart from the welter of contemporary prose tracts and warrants the attention given to their forms. While other writers such as Richard Overton ... assume personae or interject witty jibes, their efforts do not rise above the *ad hoc* attack of animadversion."[4] This judgement both over-estimates the degree of polish in the Marprelate tracts and under-estimates the content of Overton's writings.

Very little is known of Overton's life. Born perhaps in 1615, he may have studied at Cambridge and performed in plays there. He may also have witnessed in some capacity the Bishops' War against the Scots in the late 1630s. None of this evidence can be used with certainty. The first definite news we have of him is his publication of a series of short anti-episcopal, anti-Laud pamphlets in 1641 and 1642.[5] These are pseudo-dramatic in form, and contain many of the strategies of satire and inversion which feature in the later Marpriest tracts.[6] At this point, Overton's work was part of a fairly crude satirical and witty style, itself part of the general anti-episcopal furor of the very early 1640s. No religious or political radicalism was apparent in these publications beyond a ridicule of Bishops and King.

According to Marie Gimelfarb-Brack, Overton then disappeared from the pamphleteering scene in London during two periods in 1642 and 1643. The first was in April 1642, a silence of eight months, after which Overton reappeared in January 1643 to help publish a reprint of a tract associated with Marprelate entitled *The Character Of A Puritan*.[7] The second disappearance followed in 1643, when it seems that Overton went to Amsterdam and converted there to Mennonite Anabaptism. Returning to England, he published in January 1644 an argument for the mortality of the soul, *Mans Mortalitie*, a work written under Anabaptist influence.[8]

The increase in the Presbyterian persecution of sectarians led Overton to speak out against oppressive ecclesiastical powers, but this time not the Bishops. Parliament had established the Assembly of Divines to discuss and recommend a reformed church discipline for the country. This body consisted of clergymen of different parties. The Presbyterians had attempted to establish their own model of church discipline, based upon a national hierarchy of assemblies, by act of Parliament. This was against the preference for a less hierarchical structure of locally-governed congregations favoured by the Independents. In *A Sacred Decretall* (p. 12), Overton recounts how the Presbyterians had requested in the early 1640s that the separatists Green and Spencer suspend their open and public meetings in order to stop fears of the rise of heresy, and therefore to hasten the overthrow of the Bishops. Green and Spencer had been promised liberty to worship later on, but in 1645 the Presbyterians urged their suppression. Overton's voice was but one among many here, though he spoke on behalf of the more extreme sectarian and tolerationist positions, as opposed to the Independent ministers who sat in the Westminster Assembly. He addressed the central issues of complaint against the Presbyterians: the Ordinances for the ordination of ministers, tithes (compared to a soap monopoly and related to fluctuating prices), the Directory for Public Worship, and press censorship. Despite the considerable debate between Presbyterians and Independents within the Assembly, the Presbyterians did try to silence the opposition of the Independents, and those groups to the left of them, by censoring the anti-Presbyterian press.[9] Overton launched his own attack on the Presbyterians in the Marpriest tracts, starting on 8 April 1645 with *The Araignement Of Mr. Persecvtion*.

The Marpriest tracts had two objectives: to discredit the Presbyterian objection to the liberty of conscience in speech and in the press, and to attack the continued Presbyterian insistence upon an ordained ministry only, maintained by tithes. In so far as Overton attacks the idea of Presbyterianism existing *jure divino*, he could be said to agree with the Erastian party in Parliament, which argued that any reformed church should be subject to the civil power. However, Overton advocates a degree of toleration which most Erastians would not have permitted.

The pamphlets themselves were printed on a press established by Overton and William Larner, another opponent of episcopacy who would become a Leveller. In the second half of 1645, this press published tracts by John Lilburne, and Sir Henry Marten, the republican member of the Commons who was associated with the emergent Levellers at this time. Here, the first statements of the Leveller campaign for the establishment of fundamental political rights and equality were made.

The success of the Marpriest tracts is evident in the way that they scandalised the Presbyterians during the following months. Martin Marpriest became one of a series of stylistically distinct voices speaking in defence of the individual rights of citizens and the entire separation of church and state. Both of these ideals appealed at the time, though not permanently, to most of the radical religious groups in London, the milieu from which the Levellers drew much of their early support. Such was Overton's success in obscuring the real author of the Marpriest tracts that he was able to escape the attention of the authorities for several months. However, he was finally apprehended by two members of the Stationers Company hostile to him, and brought before the House of Lords in August 1646.

The works which offended the Lords were *An Alarum to the House of Lords* (31 July 1646), *The Last Warning* (20 March 1646), written by Lilburne and Overton together, and later on, *A Defiance Against All Arbitrary Usurpations* (17 August 1646), but the informers also said that they had found other books in Overton's house.[10] These books may have been copies of the Marpriest tracts. The Lords interrogated Overton, he refused to answer questions, and he was committed to Newgate. The publishing, however, continued, including appeals to the House of Commons by Overton for his release. In fact, the forms employed by Overton in his tracts changed as his conditions of personal liberty altered. Further imprisonments continued, including that of Overton's wife and his younger brother. This situation continued until the release of Overton on 16 September 1647, in the context of Army pressure upon Parliament, including soldiers' petitions for the release of Lilburne and Overton. Lilburne, however, remained in prison, and this state of affairs was the point where Leveller activity began properly, with tensions between the Army and Parliament, and between agitators and commanding officers within the Army.[11]

II

By 1645, Overton was a very experienced pamphleteer. He had mastered a popular satirical form (which was not without its imitators), and he had penned one of the most potent statements of radical religious theology to appear during the century. His choice of strategy in April 1645 was itself a deliberate response to the context in which he found himself. There were seven pamphlets in the series: *The Araignement Of Mr. Persecvtion* (8 April 1645), *A Sacred Decretall* (31 May 1645, though the date mentioned in the text itself is 6 June), *Martin's Eccho* (27 June 1645), *The Nativity of Sir John Presbyter* (2 July 1645), *The Ordinance For Tythes Dismounted* (29 December 1645), *Divine Observations* (24 January 1646), and finally *An Arrow Against All Tyrants* (12 October 1646). Apart from their polemical purpose, the Marpriest tracts were also an attempt to refashion the tradition of Puritan writing founded by Martin Marprelate, in terms of the more overtly dramatic ridicule of Overton's earlier pamphlets. Overton clearly saw parallels between his own situation and that of Marprelate. He might also have known of the strategies of a pamphleteer like Thomas Scot, whose attacks on James I's Spanish marriage policy led to his persecution and eventual assassination, and who also employed dialogue techniques in his pamphlets.[12] All three pamphleteers owe a general debt to the traditions of Medieval complaint satire. In fact, one of the Marpriest tracts contains a comparison of the persecution of religious radicals by the Presbyterians in the 1640s with the intimidation of the Elizabethan nonconformists, Barrow, Greenwood and Penry, by the Bishops.[13] The Presbyterian faction in Parliament had tried to staunch the flow of sectarian literature with the 1643 Licensing Ordinance which sought to impose a censorship by requiring the licensing of all publications. This was immediately ignored by many radicals. Like Marprelate, Overton wrote against censorship, making that censorship a central issue in each pamphlet. To do this, Overton followed Marprelate in adopting a disguise, so hiding his true identity from the gaze of a censorious authority. This very strategy had a radical destabilising effect upon the accepted and expected notions of readership and the persuasive power of the author. Like Marprelate too, Overton was aware that the strategies he was using were abhorrent to most Puritans, even the radical ones.

In fact, Overton may have been connected with the re-publication of two Martinist tracts in 1640 and 1642 (*A Dialogue Wherein Is Plainly Laide Open the tyrannicall dealing of L. Bishopps against Gods children* [1589, 1640], issued again as *The Character Of A Puritan* in 1643, and *Reformation No Enemie* [1641], a retitled *Hay any worke for Cooper* [1589], published again under its original title in March 1642). Only the seventeenth-century versions of *A Dialogue* are signed by Martin Marprelate, though it is now argued that the author of the Marprelate tracts and of *A Dialogue* was the same man, Job Throckmorton.[14] Marprelate was taken in the 1640s, then, to be the author of a far more dialogue-oriented style, as well as the familiar jesting *persona* of Martin, and this too influenced Overton. Both tracts seem to have been reprinted in a general anti-episcopal cause. However, Marprelate could not be reproduced to attack the Presbyterians, since it would not be apt. Overton had to develop a different mode.

Most Puritans regarded Marprelate's techniques with horror. Using the pattern supplied by jest books, and elaborating upon methods of ridicule in humanist dialogue, Martin Marprelate had broken the codes of Puritan rectitude and plainness.[15] He took his rhetorical dictum of *decorum personae* from Horace and Erasmus, where the author impersonated the object of attack, in order to ridicule that object.[16] The degree of ridicule was determined by the extent of the impersonated target's guilt or immorality. Obviously, the satirist himself could determine entirely the seriousness of the crime. The rest of Marprelate was an explosive form of humour where Elizabethan Bishops, like John Bridges, were seen to degrade themselves, and lose the dignity associated with their role and status at the hands of jesting, teasing Martin. Throckmorton was familiar with comic forms through his humanist education.[17] Not being a member of the clergy or a very strict Puritan, he found no difficulty in producing a potent satire which was to have a resounding influence upon the literature of the 1590s and afterwards.

The Puritans were offended by Marprelate because they felt he had discredited their cause by using a literary form which was in direct contradiction to their moral and ethical programme. For instance, the Independent minister Sidrach Simpson expressed the view that the godly should be in the business of persuasion and exhortation, not the subversive techniques of Marprelate, to achieve their ends.[18] Simpson was writing in the 1640s, but his attitudes are representative of a view which prevailed when the Marprelate pamphlets were first published. In Puritan eyes, Marprelate stood for a kind of imaginative transgression, an engagement with the darker, devilish side of the human psyche and will. In his *Gangraena* (1646, I, p. 38), the outraged Thomas Edwards noted the blasphemy of Marpriest in showing how the Holy Ghost left Scotland for England in a "Cloakbagge," and how a prayer in *The Araignement* scoffed at the "Passion, Death, Resurrection and Ascension of Christ." This mode of expression and observation defied the uncomplicated black and white vision of good and evil through which Puritans viewed the world. There is a more well-known example which can help there. When Bunyan published *The Pilgrim's Progress* (1678), he was reprimanded by some of his fellow dissenters for publishing an allegory which borrowed its form from popular heroic literature. The "carnal" imagination had been used to talk about a godly subject. Critics have for some time also supposed that Bunyan may have taken some of his allegorical form in *The Pilgrim's Progress*, and the trial scenes in *The Pilgrim's Progess* and *The Holy War*, from Overton's *The Araignement Of Mr. Persecvtion*.[19] If this was the case, then in some sense Bunyan was using an imaginative form which transgressed against the dominant frame of Puritan literary imperatives.

If the harshness of non-Martinist sixteenth-century Puritan writing is compared with the pyrotechnics of Martin, the shock which the latter must have had upon contemporary readers is apparent:

> To the ende then it may appeare what that reformation is which we seeke for, and which these men do account the enemie of our state; it is to be vnderstood, that by reformation we mean nothing els, but the remouing of all those vnlawful callings which are maintained in our Church and ministrie, contrarie vnto the reuealed will and written word of the Lord our God, and the restoring therunto of all such offices and ministries.

> Well fare old mother experience yet / the burnt childe dreads the fire: his grace will cary to his graue I warrant you / the blowes which M. Cartwright gaue him in this cause: & therefore no maruell though he was loth to have any other so banged as he himselfe was to his woe.[20]

Marprelate's voice is astonishing for its direct colloquial tones and imitation of verbal gestures. Marprelate has the ability to anticipate the reader's response, and turn it to his own ends. The effect, when coupled with the painstaking quotation of sections from episcopal pamphlets, is overwhelming:

> Would you haue the naturall eies put out (as your brethren the bishops haue don in the church of England / euer since John of Canterbury urged his wretched subscription) and unnatural squint gogled eies put in their steede: when the body cannot see with any eies? but with the natural eies thereof.[21]

This was an early example of *calumniation*, the distortion of the substance of one's opponents' arguments in the very process of controversial exchange. Significantly, this was to worry Puritans greatly in the 1640s, when Presbyterian and Independent battled in the Westminster Assembly of Divines, called by Parliament to settle the religious affairs of the kingdom. Here is Sidrach Simpson again:

> There are two too usuall errours in handling Controversies. One to make the difference voluminous and many-headed, that so it may appear more horrid, monstrous and irreconcileable: the other to make the Opposites odious, by charging their reall or supposed faults upon their Tenents; for every man is glad to heare something against those they hate, and ready to believe it without any, or on very slight examination.[22]

III

Overton built upon Marprelate not simply through a direct textual imitation. Rather, we see the transformation of a polemical *persona*. For Overton, it was first necessary to signal his relationship to Marprelate by constructing a genealogy. "MARTIN MAR-PRIEST" is son to "old MARTIN the Metropolitane."[23] "MARTIN MAR-PRIEST" promises something of the same, but with a slight difference. As with most controversial writing of this nature, the success of any one attack is based upon the tensions between identities. In *Martin's Eccho*, Martin speaks of himself in the third person, as if to aggrandise his status, as well as to parody this form of authority. The invisible author exploits the relationship between him or herself, the speaking *persona* in the text, and the reader. Martin is presented as a chip off the old block. This time, however, "Mar-Priest" is more distinctly a figure of Christian folly, the words on one title page actually invoking the relevant passage from 1 Cor. 1.20.[24] Martin takes on a number of roles and disguises in the pamphlets which are dependent upon this wise fool identity. Not surprisingly, these other roles are determined by the particular context, though we should also note that they are made quite distinctly. So, Martin becomes, in *A Sacred Decretall* (p.17), a "Tell-tale," who perceives the truth with a greater clarity than most. He is a martin, according to his fictional opponent, the bird which sees more clearly than others. This is especially true with regard to the issue of whether ordination is necessary before an individual may preach. At the same time, Martin is, of course, more honest, in order to gain the maximum persuasive purchase (p.18).

In the sequel pamphlet to *A Sacred Decretall*, entitled *Martin's Eccho*, Martin appears as the correct adviser for the reader, through his sarcastic expounding of Presbyterian aims: "cease not to possesse both Parliament and People, that all that oppose you by word or writing (*though never so conformable to Truth*) are unnaturall enemies and Rebells to their Countrey, and insufferable in a Common-Wealth."[25] In *The Araignement*, Liberty of Conscience speaks with a Martinist voice, thereby enhancing the direction of the criticisms (p.26). This voice is characterised by its ability to perceive absurd logic in its opponents' statements, from which iniquity arises. The Presbyterian heresiographer Thomas Edwards was the scourge of the sects. His arguments are here rendered thus: "*States-men must weare Bells about their neckes, because antient Divines say, Kings are but Packe-horses to the Clergie*" (p.19). There is an irony here, as Martin is referred to as "Dr. Martin," though he is speaking on behalf of the unlearned lay preachers of the sectarians. This paradox points up Overton's claim for the spirit, but he makes it in terms of the ecclesiastical hierarchy being attacked. The result is a freeing of the reader's sense of play and fun, as Martin gains an imaginative victory, contrasting both what he stands for, with the terms, apparently, of his opponents. Yet ironically again, Martin appears in Presbyterian eyes as a Protestant emblem or icon. If he will join the Presbyterians, Martin will become a greedy, oppressive giant with St. Peter's keys and St. Paul's "*Back-sword*," as well as "*Scotch-Dagger*" and a "Classical Club." This image of violent greed, a negative image of the real Martin, is juxtaposed with the genuine power of God's vengeance which will act in the name of liberty of conscience.[26]

By contrast, the reader is subjected to the excruciating characters of Sir Simon Synod and Sir John Presbyter, both of whom speak in the tracts, and are represented dramatically or pictorially. Using the title of knight was a way of ridiculing any foolish priest at the time, while the latter name as a whole might be an ironic parody of the revered figure of Prester John. The theatrical association of the Martinist pamphlets with the Shakespearian representation of the foolish priest, Sir Oliver Mar-text, is apparent. Indeed, the Presbyterians are seen to behave precisely as hedge-priests, from the *Commedia dell'Arte*, but in a negative way: "why did you your selves put to your hands with such violence to break down the HEDGE by pulling up the *Hedge-stakes* thereof, the Lord Bishops, &c. as was evident by your

Petitioning and Preaching against them.'' This is especially so given the frequency with which Presbyterians referred to the vineyard as an image of the place which God's husbandmen, the Presbyters, had to cultivate. There may also be associations with genuine leading Presbyterians, like Simeon Ashe, though he is referred to in the tracts in his own right.[27]

As with Martin, the mutable nature of these characters is evident. They are both allegorical personifications of the Presbyterian movement, and vice characters, whose recognisable mannerisms figure forth the short-comings of the Presbyterian ideal. The impression is one of fearful, miserly lowness, which is devilish in its gluttony: "O how we gloz'd and fawn'd upon them! were fit to stroake them on the heads, and call them our *white Boyes*, while neatly we flatter'd them out of their Liberties; (*O divine pollicy!*) and cozen'd the fooles of all, (*Hoh, hoh, hoh, The Divell he laugh'd aloud:*).''[28] Sir John appears as a *miles gloriosus* of sorts in *The Araignment Of Mr. Persecvtion* (p. 9), though in the following pamphlets, *A Sacred Decretall* and *Martin's Eccho*, he is made into a young baby with one of the chief English Presbyterians, John Bastwick, and the Scot, Jockey, as his godfathers, and the Whore of Babylon as his godmother, an inverse parallel to Martin Marpriest's own genealogy. He is given a *corall*, a teething ring, to stifle his miserable wailings, the *corall* standing for the Ordinance for Tithes passed by a Parliament in which the Presbyterians had considerable influence.[29] Again, a Swiftian disproportion of roles is apparent as the source of the comic effect, a ridiculing by diminishment, by describing Presbyterian motives in terms of another set of human relationships.[30] The ecclesiological and the political are transformed into the domestic. Presbyterian claims are made to appear as both selfish and helpless. Sir Simon Synod displays a hatred of the common people. There is also a sense of great power being wielded by dangerous and unbalanced immaturity. The restless child, Sir John, controls the City of London with its powerful levy of merchants and aldermen, many of whom were sym-pathetic to the Presbyterians. While Martin has a strong voice, Sir Simon Synod, who speaks throughout *A Sacred Decretall*, has a slimy voice which is superstitious and incapable of disguising or suppressing his evil intentions. His voice is vain, negative and marked by false incantatory phrases which are self-evidently hollow: "O that profane *Martin*! that cursed *Martin*! that wicked *Martin*! wring off his neck, for *ever and ever, And let all people say, AMEN.*''[31]

What should be noted here is the flux of identities, not only as each character is metamorphosised for the sake of the satirical attack at any particular point, but also because of the way in which each character renames the others. Here, we see the calumniation process going on in front of us within the pamphlets. The author is making the reader aware that he knows what is going on, and that he wants the reader to be aware too. Martin successively enhances our sense of the real folly and knavery of Sir John, whose status is diminished by the lunacy of his judgements.[32] Sir Simon becomes *Simon Suck-egge*,[33] a reference to the Presbyterian greed for tithes, but paranomasia is also used to identify the Presbyterians with the notorious Cavalier poet, Sir John Suckling (see also *Vox Borealis* (1641, Sig. C2r)). Martin, though, is characterised by Sir Simon and Sir John as both a violent bull and a disease.

The animalising tendency is of course an attempt to reduce rational men to beasts. Martin is a dog whose bark is louder than the Presbyterians *"Blurting."* There is also a play of identities upon bulls here. If Martin is an angry bull in the china shop of Presbyterianism, the Presbyterians are likened unto the *"Bulls of Bason"* (Ps.22.12), the traditional symbol of an oppressor, later applied by Overton and others to Cromwell. The allegory is fastidiously precise as it is explained in the text: Martin's right horn is for tithes, and his left horn for the Directory. The Presbyterians become wolves or foxes, the identifications usually applied to Papists, and again a potent part of English Protestant propaganda. The Presbyterians are also cormorants or young cubs in their greed, unclean birds in their attitudes towards church discipline, or "croaking skip-jacke" toads as they had just been cast up from the stomach of the dragon. On the other hand, domestic or pastoral animals exist as an image of social harmony, though the final balance is an impression of threat rather than harmony as the martins, cuckoos and swallows are forced to migrate (go into exile) by "Church-owles," "Jack-Dawes" (Sir John Presbyters), "blinde *Batts*" and "Presbyterian *Wood-cocks*." [34]

Who, though, is the more violent here? Martin has a justified *holy violence*, because he is exposing the weakness, evil and folly of that neo-Papist religion, Presbyterianism. The woodcut which prefaces *A Sacred Decretall* shows Martin as a bull, seated at table, writing a tract, and in the act of writing, tossing a Presbyter, perhaps Sir Simon or Sir John, over his head and into a fire (Sig. *2r; see Fig. 1). It is all a big joke: the bull perhaps winks at the viewer, as if to confirm his descent from the jesting figure of Martin Marprelate. Moreover, there is, it can be argued, a visual insight into the conditions of surreptitious pamphleteering at this time. Martin the bull would seem to be sitting in a small room within just a few texts on a shelf above the table. The horns give Martin a superior power over the Presbyterians since they are associated with the horns of Moses, while the horns signify the jealousy of the cuckold, deprived by the Presbyterians of the true relationship with Christ. In *A Sacred Decretall* a hilarious parody of the Assembly of Divines is developed as an ironic parallel to Martin's horns and true Christian worship. From a reference in a sermon by Matthew Newcomen which refers to the Assembly waiting daily upon the Angel in the Mount, Overton develops the picture of the Assembly as the mount of dunces, on top of which the Earl of Holland, a leading Presbyterian aristocrat, waits like Moses. The angel is a Scotsman, the Kirk, with whom the Earl has wrestled in the past on the verges of the mount, presumably a reference to the Bishops' War. The joke returns to the issue of Scriptural interpretation: in Scotland, the mount is called *"Dunce-Hill,'* but in England it is deceitfully rendered as *"Mount-Sion,"* referring to its popular name, Sion College. There is a sense of modesty and secrecy, as though Overton were trying to show the state to which the censorship has pushed

Fig. 1.   Richard Overton; *A Sacred Decretall* (31 May 1645), Sig. *2r.
Bodleian Library, 4°V.8.(13) Th.Bs.

radical religious writers. There is also a visual impression of overthrowing, suggestive of the phrase *overturning* which was to become so popular with the radicals in the later 1640s and the 1650s.[35] Presbyterianism, Popery in disguise, is thrown over as part of the old order. Overton's name, a homonym of *overturning*, signifies his aptness for his active role in this usurpation.

In fact, the Marpriest tracts repeatedly enforce "God's Vengeance" as the apocalyptic power which passes final judgement upon the Presbyterians. Overton is possibly trying to make capital out of the emergent popular millennialism at this point.

On the other hand, Sir John Presbyter is violent not in terms of reformation, but in terms of consumption. In an earlier pamphlet, *A New Play Called Canterburie His Change of Diot* (1641, Sig. A2r), Overton had comically represented Laud's persecution by shewing the Archbishop and accomplices dining on the ears cut from the Puritans Bastwick, Burton and Prynne in 1637. Consumption both ridicules and makes more horrific the presence of tyrannical violence. Overton's works of 1645 locate the Presbyterians in the tradition of greedy materialist Papists, the representation of a corruption which goes back to the very roots of the Reformation. Sir John becomes a machine-like cannibal who threatens to gnash people between his teeth as the Presbyterian favouring of tithes deprives people of that which enables them merely to survive:

> O all ye holy ravenous Order of *Syon-Jesuites*, pluck off his feathers, teare him in pieces, rend his flesh, crush his bones with your great *Iron Teeth*, make no more of him then you would of a *Tith Pigge*, be sure to devoure him, but you must have a speciall care to chew him well, for he is a tough *Bitt*.[36]

Overton is in no doubt that such appropriations cause real hardship: poor widows and orphans cry out while Presbyters endow their wives with fine clothes. Overton notes that the Presbyterian ministers are well paid: Cornelius Burges was settled as lecturer in St. Paul's Cathedral at a rate of £400 per year. The very titles of *Sir* Simon and *Sir* John reveal the link made between Presbyterianism and the gentry, many of whom were in favour of keeping tithes since they were often impropriators, and were allowed to keep a portion of what they collected for themselves.[37] The champing teeth have to be pacified with a *corall*, a child's teething ring.[38] The *corall* is the Ordinance for Tithes of 8 November 1644 and it is given by Parliament.[39] This fit of consumption is marked by a repeated usage of keywords which emphasise the greed: the tithes are to be paid not only in money, but more traditionally as lambs, geese and pigs.[40] Presbyterians have huge bellies, so that the collective body of the Assembly of Divines, even though it was not purely Presbyterian, still has an insatiable appetite. Here, Overton falls back upon a version of the body politic metaphor, a habitual means of representing metaphorically the political process in this period. Persecution is seen as a means of the destruction of the body politic in *"dissentions, mutinies, tumults, insurrections, uproares*, and *divisions."*[41] It is also another point at which the festive inversion can be made plain in these pamphlets. While Sir John and Sir Simon have *classicall clubs*, as if they were stock braggart warriors, they will be contested by the *Independent hammer* of the sectarians. Such figures become associated with the Philistines.[42] Here, ecclesiastical debate is portrayed as a kind of Punch and Judy show, with Sir John as a ridiculous Hercules with his club, or equally, like a version of the tyrant Nero.[43]

However, these metaphorical envisionings of dissention, disruption, want, suffering and disfigurement alternate with a descriptive register which blatantly sets out the effects of religious oppression and civil strife. Against a background of European-wide violence in the Thirty Years' War, Overton exposes the stupidity of mutually opposed enemies, Papist and Protestant, who will always torture and maim in order to force the consciences of each other. Human history becomes a list of horrendous punishments, a condensed Foxe:

this *Savage Blood-thirsty* Wretch *Hangeth, Burneth, Stoneth, Tortureth, Saweth a sunder, Casteth into the fiery* Fornace, *into the Lions Denne, Teareth in peeces with* Wild Horses, *Plucketh out the eyes, Roasteth quicke, Bur*[i]*eth alive, Plucketh out the* Tongues, *Imprisoneth, Scourgeth, Revileth, Curseth, yea, with* Bell, Booke *and* Candle, *Belyeth, Cutteth the* Eares, *Slitte*[t]*h the* Nose.[44]

The expansion on p. 44 of the second edition of *The Araignement* connects this violence specifically with Scotland and the Solemn League and Covenant, the agreement taken by Parliament upon which the Presbyterian party was staking its claim. In *A Sacred Decretall*, the two indexes are merged, mixing mockery and horrific violence when Sir Simon Synod says that *"rods in pisse"* have been laid for a future whipping of Cromwell.[45] This dense recounting of violence is a response to persecution as well as a means of rousing people against it.

The modes of inversion here extend from the body politic metaphor to a series of plays upon surface appearances. The organising principle here is metamorphosis, fantastic transformation or metempsychosis, but applied to a base material subject. A similar technique had already been used against episcopacy by Sir Edward Dering in 1642.[46] Thus, particular attention is paid to the changing appearance of Sir John. Inside, or beneath the surface, he still *is* an oppressive Roman power, or a Jesuit.[47] As Overton was to say later in the narrative of his arrest and imprisonment, he would stand up and oppose tyranny in whichever *form* it occurred. Sir John has simply changed his dress, so that he is now disguised as a Presbyter. In *The Araignement*, Persecution is shown to have moved through several forms of tyranny, while maintaining the presumption of the "median posture." Sir John now has the characteristic *blew capp* and the *cloak-bagge*, the marks of a Presbyter. This is a clear development from Marprelate, where Bishops are distinguished by the "cater-caps."[48] From the *cloak-bagge*, all other disguises may come: you can never trust a Presbyter.[49] This is juxtaposed again with the simple, plain cassock of Martin.

Moreover, the metamorphosis motif is also applied to the linguistic and Scriptural procedures of the Presbyterians. They are guilty of perpetrating false glosses and sophistications in their writings, "Castles in the Ayre," as well as incorporating metamorphosis itself in their own language, something which is equivalent to the deceitful disguise exhibited in their dress. The opening passage of *The Araignement* traces Persecution through the name of Spanish Inquisition, the casting off of episcopal garments for the sake of Presbytery, jumping down from Scotland to England, disguised "with a Sylogisticall pair of Britches (saving your presence) in *Bocardo*, and snatching a Rhetoricall Cassok he girt up his loynes with a Sophisticall Girdle, and ran into the wildernesse of *Tropes*, and *Figures*." Like quick-fire spreading, the passage accelerates as the figures of sure perception and judgement follow Persecution through the churches of the land until he is cornered in the Assembly of Divines, but in self-defence, he turns himself into a *"reverend Imprimatur,"* silencing his critics. Such a highly wrought *peripeteia* serves to explain aptly, in its concentration upon the Presbyterian use of metaphor, the nature of the trial which follows, for the trial is none other than an allegory of the paper war in which the arguments for the liberty of conscience were put forward in the early 1640s.[50] It is, of course, a judgement and set of perceptions which is imposed by Overton: *decorum personae* had become *decorum rhetoricae* also. In a sense, Overton is also fighting for a truth-status which he knows will be challenged because of the very nature of his satirical strategy. In an attack upon the Marpriest pamphlets, John Vicars singled out the deceitful rhetoric and allegory which Overton uses in his own pamphlet as a figure for the transformation of persecution.[51]

These forms are organised in *The Araignement Of Mr. Persecvtion* by the appealing device of the trial. The trial was to have an influence upon Overton's writings after the overt usage which it received in *The Araignement*. For instance, the title page of *The Inditement of Tythes* (Feb., 1646) (perhaps assembled by Overton) has echoes of a trial document, so that the sense of the reader being invited to share with the author a judgement upon Presbyterianism is compounded. It is also made more effective by its juxtaposition with other recognisable voices of radical religious or Leveller complaint, and the general claim that the Presbyterians use the law to deceive the common people, who have no skill in legal tactics.[52]

The Araignement Of Mr. Persecvtion itself is a substantial success as a trial pamphlet. It is only from this strength that the sequel pamphlets gain their credibility. The voices of ridicule and good sense are built up carefully, sanctioning in the reader's mind, as it were, the more flamboyant strategies of the later pamphlets. Dialogues, including trials, were by 1645 very much part of the sub-genres which prevailed in popular pamphlets, though the way in which *The Araignement* talks about a religious subject in such depth, and incorporates skilfully so many radical religious standpoints and personalities, was something of an innovation. Like impersonation and disguise, trials allowed opponents to be denigrated and for those opponents to be seen to denigrate themselves, only with the impression of fairness or righteousness which the properly conducted trial gives.[53] In the dialogue, Overton can be seen writing in a deliberately popular mode, which draws from both religious and secular traditions. There might also be a dramatic influence in the manner in which the characters are laid out like a *dramatis personae* list (p. 3), while this list also resembles loosely the *schema* which were often attached to works of devotion. On this level, the pamphlet again conflates the sacred with the secular at a deliberately profane and popular level.[54]

The identities of the characters in the trial are established by the application of both allegorical and political names to the characters in a Court of Assizes. The prisoner, Persecution, may seem to receive a rough deal because the jury is composed almost wholly of *good* characters, while the persecutor is the apocalyptic *God's Vengeance*. However, during the trial, Sir Simon Synod tries to organise an alternative jury consisting of members abhorrent to the Independent and sectarian cause. So, the trial manifests the continuing deceit and unfairness of the Presbyterians, while being set in a moral context in which good and evil, white and black, are established *a priori* in the *dramatis personae* (pp.2–3).

Above all, it is a tension between the juridical role of the characters and their allegorical significance, both political and religious, which bolsters the appeal of the pamphlet. In this, Overton reveals himself to be a not unsubtle witness to the make-up of English social fabric, and the way that fabric was perceived by contemporaries. Thus, the members of the committee for the Grand Inquest include Mr Nationall Strength, with a play on *notional*, to point up the way in which people are initially concerned only with forms, outsides, rather than insides, or substances. Accordingly, Mr Nationall Strength thinks in similitudes of the body politic. Persecution has ruptured the *naturall skin* of the *one politicke body*, ruining a model of harmonious behaviour in the country. It is not simply that Persecution has sought social disruption, but that he has wreaked havoc upon the way in which the people think about the peace and unity of the nation. Despite the concern with surfaces, this aspect of people's habitual ways of thinking is seen to be continuous with other, more material, modes of oppression.

So, in allegorically elaborate and complete terms, Persecution is indicted and tried. He is defended by Sir John Presbyter and Sir Simon Synod, who are prevented from rigging the jury by the presiding Justices, Reason and Humility. Persecution is testified against by Gaffars Christian, Martyrs and Liberty of Conscience. The last, Sir Simon tries to keep out of the courtroom, a dramatic representation of censorship. Despite a further alliance between the Knights of Presbytery and the third justice, Conformity, Persecution, Sir John and Sir Simon are eventually punished by being kept in custody by Parliament until the final pronouncements at the Day of Judgement.

The main body of the pamphlet falls into two parts. The first belongs to the festive technique, and is concerned with the play and transformation of identities in order to ridicule Presbytery at the expense of Independency and the sects. The second is the expounding of the arguments of the two sides within the context of the trial scene.

IV

The writing of inversion itself is a kind of endless, energetic stream which could be appropriated for any standpoint. As Terry Eagleton has noted, carnival, like inversion, stands for little itself in terms of content, an *empty semiotic flow* which signifies only *comradeship* in the barriers it breaks down between reader and speaking voice.[55] As *The Araignement Of Mr. Persecvtion* progresses, this element is reduced, to make way for the serious statement of the opposition to persecution.

If the exchanges in the pamphlet wars of the 1590s were characterised by men, like Thomas Nashe, who wrote for a living, and who would invent the next trope in order to gain a penny, then it could be argued that

Overton's style in part derives from the attitudes behind this method. Like Marprelate, Overton adopted such a rhetoric for a religious purpose, though it should be said also that Marprelate is generally held to have had an influence upon exactly those pamphleteers, like Nashe, who were hired to attack him.[56] It is logical enough, given that Overton is posturing as someone *low* attacking something *high*. It is here that the assuring voice of Martin which we have heard elsewhere in the Marpriest tracts turns into a racy voice of condemnation, the accretive qualities of the style matching the trading habits of the Presbyters.[57] According to William Prynne, that unrelenting opponent of Independency, Marpriest was guilty of "unchristian, uncivill, approbrious, Billingsgate tearmes, as (I am confident) no *Oxford Aulicus* or satyricall *cavaleere* is able to paralell." Prynne also disliked the belittling, instanced in the likening of Parliamentary Ordinances to toys.[58] This relies upon a hasty syntax, which exploits the typography of print, and defies a sense of reason in the swift connections of thought, and the repeated exclamations which seem to parody a sermon. Here, both Presbyterian braggadocios speak:

> Woe *unto those* Anabaptists, Brownists, *&c. those cursed Heretickes, for those* presbyterian Feinds *expect but the* word of command, *to devoure them up*: But Mr. William[s], *all this will come to nothing, if this Prisoner be put to death, you see those Sectaries have had such freedom of speech that my Son Iacke and I can doe no good; now, there being not such a considerable person in this County as your self to prevaile.*[59]

However, this is not a Presbyterian sermon. It does not fit with Abraham Wright's imitation of Presbyterian sermons,[60] and also, Martin derides implicitly those preachers who are trained at university. The syntax achieves here its own metamorphosis, paralleling that which is taking place in Persecution's change of clothes.[61] This particular style is taken on throughout the pamphlet by various other voices of good sense. Though in *A Sacred Decretall*, Sir Simon Synod talks in a deliberately oily fashion (p. 17), verisimilitude to the legal setting in *The Araignement* is enhanced by the cool manner in which Persecution speaks, the way that he tries, in a voice of reason, to smear the Grand Inquest and Gods-Vengeance, even in the light of equity. Here, Sir Simon adopts the same description of the metempsychosis of Persecution, from his own point of view, that we witness at the beginning of the pamphlet, from Overton's point of view. The sense of pattern makes the writing more persuasive, as we see the gap between reality and naming: "his true *and* proper name *is* Present Reformation, *which by Interpretation, is, Presbyterian Government.*"[62]

In fact, the codes here reveal much about the context of pamphleteering in the period. Unlike in Marprelate, there is no studied attempt to create a *persona* through specific, especially colloquial, phrases. There is a limited use of these in Overton, such as the occasional Marprelate-like laughter, "Ha, ha, ha." However, Overton insists largely on the clash of different personal and public voices. The clash of different styles must have been intended to signal to readers a particular stance, or simply a distinct interest, perhaps of an iniquitous nature. This is brought out well in *A Sacred Decretall*, where the style becomes self-consciously one of conspiracy. There may be a case for believing that Overton may have played conspiratorial roles himself, beyond pamphleteering. We know that later in 1652 he engaged surreptitiously in negotiations with Royalists, and his references in *Vox Borealis* (1641) to the speakers of the tract as spies (*scouts*) may be related to his experiences.[63]

In establishing each coded speech, keywords are important, for they define the terms of political and religious debate. Gaffar Christian knows, for instance, by *woefull experience* what persecution has done, *experience* here referring to the Puritan word for spiritual knowledge of the divine and of saving grace for the individual.[64] Though the Presbyterians did not interrupt the meetings of the Independents and sectarians, where confessions of *experience* might have been given in front of a congregation as a requirement of joining that church, the echoes implicit in *experience* associate the Presbyterians with the sometimes brutal interruption of separatist conventicles by Laudian or episcopal authorities.[65] Tonally, this is supported by the repeated apostrophes. The *O*s can become tedious, though they are presumably directed towards gathering a popular appeal. They do not feature greatly in other writing associated with radical religious pamphlet controversy, apart from the sermon. But again, they operate to destroy the sense of reason, expounded in Presbyterian pamphlets, and to invite the reader to share in Martin's play. After all, we are not so much listening to Martin's arguments as enjoying the sense of power released for the speaking voice and the reader in the destruction or containment of Persecution, Sir John, and Sir Simon. This is compounded by the use of proverbs, which enhance the popular impulse of Martin. In proverbs, there is no immediate or sustained thought-out sense, but a nugget of inherited wisdom cast in crude gnomic grammar. Alluding to the Chinese story, Overton refers to the proverbial long spoon necessary to eat with the devil.[66] Again, it is an opportunity for us to appreciate the sheer rightness of Martin. The same is true of the extensive classical allusion. There may be republican overtones in the quotation of the lamentation from Horace's first *Epistle*, lines 1–2, "*O Cives, Cives, quarenda pecunia primum, / Virtus post nummos.*"[67] In a culture based upon the higher truth residing in ancient wisdom, and the decay implicit in all contemporary learning, the quotation of classical literature has the same effect as the use of proverbs, except in a higher mode, as it were. At the pinnacle of this method is Overton's ridicule of the Presbyterians by suggesting that they are superstitious conjurors. *A Sacred Decretall* begins with a page of Latin conjurations which call down divine power in order to reveal Martin Marpriest's true identity. All that Sir Simon reveals is the figure of the bull tossing Sir John Presbyter on his shoulders. As Martin notes later in *Martin's Eccho*, the significance of this is that the truth is always revealed through any process of divination. The accusations of blasphemy and profanity in Martin's works is really an account of Sir Simon himself:

"*mutatio nomine de te fabula narratur.*"[68] The doctrine of *decorum personae* is again justified.

The process which is articulated by these techniques is part of Overton's presentation of the process of *calmuniation*, as we have seen already. To identify the Presbyterians with the Papists is to indulge in a form of metonymy, whereby the one is a part of the other, or rather, the Presbyterians are substituted for the Papists. In terms of the way Martin represents this, it is a process of metempsychosis or metamorphosis of the form of carnal Rome through Episcopacy into Presbyterianism. But underneath this, the terms of identity operate through metonymy. By the same token, Overton as Martin complains at the way in which Anabaptists, Brownists and other sectarians are lumped together and pejoratively condemned as one rebellious group.[69] In fact, the Anabaptists and Brownists, on the evidence of their own confessions, says Overton, are full of piety and sincerity. Such a perspective, which Overton presents as the way things are, seems to be the root of all things in the sphere of public debate: thus we see two versions of Scottish history throughout the Marpriest pamphlets, and appreciate the falseness of the Presbyterian view of Scottish history. Again, on the other side, the Scots (where Presbyterianism had taken its strongest hold) are ridiculed in terms of their accents, as *Jemmy* is spelt to imitate Scottish speech.[70]

These figures are nevertheless related closely to the reality of politics and religion. Overton finds the convenient example of the Jesuit Lysimachus Nicanor's (alias the Scottish anti-Presbyterian John Corbet) letter of congratulation to the Scottish Presbyterians.[71] Martin's logic of perception, incorporating this metonymy, sees the connection between worship and necessity, it being an issue which brings liberty of conscience to the foreground. The Presbyterians support the Ordinance for the ordination of all ministers because it will stifle the sectarian preachers in the Parliamentarian army (Cromwell's soldiers are named here). However, for Martin, the fact that the soldiers are responsible for the victory of Marston Moor makes liberty of conscience a pre-requisite for internal unity if the larger, external forces of royal tyranny are to be beaten.[72]

The effect of this metonymy (as it were) was not merely a technique of public persuasion. Rather, it was a part of the genuine political and religious situation of the 1640s, when differences arose between parties and factions over different interpretations of Scripture or legal agreements. Here, the Presbyterians are seen to be distorting the Solemn League and Covenant of 1643 in their attacks upon liberty of conscience.[73]

Each of the soon-to-be Levellers had a device here, however, which enabled them to override the balancing of perspectives which the *calumniation* effect had. This was to present themselves as martyrs, thereby focussing upon the very point where calumniation occurs. Lilburne was perhaps the master of martyrological self-presentation, but Overton was not untalented in this mode. Martin is identified with the persecuted among the Puritans in the 1630s: "my voyce is no other then the *cry of blood*, even of the Prophets and Martyrs of Iesus."[74] "*Synodean coales*" are recommended for Martin by Sir Simon Synod.[75] This, of course, was allied to Leveller philosophy concerning natural rights, and so aids the power of the strategy. Emerging from the sense of oppression, the self is presented as a free commoner, while expression is seen as part of an activity guaranteed in natural or fundamental law, which guarantees the status of the self.[76] The concern with the liberty of the subject, especially with regard to issues of religious toleration was, as Overton admitted, to lead naturally to the more fully articulated Leveller ideas of guaranteed rights. In 1645, Overton's insistence upon the subject's liberties and *salus populi* is rendered within the satire with great clarity. The argument for Presbyteries by divine right as opposed to *de jure humano* is seen as an essential problem, leading to the Presbyterian desire to appropriate land and wealth from the Irish. By setting themselves above the magistrate, the Presbyterians are not only alienating the principles of civil power, but also in spiritual terms, the royal prerogative of Christ.[77] In the 1630s and the 1640s, the individual literally was the object of oppression. Hence the concern with martyrology, a tradition which, when used by the Levellers, put them in line, of course, with the greatest Protestant account of the sufferings of the righteous at the hands of tyrants and the Papacy, Foxe's *Book of Martyrs*. So, using the apt metaphor of struggle, liberty of conscience is described as a building which may be pulled down by the oppressor.[78]

Part of this concern with oppression, suffered by the self, or the writer, put Overton as Marpriest directly in the Marprelate tradition. This was the issue of press censorship. The advent of the printing press had created a new context for criticism of princes and the church, and demanded new ways of controlling such printed material.[79] Marprelate was the first Elizabethan Puritan to make the issue of press freedom part of the content, and the satirical strategies, in his pamphlets. Overton carried on with this method. The Presbyterians had tried to silence the sectarian presses in an Ordinance of 14 June 1643, which demanded that all publications be licensed, a group of censors for different subjects being appointed.[80] The Martinist exposure of this iniquity starts with a pun, *"Pres-byters,"* while the Marpriest tracts are spotted with references to works speaking out for freedom of conscience, William Walwyn's *The Compassionate Samaritane* (1644), Roger Williams' *The Blovdy Tenent of Persecution* (1644), and Overton's previous works, including those in the Marpriest series.[81]

The Stationers Company had controlled the press by a royally-granted monopoly until the 1640s, so that Overton's anger is directed at tyranny and monopoly, in a manner similar to his attack upon the greed of the Presbyterians. Whether Milton's own plea for freedom of speech and of the press, *Areopagitica*, can be said to have influenced Overton, is a difficult matter to answer. What both Milton and Martin Marpriest have in common is a use of the very issue and language of the debate regarding press censorship as a central element in their arguments, thereby speaking out at the very point of repression, while using censorship, like disguise, as a means of avoiding the gaze of the censor. This is a form of the militant and hilarious subversion, instanced in Martin Marpriest's mimicry of imprimaturs: "This is Licensed, and printed according to Holy Order, but not Entered into the Stationers Monopole."[82] Here, Holy Order is the unlicensable spirit and religious conviction of the sectarian and Independent congregations, so putting the imprimatur in radical religious terms, but still in the form of episcopal, Presbyterian or legal phraseology. The refusal to enter it in the Stationers Monopole is a simple statement of what the liberty of the press and religious toleration should mean. Other forms of subverting *official* printed forms also occur in the Marpriest tracts: apart from the self-mocking tones of *The Epistle Dedicatorie* in *The Araignement* (sig. A4r), Martin provides a notice of appointment, such as the House of Commons would attach to Parliamentary sermons, authorising their appearance as printed books (sig. A4r). Here, dated Saturday, 6 April 1645, Martin has the Presbyterian divines Henry Roborough and Adoniram Byfield (demoted by Martin to the posts of *scribes*) sign an order from the Assembly of Divines. The order demands that the leading Presbyterian, Cornelius Burges, and the Presbyterian heresiographer, Thomas Edwards, thank Martin for his pious pamphlet, and stipulate that the pamphlet should be printed, as a *divine Hand-Maide* to the *Directory*, the Presbyterian rules for church discipline and public order authorised by Parliament. Through impersonation, Martin again takes control, and there is a final joke, for by seizing the reins here, Martin has the Assembly of Divines allow him to authorise whoever he wants to print *The Araignement*. After the command, Martin says that only Martin Claw-Clergie (possibly Overton's cousin, Henry Overton, or more possibly, William Larner) may print the tract. By calling Martin Claw-Clergie printer to the Assembly of Divines, Overton is saying that the Assembly need such a printer to cure them of the Presbyterian malaise.

It is not too out of place to raise here the significant role which the actual mentioning of texts performs in Overton's persuasive patterns. Again, because liberty of conscience and expression is at issue, any statement at all is bound to draw attention to the possibility of its own illegality. Such is the case with the quoting of passages from various hostile works, a strategy which is quite different from the Presbyterians' quoting of Martin in order to show what to them is self-evident error.[83] The ultimate manifestation of this is when the greatest statements for liberty of conscience made in the 1640s appear, with their authors, as actual characters in the trial of *The Araignement*.[84] At the same time, throughout the Marpriest tracts, Overton spares no effort in quoting directly, and in most cases accurately, from the works of opponents, both heresiography and sermons. The jesting voice of Martin or the foolish voice of the Presbyterian knights is vindicated precisely because of the presented quotations, while the hypocrisy of Presbyterian language here can also be exposed. By quoting a phrase from a 1641 anti-episcopal sermon by Cornelius Burges, Overton is able to show the inconsistency of the Presbyterians (who once railed against persecution but who now give it sanction), and to expose the very violence in their language, personalities and policies: "*those Whips of Scorpions, the back-breaking, heart-sinking Courts, which are now broken downe and dissolved.''*[85] In such a situation, the laments of Burges and Ephraim Pagitt for the wrecked vineyard of the Lord, the Church, become crocodile tears. The almost contradictory use made of quotation here is noticeable. On the one hand, a passage from a sermon by Matthew Newcomen inviting punishment from the people if the Presbyterians fail is quoted with the obvious point. On the other, without the same irony, the Ordinance for Tithes is ridiculed for being taken as a Scriptural text: "onely I shall presume ... to ranck it for the present amongst the *Apocrypha Writings*, as *A Divine Appendix to the Famous* HISTORY *of* BELL *and the* DRAGON.''[86] Working within the pervasive food frame of reference in these tracts, Presbyterian books and laws, like the Solemn League and Covenant, become bait on which to hook the people, large phrases with which to dupe the minds of the population: *"Huick discipline omnes orbis principes & Monarchas fasces suos submittere & parere necesse est.''*[87]

There is a degree of anxiety on Overton's part even here, however, for he fears, as Martin says in *The Postscript*, that a "Synoddicall misconstruction" will distort some of his meanings.[88] Martin does not wish to defame the Parliament, the Scots or the union of peace between the two kingdoms. He is simply interested in attacking the Presbyterian operation in these areas. Also, his imitation of the Order of Parliament is only "to shew the ostentation, pride, and vaine glory of the boasting Presbyters.''[89] The omission of the explanation of satirical principle and practice between the imitation of the Order and the effect Overton wishes to make is an admission, implicitly, of the comic tradition working here. It is habitual and therefore does not need to be explained. Still, censorship is, in terms of the metamorphosis of the spirit of Persecution, the last straw. The genesis of *The Araignement* (p. 2) itself is explained as the frustration with the last resting place of Persecution — in the Presbyterian control of the press — leads to the Independent press going underground ("privately"). Through *dangerous labour* and *through a deliverance*, Overton was able to bring Persecution to justice; which is to say, in the printing of the pamphlet, and the trial which it contains. Clearly, unlicensed printing is considered by Martin to be good for the people,[90] while the habit of challenging authority by printing it within one's own frames of reference is repeated in *An Arrow Against All Tyrants*, when the 1646 Ordinance for arresting Overton *for printing scandalous things against this House* is reprinted *in toto*, under the imprimatur *Rectat Justitia* (p. 18, Sig. A1r).

V

How significant and successful were the Marpriest tracts? It is, of course, difficult to be precise in determining just how widely these pamphlets were read, what sort of effects and responses they generated, and how they compared with other contemporary polemical and satirical writings. However, there is a certain amount of evidence which enables us to see the complex response which Overton's tracts evoked. This itself sheds new light upon the content of the tracts and upon 1640s Puritanism in general.

There was in fact nothing special about the jesting style, be it used by Royalists or Parliamentarians, though it should be remembered that Overton was a very distinctive stylist. The tradition of jesting as a means of commenting upon political or religious events was fairly commonplace. One such work was *The Cow-Ragiovs Castle-Combat* (1645) by James Fencer and William Wrastler, alias the Cambridge wit John Gower, a work which had already appeared under the title *Pyrgomachia*; *Vel potius Pygomachia* (1635). The Royalist news journal, *Mercurius Aulicus*, was run by Sir John Birkenhead, while the Parliament issued *Mercurius Britannicus*. Both employed techniques of jest and ridicule. All of these types of political writing were attempts to popularise particular points of view. It has been suggested recently that the forms of symbolic and ritual humour which are found in these pamphlets were borrowed from social rituals, like carnival and charivari, and that these rituals were a way for those not in the political nation of partaking in pervasive moral and political debates.[91] If this is the case, and such elements can be detected in the Marpriest tracts, then it is also the case that these symbolic forms had been adopted by a fairly sophisticated argumentative mode. They could not possibly be used simply as social gesture, since they are part of a different language, a much more complex and non-symbolic critical argument. Many satirical pamphlets do not employ such arguments. Instead, they rely upon their wit. What makes Overton remarkable is the mutually enhancing satirical strategies and the detailed and extended argument, very much akin to Marprelate.

There was a series of complaints by Presbyterians and other opponents of toleration in the two years following the first publication of *The Araignement of Mr. Persecvtion*. The first category of these were outraged remarks in the heresiography of Thomas Edwards and the Erastian William Prynne. There were also attempts to answer Martin in his own terms, but, of course, Martinist language for the Presbyterians was forbidden because it was profane. Instead, in two broadsheets, *Proper Persecution, or the Sandy Foundation of a general Toleration* (22 December 1646) and *Reall Persecution, or the Foundation of a general Toleration, Displaied and Portrayed* (13 February 1646/47), as well as in the lengthier elaborations of Prynne, sections from the Marpriest tracts, especially *Martin's Eccho*, were reprinted under phrases which condemned them as "hellish, heathenish and cursed carnal practices."[92] Interestingly enough, the pictures of inversion could be used in this mode, and one woodcut does show Martin Marpriest being ridden by a fool in a sort of charivari procession, as if it were an inversion and punishment for the picture at the front of *A Sacred Decretall* (see Fig. 2). It has not previously been noted, but Lilburne was erroneously thought by some to have been the author of the Marpriest tracts. The figure in *Reall Persecution* bears some resemblance to portraits of Lilburne in other pamphlets. Whether Lilburne was being pointed at here, or not, the identity of Martin remained as obscure as ever.[93]

Fig. 2   *Reall Persecution, or the Foundation of a general Toleration, Displaied and Portrayed* (13 Feb. 1646/47).

Overton did spark off a range of imitators, including an entire sub-genre of Sir John Presbyter pamphlets, and he may also have contributed further pamphlets himself.[94] The figure of the anti-tolerationist as braggadocio caught on and was applied to Prynne personally in *The Falsehood Of Mr. William Pryn's Truth Triumphing* (8 May 1645, p. 6). However, it is unlikely that all of these were written by Overton himself, if only for the simple reason that they do not seem to carry the same types of argument as the Marpriest tracts proper, even though many of the jesting features are similar to Overton's, especially in respect of disguise. The Royalist John Crouch's use of Overton's style, his possible acquaintance with Overton, and his possible interference with one Overton tract, has been mapped out by Marie Gimelfarb-Brack.[95] One can say with more certainty that other Royalists, such as John Cleveland, and not Parliamentarians, were influenced by Marpriest's style. Cleveland's poem, "The Hue And Cry After Sir John

Presbyter,'' though drawing a sophisticated picture of the Presbyter, seems
at first to dwell upon the image on the front of *A Sacred Decretall*, especially
the description of the moustache: "The *Negative* and *Covenanting* Oath, /
Like two Mustachoes issuing from his mouth" (see Fig. 1).[96] But then
there is an unmistakeable reference to *Martin's Eccho* as it gives indigestion
(the complaint of Sir Simon Synod) to the Assembly of Divines, which met
first at King Henry VII's Chapel, here envisioned as a decayed abbey:

> *So by an Abbyes Scheleton of late,*
> *I heard an Eccho supererogate*
> *Through imperfection, and the voice restore*
> *As if she had the hicop or'e and or'e.*[97]

Martin's vulgarity "supererogates" the purpose of the Presbyterians in the
Assembly of Divines. Cleveland makes no statement of affinity with Martin:
he would not of course have held with liberty of conscience. Ironically, while
Overton went on finally to different modes of expression (though he may
have written Marpriest pamphlets later on in the 1640s), his influence in
the Marpriest style seems largely to have been upon the greatest opponents
of toleration, the Royalists.

A sensible objection to the analysis which has just been presented would
be that the complex patterns of satire and manipulation present in the
texts were simply not understood with that detail in the mid- to late 1640s.
The Marpriest tracts scandalised their opponents but because of their very
nature, they made an easy target for immediate dismissal as blasphemous.
The method of satire did not matter. This is a worrying conclusion, since
it leaves the effect of these pamphlets still largely unexplained. It seems,
from their statements, that the Presbyterians and Prynne understood the
danger of Marpriest's satire, and were sufficiently troubled by both the
extreme statements for toleration and rights, to quote sections from the
tracts, without stooping to Martin's level in order to answer back. It was
impossible for them to put their arguments for tithes, ordination, censorship
and so forth, into the jesting mode, in order to answer Martin in kind.

Martin was first of all a weaver of fictions by means of the associative
anarchy of the mind: his argument was effected in the first instance through
that. But simply by quoting Martin within a general frame of condemnation,
the Presbyterians were allowing Martin further space in the entire body of
published materials. Marpriest had outflanked his enemies in terms of
strategy, thereby winning the battle for toleration through his method at
least: certainly for the rest of the 1640s, liberty of the press remained to
a large extent, even if tithes remained, and persecution was still a reality.
Yet, just like his father, Martin Marprelate, Martin Marpriest was to have
his greatest direct influence upon those who were the farthest away from
him in terms of the political and religious stances of 1645.

NIGEL SMITH

NOTES

I should like to thank Dr Thomas N. Corns, Professor William Lamont and Dr Blair Worden for reading and commenting upon earlier drafts of this essay.

1. Joseph Frank, *The Levellers* (Camb., Mass.: Harvard U.P., 1955); H. N. Brailsford, *The Levellers and the English Revolution*, edited and prepared for publication by Christopher Hill (London: Cresset Press, 1961); G. E. Aylmer, ed., *The Levellers in the English Revolution* (London: Thames and Hudson, 1974); Marie Gimelfarb-Brack, *Liberté, Egalité, Fraternité, Justice! La vie et l'oeuvre de Richard Overton, Niveleur* (Berne: Peter Lang, 1979). I am greatly indebted to Dr. Gimelfarb-Brack's work in this article.
2. Margot Heinemann, *Puritanism and Theatre: Thomas Middleton and Opposition Drama under the Early Stuarts* (Cambridge: C.U.P., 1980), pp. 239–52.
3. Gimelfarb-Brack, pp. 337–436.
4. Raymond A. Anselment, *"Betwixt Jest and Earnest." Marprelate, Milton, Marvell, Swift & the Decorum of Religious Ridicule* (Toronto: Toronto U.P., 1979), p. 160.
5. See Gimelfarb-Brack, pp. 21–74. For an analysis of some these early works in the contexts of the drama, see Heinemann, pp. 239–52, and Martin Butler, *Theatre and Crisis 1632–1642* (Cambridge: C.U.P., 1984), pp. 238–42, 246–7, 280.
6. For instance, in *Articles Of High Treason Exhibited against Cheap-Side Crosse* (London, 1642), p. 4, the cross is seen to crucify itself, a reference to its demolition, because it was seen as an idolatrous symbol: "Oh dismall doome, oh more accursed fate, / The *Crosse* in *Cheap-side* quite *crost out of date*." The self-performed denigration is typical of the behaviour of the Presbyterian *personae* in the Marpriest tracts.
7. See Gimelfarb-Brack, pp. 123–4. The suggestion that Overton was involved in these reprints comes from the appearance of the Latin phrase, *"Angliae MARTINIS disce favere tuis,"* on both *The Character* and *The Araignement Of Mr. Persecvtion* (London, 1645). There is no conclusive proof here, and it may be that Overton was merely copying the Marprelate printer, again signalling his filiation.
8. See Overton, *Mans Mortalitie* (Amsterdam, 1644), edited by Harold Fisch (Liverpool: Liverpool U.P., 1968); Gimelfarb-Brack, pp. 84–116.
9. See Ernest Sirluck, "Introduction," *Complete Prose Works of John Milton*, II (New Haven: Yale U.P., 1959), pp. 53–136. For an explanation of the movement of the Independents in the Assembly of Divines to a tolerationist stance, and not one of "accommodation" (toleration for those Independents only), see Robert S. Paul, *The Assembly of the Lord. Politics and Religion in the Westminster Assembly and the "Grand Debate"* (Edinburgh: T. and T. Clark, 1985), pp. 32, 49–51, 262, 540, 466, and especially pp. 477–8.
10. *Journals of the House of Lords*, VIII, 451, 457, 458, 491; John Vicars, *The Schismatick Sifted* (London, 1646), p. 26.
11. *Journals of the House of Lords*, VIII, 648.
12. See Christopher Hill, "Radical Prose in 17th Century England: From Marprelate to the Levellers," *Essays in Criticism*, 32 (1982), 95–118; for Scot, see S. L. Adams, "The Protestant Cause: Religious Alliance with West European Calvinist Communities as a political issue in England, 1585–1630" (unpublished D. Phil. thesis, University of Oxford, 1972), Appendix III, "Thomas Scot and Bohemian Propaganda," pp. 448–62.
13. *Martin's Eccho* (London, 1645), p. 3.
14. Leland H. Carlson, *Martin Marprelate, Gentleman. Master Job Throckmorton Laid Open In His Colors* (San Marino, Calif.: Huntington Library, 1981), especially pp. 158–209.
15. I am grateful to John Benger for sharing with me his knowledge of 16th century Puritan literature.
16. On *decorum personae*, see Marprelate, *Oh read ouer D. John Bridges* (East Molesey, 1588), p. 1; John S. Coolidge, "Martin Marprelate, Marvell, and *Decorum Personae* as a Satirical Theme," *PMLA*, 74 (1959), 526–32.
17. Carlson, pp. 100–1.
18. Sidrach Simpson, *The Anatomist Anatomis'd* (London, 1644), p. 3.
19. William Haller, *Tracts on Liberty in the Puritan Revolution, 1638–47*, 3 vols. (New York:

Columbia U.P., 1934), p. 97n.; Heinemann, p. 251. For Puritan ideas of style, see Harold Fisch, "Puritanism and the Reform of Prose Style," *ELH*, 19 (1952), 229–48.

20. John Penry, *A Treatise Wherein Is Manifestlie Proved, That Reformation And Those that sincerely fauor the same, are vnjustly charged to be enemies, vnto hir Maiestie, and the state* (Edinburgh, 1590), Sig. B2v; Marprelate, *Oh read ouer D. John Bridges*, p. 2.

21. *Hay any worke for Cooper* (Coventry, 1589), pp. 7–8.

22. Simpson, p. 3. On the effects of calumniation, see John K. Graham, "'Independent' and 'Presbyterian'. A Study of Religious and Political Language and the Politics of Words During the English Civil War, c. 1640–1646" (unpublished Ph. D. dissertation, Washington University, 1978).

23. *The Araignement Of Mr. Persecvtion*, Sig. A2r. Margery Marpriest's *Vox Borealis* (London, 1641, ?1639) has also been attributed to Overton (see Gimelfarb-Brack, pp. 124–6) but it awaits a full analysis of its ingenious satire on the Bishops' War in terms of Cavalier culture and the politics of drama in the late 1630s.

24. *Divine Observations*, Sig. A1r.

25. *Martin's Eccho*, p. 8.

26. *A Sacred Decretall*, p. 24; *The Araignement*, pp. 9, 12–13. A "back-sword" is a broad sword with one cutting edge only.

27. See Shakespeare's *As You Like It*; *Martin's Eccho*, p. 7; for vineyard images, see John Vicars, pp. 1, 4. For the connection with the erosion of the sense of parish boundary by enclosures, see David Underdown, *Revel, Riot and Rebellion. Popular Politics and Culture in England 1603–1660* (Oxford: Clarendon P., 1985), pp. 80–1.

28. *A Sacred Decretall*, p. 13.

29. Ibid., p. 21.

30. *Martin's Eccho*, p. 3; *A Defiance Against All Arbitrary Usurpations* (London, 1646), p. 1.

31. *A Sacred Decretall*, pp. 17, 5, 10, 13, 8.

32. *The Araignement*, p. 19.

33. *Martin's Eccho*, p. 5.

34. *The Araignement*, Sig. A3v, pp. 15, 16; *A Sacred Decretall*, pp. 3, 9.

35. The Biblical reference here is Ezek. 21.27. See N. Smith, "'The Interior Word': Aspects of the Use of Language and Rhetoric in Radical Puritan and Sectarian Literature, c. 1640–c. 1660" (unpublished D. Phil. thesis, University of Oxford, 1985), pp. 387–8.

36. *A Sacred Decretall*, p. 8. In *The Araignement*, p. 43, Overton gives the Biblical root of this image in Dan. 7.7.

37. *The Araignement*, p. 43.

38. *The Araignement*, p. 21.

39. See C. H. Firth and R. S. Rait, *Acts and Ordinances of the Interregnum, 1642–1660*, 2 vols. (London, HMSO, 1911), I, pp. 567–9.

40. *The Araignement*, p. 18.

41. *The Araignement*, p. 27.

42. *The Araignement*, pp. 22, 31.

43. *The Araignement*, p. 22; *Martin's Eccho*, p. 13.

44. *The Araignement*, p. 10.

45. *A Sacred Decretall*, p. 16.

46. Sir Edward Derling, *A Consideration And A Resolution* (London, 1642), pp. 5–6, where the transfer of votes from convocation to synod is ridiculed by comparison with metamorphosis, metempsychosis and transubstantiation.

47. *A Sacred Decretall*, p. 6.

48. Martin Marprelate, *Oh read ouer D. John Bridges*, p. 50. Catercaps were four-cornered academic caps.

49. *A Sacred Decretall*, p. 20; see also John Milton, *Paradise Lost*, III, *ll*. 474–97, for a comparison of this dress with the habits of those in limbo.

50. *The Araignement*, pp. 1–2, 16–18. "Bocardo" is a singularly apt word because it meant both prison and a difficult stage in syllogistic argument. So, Presbyterians are trapped by their apparel, both in body and in mind.

51. Vicars, pp. 2, 32.

52. *Martin's Eccho*, p. 9.

53. *The Araignement*, pp. 31, 33–34.
54. The most famous and influential religious dialogue of the 17th century was Arthur Dent's *The Plain Mans Pathway to Heaven* (London, 1601).
55. Terry Eagleton, *Walter Benjamin or Towards a Revolutionary Criticism* (London: Verso Editions, 1981), p. 146.
56. See Sandra Clark, *The Elizabethan Pamphleteers. Popular Moralistic Pamphlets 1580–1640* (London: Athlone P., 1983), pp. 25–8.
57. *The Araignement*, p. 36.
58. William Prynne, *A Fresh Discovery* (London, 1645), p. 15.
59. *The Araignement*, p. 41.
60. Abraham Wright, *Five Sermons, In Five several Styles* (London, 1656), "The Fourth Sermon, Which is that in the Presbyterian Style, or Way of Preaching," pp. [67]–159.
61. *The Araignement*, p. 1.
62. *The Araignement*, p. 34.
63. See Brailsford, p. 624, and for full details, Gimelfarb-Brack, pp. 287–304. Prior to his exile in Holland in the later part of 1654, Overton also offered his services to the Protectorate government, as he feared a conspiracy of those "of great abilities and interest agn.t the Governm.t": Bodleian Library, MS Rawl. A. 18, fol. 74.
64. *The Araignement*, pp. 13–14.
65. *The Araignement*, p. 2.
66. *A Sacred Decretall*, p. 4.
67. *The Araignement*, p. 45.
68. *Martin's Eccho*, p. 15.
69. *Divine Observations*, Sig. A1r.
70. *A Sacred Decretall*, pp. 17–18.
71. *A Sacred Decretall*, p. 19. See [John Corbet], *The Epistle Congratulatorie of Lysimachus Nicanor Of the Societie of Jesu, to the Covenanters in Scotland* (?London, 1640).
72. *A Sacred Decretall*, p. 14. See also *The Araignement*, p. 42.
73. *The Araignement*, p. 34.
74. *The Araignement*, p. 17.
75. *A Sacred Decretall*, p. 9.
76. *The Araignement*, p. 34.
77. *The Araignement*, p. 28.
78. *Divine Observations*, p. 6.
79. See F. S. Siebert, *Freedom of the Press in England 1476–1776* (Urbana, Ill., Univ. of Illinois P., 1952), pp. 21–233.
80. Firth and Rait, I, 184–7.
81. *The Araignement*, pp. 32, 41; *A Sacred Decretall*, pp. 1–2.
82. *The Araignement*, Sig. A1r.
83. *A Sacred Decretall*, pp. 6–7.
84. *The Araignement*, p. 37.
85. *Martin's Eccho*, p. 11.
86. *The Ordinance For Tythes Dismounted*, p. 38.
87. *A Sacred Decretall*, p. 7.
88. *The Araignement*, p. 46.
89. *The Araignement*, p. 46.
90. *A Defiance Against All Arbitrary Usurpations* (London, 1646), p. 18.
91. See Stuart Clark, "Inversion, Misrule and the Meaning of Witchcraft", *Past and Present*, 87 (1980), 98–127; Underdown, pp. 39, 55, 100–1, 178, 254.
92. *Proper Persecution, or the Sandy Foundation of a general Toleration* (London, 1646).
93. For the suggestion that Lilburne was the author of the Marpriest tracts, see William Prynne, *The Lyar Confounded* (London, 1645), pp. 6, 10.

94. See especially *The Ghost Of Sr. John Presbjter* (London, 11 August 1647) and *The last Will and Testament, Of Sir Iohn Presbyter* (London, 22 July 1647).
95. Gimelfarb-Brack, pp. 437–69.
96. John Cleveland, *Poems*, edited by Brian Morris and Eleanor Whithington (Oxford: Clarendon P., 1967), p. 45. A date not earlier than 1646 is offered for this poem by Morris and Whithington: Cleveland, p. 167.
97. Cleveland, p. 46.

Figures 1 and 2 are reproduced by kind permission of the Bodleian Library and the British Library.

How to be a Literary Reader of Hobbes's Most Famous Chapter

Chapter thirteen, "Of the *Naturall Condition* of Mankind, as concerning their Felicity, and Misery," is rightfully *Leviathan*'s most popular, anthologized chapter. It is overtly philosophical in content and representative of a substantial part of Hobbes's thinking. Its popularity, though, particularly its famous paragraph on "the life of man" in the state of nature, can be attributed in part to the high quality of the writing nearly throughout. The chapter can be something to a variety of readers with different scholarly interests. To characterize it generally, like many chapters in *Leviathan* chapter thirteen can be viewed as a separate and autonomous essay as well as related to the large-scale plan of the book. However, to recognize the essay style of the chapter is only to begin to understand why it has proved to be so compelling.

A little like Donne before he appeared in Herbert J.C. Grierson's popular 1912 edition, Hobbes is for the most part unknown and uncharted as a literary quantity. Bibliographies of writing about Hobbes reveal a striking fact: the least discussed aspect of Hobbes's work has been the writing itself.[1] Writing on "Sixteenth and Seventeenth Century Prose," John Carey observes that Hobbes's writing can be exhilarating and "poetic."[2] John Richetti notes the "dramatic concreteness" of Hobbes's writing and his "dramatization of ... thought by means of style."[3] Michael Oakeshott calls *Leviathan* "the greatest, perhaps the sole, masterpiece of political philosophy in the English language." Moreover, *Leviathan* is a "masterpiece of ... language."[4] However, for most students of literature and philosophy Hobbes's writing is a sleeping giant yet to be discovered.

Hobbes's *Leviathan* (1651) may be the most widely read, acclaimed and accessible of his works precisely because it is his most literary, even though this quality is not widely recognized. He writes at the end of his book "if there be not powerfull Eloquence which procureth attention and Consent, the effect of Reason will be little."[5] To achieve such "Eloquence," in *Leviathan* and many other works, Hobbes cannot write without rhetoric, which he himself defines as "that Faculty, by which we understand what will serve our turn, concerning any Subject to win belief in the hearer."[6] All writing may be considered rhetorical but Hobbes's writing is rhetorical to a degree that is expected from works of literature more than of philosophy. Nevertheless, even though Hobbes's writing has been recognized as rhetorical, his use of rhetoric is not much discussed or is avoided; as if it is simply a kind of excess that one will be interested in or tolerate from poets, playwrights or novelists but not from political scientists or philosophers. However, Hobbes's philosophical ideas should not necessarily be considered essentially separate from his rhetorical expression of them. When we abstract, quite literally, Hobbes's ideas from their rhetorical expression we destroy not only his "Eloquence"; we may destroy (or at least deconstruct) his ideas themselves. Not only does Hobbes realize the necessity of "powerful Eloquence which procureth attention and Consent" for his writing; he understands, as he writes in *De Cive*, that eloquence is twofold. One part of it is the

> cleare expression of the conceptions of the mind; and riseth partly from an understanding of words taken in their own proper and definite significations. The other is a commotion of the passions of the mind, such as *hope, fear, anger, pity*; and derives from the metaphorical use of words fitted to the passions. That forms a speech from true principles; this from opinions already received, what nature soever they are of. The art of that is logic, of this rhetoric; the end of that is truth, of this victory. Each hath its use; that in deliberations, this in exhortations... .[7]

There is, of course, much that is *unliterary* about *Leviathan*. Generations of scholars in philosophy and political science have not been totally misguided in their analyses of Hobbes's work. However, Hobbes's own advice in *Leviathan* about how to be persuasive in writing about ideas suggests that in theory, if to a lesser degree in practice, he knows when he wants to employ literary artifice and when he does not; when he wants his writing to appear "deliberative," and when "exhortative"; when, to invoke the criteria of Hobbes himself in the "Review, and Conclusion" of *Leviathan*, he wants his language to exhibit "Severity of Judgment" and when "Celerity of Fancy" (717); or when, in comparing himself in writing *Leviathan* with the "Israelites in Egypt," he is "fastened to ... labour of making bricks, and other times ... ranging abroad to gather straw" (718). To see the *literary* quality of *Leviathan* is no doubt to emphasize, along with its extensive theoretical discussions of language and imagination, those exhortative passages of "Fancy" or "straw" or, as Hobbes himself says, the ways that the book will "please for the Extravagancy."

Not only chapter thirteen, *Leviathan*'s most famous chapter, can be read as a literary text, but all of *Leviathan*'s forty-seven chapters and the book's dedicatory epistle, introduction, table of contents, and conclusion can be considered similarly. Needless to add, the following commentary is only one way to discover yet only to begin to understand the literary *Leviathan*. The history of literary criticism and particularly its flux suggest that works of literature benefit from many different kinds of literary readers, rather as Hobbes's works have ultimately benefited by having readers from various scholarly disciplines. Nevertheless, the time is overdue for readers primarily of literature to receive the benefit of reading Hobbes closely and to elucidate his style.

Chapter thirteen's formal, awkward title — "Of the *Naturall Condition* of Mankind, as concerning their Felicity, and Misery," — seems to be at least in part forgotten by Hobbes as the essay's paragraphs accumulate under his hand. For him, to write on "The *Naturall Condition* of Mankind" is to write primarily about "Misery." Little if any human "Felicity" is discussed. Though "Felicity" is spontaneously and unpredictably cut out of Hobbes's picture of man's "Naturall Condition," the chapter is for the most part carefully constructed. Strongly yet smoothly, Hobbes's tone modulates from "deliberative" to "exhortative" and then back to "deliberative." Perhaps in no other chapter in *Leviathan* does Hobbes sound as much in control of his argument. Its cumulative effect is persuasive. He puts forth a number of concise yet bleak propositions about a human being's "naturall" predisposition and its consequences, and that they should amount to nothing but "Misery" seems inevitable.

The first paragraph establishes the relative equality of physical strength in human beings; "the weakest has strength enough to kill the strongest" (I. 13, 183). The second paragraph regards "the faculties of the mind" and asserts "yet a greater equality amongst men than that of strength." Plainly expressed, such notions starkly reveal Hobbes' powers of "deliberation." They also display his rhetorical sensitivity, immediately anticipating the reader who will find unbelievable what Hobbes states so matter-of-factly. He writes that to

> make such equality incredible, is but a vaine conceipt of one's owne wisdom, which almost all men think they have in a greater degree than the vulgar: that is, in all men but themselves, and a few others, whom by Fame, or for concurring with themselves, they approve. (I. 13, 183–4)

Each phrase of the sentence drily yet precisely opens into yet another characteristic of the vanity of human wishes.

Hobbes continues by elaborating on his own "conceipt" of human "equality" as opposed to human superiority and inferiority. For example, from human "equality of ability," physical or mental, naturally "ariseth equality of hope in the attaining of our Ends" (I. 13, 184). Rhetorically attempting to establish a kind of logical inevitability, Hobbes immediately claims that the consequence of such "equality of hope" is universal "diffidence." Previously defined as "Constant Despayre" (I. 6, 123), "diffidence" results because "two men," though their hope may be equal, may "desire the same thing, which nevertheless they cannot both enjoy" (I. 13, 184). Re-introducing the word "diffidence," Hobbes manages yet another variation on the rhetorically conventional pairing of hope and despair. This "diffidence" makes "enemies" and leads to men's "endeavour to destroy, or subdue one another." In short, as the gloss tells it, "From Diffidence Warre." Due to equality of human ability and, furthermore, "equality of hope in attaining ... Ends" (which are, presumably, "Felicity"), such "Diffidence" is inevitable and so is "Warre." Such a chain of reasoning may sound logical or illogical, depending on the reader. Yet if it sounds typically Hobbesian, this is due as much to the rhetoric as to the logic of such formulations. The links of Hobbes's argument are powerfully concise phrases like "equality of ability," "equality of hope," "Constant Despayre" or "Diffidence" and "From Diffidence Warre." They glow darkly in themselves and forged together resemble an austerely poetic "trayne of imagination," to use Hobbes's phrase. Through his "conceipt" on "equality" Hobbes concludes that "the Naturall Condition of Mankind" is "Warre." This statement in itself would not be noteworthy unless Hobbes elaborated on "Warre" as he did on "equality" in order to present his chapter's and perhaps his book's greatest and most memorable "conceipt": the state of nature.

"Warre" is the "Naturall Condition" that contains the famous "Misery" of the "state of nature." With "Warre" Hobbes sets the stage for the climax of chapter thirteen and of *Leviathan*'s entire first part. (The book, it will be recalled, is organized into four parts: "Of Man," "Of Common-wealth," "Of a Christian Common-wealth," "Of The Kingdome of Darknesse.") The first casualty of Hobbes's turning to a discussion of war as the means to his declaiming a state of nature is the chapter title's promise to discuss "Felicity." It is dispatched entirely and receives no notice until the chapter's last, brief, tacked-on paragraph. Logically however, "Felicity" has no place in the chapter or in *Leviathan*'s part one, and this is an occasion in the book when Hobbes decides to abide by rather than forget its large organizing principles. As the consequence of "equality of hope" and universal "diffidence" is "warre," so is the consequence of all of Hobbes's analysis "Of Man" thus far. For example, Hobbes maintains in chapter thirteen that "men have no pleasure, (but on the contrary a great deal of griefe) in keeping company, where there is no power able to over-awe them all" (I. 13, 185). The "power" "to over-awe them all" in the "Naturall Condition" "Of Man" is to be formally and extensively considered in *Leviathan*'s second part, "Of Common-wealth." *Leviathan*'s third part, "Of a Christian Common-wealth," further elaborates on this "power." There is no "pleasure" or "Felicity" possible without such civil and ecclesiastical "power," as these two later parts convey. Therefore, a picture of "Felicity" cannot logically be presented in chapter thirteen.

That "Felicity" is incompatible with the state of nature is not difficult to understand. The critical problem is that the title of Hobbes's chapter states that it will involve a discourse on "Felicity." Including "Felicity" in his title rhetorically to establish a balance and symmetry for humankind's "Misery," Hobbes seems unaware that he will make the logical choice not to consider "Felicity" in this chapter. Or perhaps the resolution and inexorability of his discussion of "Warre" and the state of nature make him forget "Felicity." Moreover, the critical problem of the unexpected exclusion of "Felicity" from chapter thirteen is not solved by the logical recognition that a state of nature and a state of "Felicity" are irreconcilable. The text contains more than logic. Even though Hobbes does at this point abide by his text's logic, throughout *Leviathan* he continually violates the logic of his argument, especially when he sees the opportunity for a rhetorical flourish. Hobbes' rhetoric is not subject to his logic. He deliberates with it or violates it "to win belief" and "victory" in his writing.

Reaching the point where "every man is against every man" (I. 13, 185) – and Hobbes's use of the medieval distinction of "every man" is not accidental – Hobbes could fittingly end *Leviathan*'s first part. Instead, this conclusion marks a change in the chapter from a manner of "deliberation" to "exhortation." The shift is subtle at first and appears in an analogy that seems extemporaneous and fresh because the chapter thus far is highly unmetaphorical. Hobbes is discussing "Warre" and maintaining that it exists not only in action but in "Anticipation," "not in Battel onely, or the act of fighting; but in a tract of *Time*, wherein the Will to contend by Battel is sufficiently known ..." (I. 13, 185–186). The precept is not as bluntly logical as Hobbes's previous concatenation derived from "Equality." What is now called a "cold war" and also Hobbes's way of describing it are not, to use Hobbes's own distinction, "a proper speech" or literal phrase. Furthermore, that war is a state of mind and not necessarily of physical action is a notion that Hobbes develops not logically but rhetorically. For him it is like "the nature of Weather," nasty British weather it seems: "For the nature of foule weather, lyeth not in a shower or two of rain; but in an inclination thereto of many dayes together: So the nature of War, consisteth not in actually fighting; but in the known disposition thereto ..." (I. 13, 186). Hobbes does not bother with a logical demonstration to contend that war, like a storm, can be predicted by gauging "a tract of *time*" which precedes it. For him an analogy suffices. Not the product of "deliberation," it is a subtle, easy-going form of "exhortation."

Turning to "The Incommodities of ... Warre," "where every man is Enemy to every man," Hobbes's shift in the chapter from "deliberation" to "exhortation" could not be less subtle. His picture of "the life of man" and the "misery" of the state of nature is pure "exhortation."

As a concept it is also a philosophical convention. Presenting his state of nature Hobbes conceives an original way to state and develop, in Wyndham Lewis' words (though he was speaking of Machiavelli's views), "the same black material of social truth to which hundreds of other philosophers have subscribed."[8] Scholars sometimes consider Hobbes's state of nature to be a kind of logical by-product of his essentially maintaining viewpoints like materialism, empirical rationalism, naturalistic egoism, psychological egoism, misanthropic pessimism, positivism, nominalism, atheism. Hobbes is sometimes considered prototypically modern in his disillusionment with human nature and its political institutions. But Hobbes is no more disillusioned or modern regarding human origins than the prophets of the Old Testament, most Greek and Roman writers, St. Paul, the Fathers of the Church and a host of pre-Romantic writers who consider political human nature. Furthermore Hobbes demonstrates in his writing that he knows such sources well. They are themselves an eloquent combination of logic and rhetoric, deliberation and exhortation, and they provide a rich background for Hobbes's "state of nature"; against which any list of twentieth-century philosophical "isms" is a poor foreground. To imagine a prehistoric, anarchic state of chaos and confusion in which people act like wild animals is a convention of classical literature, as in Thucydides, Lucretius or Horace.

The "Eloquence" of Hobbes's work becomes apparent through the realization that he hardly invents either cultural pessimism, which is manifest in his views on human nature in the "state of nature," or, for that matter, the political solution of absolute sovereignty and one-man rule. Hobbes's rhetorical elaborations on these conventional ideas contain some of his most impressive "Eloquence." His powers of rhetorical invention result in the significant difference between actually imagining man's life in a "state of nature" and merely feeling vague dread at the prospect of civil disorder; or similarly, in the difference between the almost inarticulate yet common need for a single, strong political sovereign, and Hobbes's elaborate, mythical delineation of the one person extravagantly named "Leviathan." Hobbes's widely praised powers of deduction are most apparent in the imaginative, creative visions of political disorder and order which he deduces from commonplace political notions.

This is not to say that the commonplace political notions which Hobbes expresses with great rhetorical flair are the only political truisms circulating through the civil turbulence of the 1640s and 1650s. Hobbes may be the heir of a major tradition in Western thought about political human nature, but that tradition consists of several, brightly contrasting strands. For example, Milton, Winstanley, Clarendon and Filmer also represent widely held seventeenth-century political assumptions or conventions and, furthermore, these writers, too, express them with great literary originality and style. Each of these writers maintains different premises about political rights, and they radically differ from what Hobbes argues. Yet precisely Hobbes's "Eloquence" in articulating his own views is what establishes his work within a great tradition of English writing that is political and literary. Hobbes may even be the greatest exponent of such a genre. His vision of the state of nature is more immediate, widely recognized, timeless and untrammeled than any viewpoint on human origins put forth by Winstanley, Clarendon and Filmer. Hobbes's view is also pithily and memorably expressed. Only Milton is more eloquent about human origins, although this is the case in *Paradise Lost* (1667) and not in *The Tenure of Kings and Magistrates* (1649). Nevertheless, the latter argues with undeniable eloquence of its own, as Douglas Bush notes, "that sovereign power resides always with the people, who may recall it and depose or even execute a monarch if he abuses his trust."[9] For Hobbes the people must relinquish this "power" unequivocally and absolutely to their sovereign monarch; otherwise they shall live and die in a state of nature or, which is almost as awful, a "Kingdome of Dark-nesse," as Hobbes calls it in *Leviathan*'s fourth part. Hobbes's view of the original political covenant between the ruled and the ruler also differs from Clarendon's. As George Miller states,

"Originally," for Clarendon, means beginning with Adam. ... He begins by rejecting Hobbes's view that outside of civil states man exists in a natural condition of war ... Man began ... not in a state of war, but a state of peace, and Adam was the "sole monarch" of the world. This absolute monarchy experienced neither "sedition" nor "civil war" until after the Flood.[10]

Robert Filmer too reads Genesis as a literal yet divine statement about human, political origins. In *Observations Concerning the Originall of Government* (1652) and *Patriarcha* (1680), Filmer argues that, again in Bush's words,

The State is the macrocosm of the family. All government is arbitrary; the only question is who shall exercise it, and God and scriptural history, reason, and nature have once and for all established the absolute monarch, the magnified *paterfamilias*, as the only real sovereign. No group has the moral authority of a sovereign, and representative government, strictly considered, is only a legal fiction.[11]

To leave aside for now just what is "fiction" or what is "magnified" in both Clarendon and Filmer's literal yet elaborate readings of the simple, sketchy Genesis narrative, to turn to Gerrard Winstanley's account of political origins and rights is again to observe how a great political writer employs a myth to substantiate or legitimatize a contemporary thesis about sovereignty. Unlike Filmer and Clarendon yet more like Hobbes, Winstanley eschews a literal reading of Genesis to create an historical political paradigm. He upholds and elaborates a vision of pristine, egalitarian pre-Norman England, a commonplace of English radical thought, which contemporary government should restore. For Hobbes there is no original historical order, biblical or Norman, to restore. Milton, Clarendon, Filmer and Winstanley offer a myth about the origins of political human nature that is more optimistic than Hobbes's view of an original, anarchic state of chaos. Moreover, because none of these writers is optimistic about the course of contemporary English politics, they hope that the rhetorical power of their arguments will "win belief" from the factions to whom they appeal.

Remaining silent about these alternative visions of the origins of political human nature, Hobbes writes in a kind of vacuum. Noting neither the Genesis account nor any verifiable historical period as a paradigm of political perfection, Hobbes generates a stark sense of absence. A reader expects more than Hobbes's state of nature to illustrate his philosophical contentions. It denies not only that a good and decent political order once existed. Excluding it from his text, Hobbes writes as if the possibility of reality conforming to such political ideals is not even worth mentioning. Filmer, Winstanley, Milton and Clarendon with their ideal visions of political origins gasp and cease to exist in the vacuum of Hobbes's state of nature. Yet his own "Eloquence" is "powerfull" and thrives in such a condition.

To consider Hobbes's idea of the "state of nature" itself is to realize that the "Eloquence" of its expression reveals Hobbes both logically and rhetorically elaborating on this philosophical convention of innate human depravity. Also apparent is that the most famous six words that Hobbes ever wrote – chapter thirteen's characterization of "the life of man" (I. 13, 186) – are indeed most widely appreciated not through accident or ignorance but because of Hobbes's "Eloquence," his unique mixture of logic and rhetoric on this matter.

Reading Hobbes, Robert Filmer argues that the republican ideals of "heathen" writers, like Aristotle and Cicero, merely represent "a conceit of original freedom" because they do not derive their political principles from life as it is represented in Scripture.[12] Classical political theorists consider man in the original state of nature to be subject to no one. For Filmer, however, man in his original state, as in Genesis, is absolutely subject to his Creator. By this criterion of Scripture, Hobbes's "horrid condition of pure nature ... called a state of war of all men against all men,"[13] to use Filmer's words again, is also a "conceit." It is imaginary and hypothetical with no actual historical or political reality and not, at least explicitly, derived from Scripture. Furthermore, this "horrid condition" is metaphorical because it can easily represent political conditions like those of interregnum England, Thucydides' Athens or any state of civil chaos. Still, although Hobbes's "state of nature" may be a classical convention, conceit, or metaphor, this does not disallow it as a philosophical "given."

In seventeenth-century literature Hobbes is not alone in presenting a "vision" or "conceit" of man's primal beginnings. He is perhaps more special in offering a post-lapsarian picture. Filmer, Milton, Clarendon, Winstanley, Richard Overton, the Levellers and the Diggers also present elaborate visions – "conceits" when compared with the original Genesis or historical accounts – of man's first state. Hobbes's "state of nature" clearly is as much a conceit about man's beginning as Filmer's "Patriarchy," Milton's "Paradise," Clarendon's antediluvian Canaan and Winstanley's pre-Norman England. Nevertheless, each writer imagines a first state in order to express what he considers to be the crucial elements of human nature and society. The political consequences when Adam the great patriarch no longer rules (Filmer) and the personal consequences of his "first disobedience" (Milton) precipitate the "Misery" of "Mankind" as found in *Leviathan*'s thirteenth chapter. Moreover, the horror of Hobbes's picture of a state of nature at the human animal's origin is similar to Winstanley's vision, presented in the Diggers' first manifesto, *The True Levellers Standard Advanced: Or, The State of Community Opened, and Presented to the Sons of Men* (1649), of the heirs of "The *Norman* Bastard *William* himself ... who still are from that time to this day in pursuite of that victory, Imprisoning, Robbing, and Killing the poor enslaved *English* Israelites."[14]

Hobbes's rhetoric in presenting this conventional idea of the innate depravity of human nature is best seen in the process of literary revision on his part that leads up to his most famous statement about "the life of man" in *Leviathan*'s thirteenth chapter. Hobbes is intent on particularly heightening the rhetorical impact of this figure of thought. In a little over a decade, that is between 1640 and 1651, Hobbes states it in print three times. In light of the political reality of the time – the killing of the king and the bloody civil war – Hobbes's decision to increase the alarming, rhetorical power of his idea seems justified. Whatever the inspiration, he manages to transform a bald "precept" into his most memorable line. Chapter one of *De Corpore Politico*, chapter one of *De Cive*, and chapter thirteen of *Leviathan*, each give not substantially different accounts of the perpetually warlike conditions of man's life "in the bare state of nature" (DC 9). Neither close nor extensive comparison of these three similar accounts is necessary to see that the *Leviathan* rendition is Hobbes's most effective rendering of "life" in this awful condition. In *De Corpore Politico* he states that in the "state of nature" man's life is "short-lived" and "the people few."[15] Furthermore, Hobbes makes this mundane, rhetorically flat statement obscure, basing it on a vague historical reference to "the experience of savage nations that live at this day, and by the histories of our ancestors the old inhabitants of Germany. . . ." In *De Cive* this same life is described as "fierce, short-lived, poor, nasty" (DC 12), and the not very specific "savage nations" are identified as "America"; however, the antiquarian flavour of "the old inhabitants of Germany" is unfortunately refined into the characterless "former ages." In 1651, the awkwardly hyphenated, colourless one word from *De Corpore Politico*, and the abstract sense and poor rhythm of the phrase from *The Citizen*, become *Leviathan*'s unforgettable "solitary, poore, nasty, brutish, and short."

Descending from his chapter's rhetorical high point on "the life of man" in the warlike state of nature, Hobbes again adopts a manner less obviously exhortative and more deliberative. "The life of man" is contained in a paragraph of two sentences which are long, sweeping, reductive, general, impersonal, climactic and formal. To elaborate on its "everlasting no" Hobbes takes a more casual, even personal approach. To elaborate further he even attempts to historicize his conceit, dropping his personal argument to sound more professorial.

To affirm the existence of the state of nature Hobbes simply asks the reader to "consider with himselfe," or look in his heart. The contrast in scale between the kind of universal state of war just portrayed and one individual is immense and startling. Yet this turn in the argument's process of "exhortation" and "deliberation" recalls the second half of *Leviathan*'s "Introduction." There too Hobbes bids his reader to analyse or read himself – "*Nosce teipsum*" (82) – and find "the same" as what Hobbes finds "in himself." In chapter thirteen Hobbes is not content with grandly stating a philosophical principle; he further engages his reader in a personal manner, thus employing several rhetorical means for the same logical end. Shifting from a kind of mythological to a personal view of "the life of man" in a state of nature, Hobbes also returns to the more proper, previously prescribed focus of part one. This first view, justifiably the famous one, actually could only be expressed, as its specific terms indicate, by invoking the context of a commonwealth of men. All of its felicities and "commodities" are subtracted through the rhetorical repetition of "No ... no ... no ... no," inextricably leading like the howls of King Lear into hopelessness. Hobbes does not care if his book is not yet supposed to be "Of Common-wealth" but merely "Of Man," and more of a particular man, like Hobbes or the reader, than man in general. Personally to exhort his reader, Hobbes asks him not to deliberate over a conceit about man's primal state but instead to consider a more mundane, practical, immediate and bourgeois set of circumstances. Hobbes asks his reader to wonder why

> when taking a journey, he armes himself, and seeks to go well accompanied; when going to sleep, he locks his doors; when even in his house he locks his chests; and this when he knows there bee Lawes, and publick officers, armed, to revenge all injuries shall bee done to him; what opinion he has of his fellow subjects, when he rides armed; of his fellow citizens when he locks his dores; and of his children, and servants, when he locks his chests. Does he not here as much accuse mankind by his actions, as I do by my words? (I. 13, 186–187).

The appeal is personal and demagogic, yet the accumulation of evidence that adds up to one large indicting, rhetorical question is calculated and forensic as it would establish that the state of nature is a common state of mind.

Having sought to establish the individual, psychological reality of the state of warlike nature, Hobbes suggests historical examples to illustrate it. However, he first states, "I believe it was never generally so" (I. 13, 187). The "I believe" perhaps represents his concern that he not be accused of denying the literal interpretation of the Creation in Genesis; that he not be typed as a neo-Lucretian, as inevitably he was, notably by Dryden. For his first example Hobbes offers a conventional European vision of "the savage people in many places of America...." As previously noted, Hobbes also employs this example in the same context in earlier works. Far more striking is his second example. It refers to "the manner of life, which men that have formerly lived under a peaceful government, use to degenerate into, in a civill Warre." While Hobbes can say that the state of warlike nature exists in every man's mind, he can not as explicitly note that it exists "Now and in England," though his remark has no more immediate purport. On *Leviathan*'s penultimate page Hobbes forthrightly states that the book is "occasioned by the disorders of the present time" (728). Hobbes's conceit of the state of nature is his artful reflection of such specific contemporary, historical "disorders." There is a counterpoint between Hobbes's sense of "the present time" and his state of nature. The latter serves as a kind of conceited or allegorical reflection of the former. Furthermore, this counterpoint frequently echoes in subsequent chapters as they allude to a state of nature and "a civill Warre" that must remain nameless in such a context.

Hobbes offers one more historical, contemporary example to suggest the reality of the state of nature, although he still admits the possibility that "there had never been any time wherein ... men were in a condition of warre one against another" (I. 13, 187). He notes that

> in all times, Kings, and Persons of Soveraigne authority ... are in continuall jealousies, and in the state and posture of Gladiators; having their weapons pointing, and their eyes fixed on one another; that is, their Forts, Garrisons, and Guns upon the Frontiers of Kingdome; and continuall Spyes upon their neighbors; which is a posture of War. (I. 13, 187–88)

As at the beginning of the chapter an individual's "equality of hope" precipitated war, so do nations suffer similar "equality." Earlier too, moreover, Hobbes considers that a state of war also exists when "the Will to contend by Battell is sufficiently known." This "Will to Contend" clearly resembles what at the end of the chapter he calls "a posture of War." Like Swift in *A Modest Proposal*, what Hobbes suggests as a repugnant social or political theory is revealed to be already popular practice.

Hobbes's portrayal of "this warre of every man against every man" in "meer Nature" (I. 13, 188) is not yet complete. While his point is clearly made, he would recycle passages from previous works about the "*Natural Condition*." He self-consciously constructs a formal, drily analytic, brick-like paragraph to contend that in a state of nature and war there is no right or wrong and there is no property.

Establishing the state of nature as a philosophical, psychological and historical reality, and exhorting his reader to agree with him, Hobbes could even more extensively elaborate on the consequences for "every man" who finds himself in the "Misery" of "meer Nature." If Hobbes does write this chapter with the similar passages from *De Corpore Politico* and *De Cive* at hand, he might also include what these works say about "meer Nature" in his *Leviathan* too. For example, he could add that "Every man's strength and knowledge" is merely "for his own use" (DCP 83). Also, "every man regards not his fellow, but his business" (DC 3). In this, "Every man's" first right is to defend himself, and thus "preserve his own life and limbs" (DCP 175). Not only does "Every man" have this "first right"; he "by nature hath right to all things" too (DCP 84). Consequently, "Every man's" right to these ends "implieth right to the means" (DCP 83), indeed "all meanes," as Hobbes adds to the portrait in *Leviathan* (I. 14, 190). Furthermore, "Every man" is "his own judge" (DCP 83), although his "desire and will" is "to hurt" (DC 7), and for the most part he is only "wont to please himself most with those things which stir up laughter," that is, his "own vain glory" (DC 3–4). Since in each of these characteristics all men are "by nature equal" (DCP 83), and all suffer equally from "pride" (DC 39), "all free congress ariseth either from mutual poverty or from vain glory" (DC 4–5). From this, it is perhaps unnecessary to add, "violence proceedeth from controversies that arise between men concerning *meum* and *tuum*, right and wrong, good and bad, and the like" (DCP 131): which quickly becomes "a mere war, and that not simply, but a war of all men against all men" (DC 11). Moreover, as Hobbes writes in *Leviathan*, although "Every man's" "perpetuall and restless desire of Power after power ... ceaseth only in Death" (I. 11, 161), this is not the only consequence of his "hostility" because "nature itself is destroyed" (DCP 84). Regardless of these and many more possibilities for elaboration, Hobbes's account of "every man" and "meer Nature" in *Leviathan* is briefer and less detailed than in previous works. He only offers a dry, bare-bones note to suggest, for example, that "consequent" "To this warre of every man against every man... . The notions of Right and Wrong, Justice and Injustice have there no place" (I. 13, 188). Although he spins a few more "consequences," he could spin many more. Instead, at the end of chapter thirteen he moves to a new topic.

Unexpectedly and arbitrarily it emerges out of "meer Nature" and is, as he notes in the chapter's last paragraph, "The Passions that incline men to Peace" (I. 13, 188). Is this the long-lost subject of "Felicity" that chapter thirteen's title promised? If so, then the chapter could not be more asymmetrical since "Peace" is presented in one brief paragraph in comparison with an entire chapter on war. Yet Hobbes promises that he "shall speak" of the "Articles of Peace ... more particularly, in the two following Chapters." He anticipates it and even seems to warm to the task, as might the reader. Nevertheless, in writing *Leviathan* Hobbes often lets his concerns of the moment subvert any grand or sustained plan that the book is supposed to follow. He does not seem to care or even to be aware that if "Felicity" and "Peace" are to be discussed in the "following Chapters," then chapter thirteen − "Of ... Misery" *and* "Felicity" − is mistitled. Furthermore, in his rush to "speak" about "Peace" Hobbes may not realize or care, though a reader might, that *Leviathan*'s second part, "Of Common-wealth," logically if not rhetorically has begun. Moreover, the ending of *Leviathan*'s first part, be it logically with chapter thirteen or rhetorically and actually with chapter fifteen is, like many other chapter endings in *Leviathan*, neither definitive nor finished but, as Valéry said an essay must be, abandoned. Hobbes abandons chapter thirteen's portrayal of "misery" with a cursory "Thus much for the ill condition," just as in *Leviathan*'s first part he ends chapters six and eight also with the phrase "thus much." But how much is "thus much"? Only a literary commentary on *Leviathan* can show how right Hobbes was in thinking that "thus much" of "the effect of Reason" and "logic" would "be little" if the book's "rhetoric" and "Eloquence" did not "win [our] Belief," "attention and Consent."

CHARLES CANTALUPO

NOTES

1. See Charles Hinnant, *Thomas Hobbes: A Reference Guide* (Boston: G.K. Hall, 1980); William Sacksteder, *Hobbes Studies (1879–1979): A Bibliography* (Bowling Green: Philosophy Documentation Center, 1982); *Restoration* 6 (1982), 86–8.

2. John Carey, "Sixteenth and Seventeenth Century Prose," *English Poetry and Prose, 1540–1674*, ed. Christopher Ricks (London: Sphere, 1970), p. 425.

3. John Richetti, *Philosophical Writing: Locke, Berkeley, Hume* (Cambridge, Mass. and London: Harvard Univ. Press 1983), pp. 65, 53.

4. Michael Oakeshott, "Introduction," *Leviathan* (Oxford and New York: Basil Blackwell, 1947), p. viii.

5. Thomas Hobbes, *Leviathan* (1651), ed. C. B. Macpherson (Harmondsworth: Penguin, 1968), p. 717. Hereafter, all citations from *Leviathan* are from Macpherson's edition and are included in the text.

6. Thomas Hobbes, *The Whole Art of Rhetoric* (1637), *The English Works*, ed. William Molesworth, vol. 6 (London: John Bohn, 1840), 424.

7. Thomas Hobbes, *De Cive* (1642), trans. *Philosophical Rudiments Concerning Government and Society* (1651), *The English Works*, ed. William Molesworth, vol. 2 (London: John Bohn, 1841), 161–2. All subsequent citations from *De Cive* are from the Molesworth edition and are included in the text. The shortened title is "DC."

8. Wyndham Lewis, *The Lion and the Fox* (1927; rpt. London: Methuen, 1971), p. 9.

9. Douglas Bush, *Milton: Poetical Works* (London: Oxford Univ. Press, 1969), p. xix.

10. George E. Miller, *Edward Hyde, Earl of Clarendon* (Boston: Twayne, 1983), p. 117.

11. Douglas Bush, *English Literature in the Earlier Seventeenth Century* (Oxford and New York: Oxford Univ. Press, 1962), p. 251.

12. Robert Filmer, *Observations Concerning the Originall of Government* (1652), *Patriarcha and Other Works of Sir Robert Filmer*, ed. Peter Laslett (Oxford: Oxford Univ. Press, 1949), p. 188.

13. Filmer, *Observations Concerning the Originall of Government*, p. 242.

14. T. Wilson Hayes, *Winstanley the Digger* (Cambridge, Mass., and London: Harvard Univ. Press, 1979), p. 147.

15. Thomas Hobbes, *De Corpore Politico* (1640), *The English Works*, ed. William Molesworth, vol. 4 (London: John Bohn, 1840), 85. Hereafter, all citations from *De Corpore Politico* are from the Molesworth edition and are included in the text. The shortened title is "DCP."

Something to the purpose:
Marvell's rhetorical strategy in
The Rehearsal Transpros'd (*1672*)

The Rehearsal Transpros'd is constructed in a complex of circumstances. The immediate literary context is the pamphlet war being conducted by conformists and non-conformists to the Church of England in the 1670s. This controversy went back to the Elizabethan Marprelate pamphlets from which Marvell derived one of his strategies, that of treating his opponent, Samuel Parker, unseriously in decorum with Parker's folly.[1] Marvell's book also exists in the context of his political work and the debates in Parliament about religious dissent, the history of which again derives from the first schisms in the Elizabethan Church. In such a situation *The Rehearsal Transpros'd* is necessarily much concerned with questions of authorian intention, both Marvell's own and those of the other participants in the controversy. The concept of authorial intention is now a problematic one: so too, though in different ways, it was in the seventeenth century. I hope to suggest that the shared awareness of difficulty is not unproductive. Looking at its situation we can say that Marvell is writing to change his readers' minds, to persuade them of the importance of religious toleration and even, if they had previously believed it to be dangerous to the stability of society, as Parker insisted, that it was, in fact, the less dangerous course for governments to take.

The question of who Andrew Marvell is, writing this book, is however, not a simple one, though not because we know, as is often said, very little about him (we have a not unreasonable amount of information): the problem lies in how we read it. To the eighteenth and nineteenth centuries he was a political writer, defender of liberty, claimed by the Whigs as their own, but by the end of the nineteenth century he became a "poet" and was emphatically confirmed in that status by T. S. Eliot and F. R. Leavis, and the "New Critics." In 1961 M. C. Bradbrook and M. G. Lloyd Thomas gave his political writing serious consideration, a concern reaffirmed notably by John Wallace in 1968 and by Annabel Patterson in 1978. But this has not been the dominant view, and in 1983 Warren Chernaik could still centre a study of Marvell's political writing on his role as a "poet," a figure he finds to have difficulty entering politics.[2] However, as David Norbrook points out, in his *Poetry and Politics in the English Renaissance*, "some of the greatest English Renaissance poets were politicians, and all of them tried to influence public affairs through their writings." Indeed, "the issue is not so much why one should politicise poetry as why critics have for so long been trying to depoliticise it."[3] In considering one of

Marvell's political prose works we need not leave aside our awareness of his poetry (though we may leave aside Chernaik's "poet" if he finds politics difficult). As Patterson chose to do, we may consider the writer who wrote both. For Andrew Marvell, the writer, in 1672 finds politics no more and no less difficult than they need to be and that is not because he could not write a poem like "The Garden" in one of the long intervals in the Cavalier Parliament (or indeed one of the short ones).

In *The Second Part* of *The Rehearsal Transpros'd*, in 1673, when he has established his ground and puts his name to his book, Marvell describes those who choose to write as "moved to it either by Ambition or Charity," to do themselves or others good. "For indeed whosoever he be that comes in Print whereas he might have sate at home in quiet, does either make a Treat, or send a Chalenge to all Readers."[4] Marvell's second book is the only one in the controversy which bears its author's name, but the man behind the book is responsible for, and present in, it regardless of whether it bears his name. A substantial part of Marvell's work is concerned with characterizing Samuel Parker both as the anonymous writer and as the powerful churchman who, because of that power, can write as he did against Nonconformists. The question of the author and the author's intention is, that is to say, a political one.

This essay, then, functions on the premise that there is a historical Andrew Marvell, involved in politics, and who wrote *The Rehearsal Transpros'd*, though this is not to say that that identity is either single or easy. As he wrote his first book, which is our main concern here, anonymously he had in some way to construct himself for his audience. This necessity he used to positive effect. As his adversary was also anonymous, only revealing his identity (though Marvell knew it before) after Marvell's first book was published, Marvell also constructs Parker. As he describes in *The Second Part*, he "intermixed things apparently fabulous, with others probably true, and that partly out of my uncertainty of the Author, and partly that if he pleas'd he might continue so" (170–171). The real Andrew Marvell and Samuel Parker are thus not simple figures, but nonetheless their debate comes from who they are. Nor is the Andrew Marvell who puts his name to *The Second Part* rendered a simpler figure by addition of the MP for Hull and ex-civil servant of the Protectorate. He is a complex person but not an incoherent one, unless viewed in the light of a notion of transcendent subject, the "poet" as Antony Easthope observes, transformed into that "unnecessary" supposition the "meta-subject" of his own text.[5] (The notion, that is, upon which Eliot based his selection of good and bad Marvell poems.)

As political writing *The Rehearsal Transpros'd* might be claimed not to be involved in the current critical argument about author and intention, but the complexity of Marvell's use and definition of authorial subject involves us in problems which purely historical or political notions of subject seem not fitted to resolve. As Bradbrook and Lloyd Thomas pointed out, Marvell's book is often a literary criticism of Parker's.[6]

Further, as David Norbrook has observed, there is a tendency for modern post-structuralist critics to follow Leavis and the New Critics in resisting "the project of reconstructing authorial intention" and finding "that the lyrics of Donne and Marvell are valuable because they do not force the reader to take sides."[7] It is perhaps the critical and not the authorial intention we should now be alert to deconstruct. It may be useful to look more closely at the passage in Antony Easthope's essay, "Towards the autonomous subject in poetry: Milton 'On his Blindness'", to which David Norbrook refers. Easthope objects to the "unnecessary and impossible search for the 'real man' behind the text," the poet, the meta-subject, that transcends it.[8] But to be behind a text is not to transcend it; as Marvell handles Parker it is to be entangled, implicated in it. The kind of transcendent subject constituted in terms of a "poet," a great writer, is certainly something which is unnecessary and impossible and indeed has been particularly useless in providing intelligible readings of Marvell's political writings, both poems and prose. That is, his political writing has not fitted the "poet" Marvell who has been constructed, through various unexamined criteria, in relation to his lyric poetry. Lyric poetry itself is a term which begs questions in this context. That is to say, the author as metasubject does not fit the historical Marvell, the real man. Since the real man behind Parker's text is also exactly what Marvell seeks to uncover in *The Rehearsal Transpros'd*, the question then is, how to define that reality. Marvell does so in terms of political position, power, manner of treating others, desires etc., a reality rooted in social and material circumstances and in history. Marvell is precisely proving that Parker, even in the role of anonymous writer, is not a transcendental subject whose words carry some pure meaning but a real man with interests.

To imply, as Easthope does, that the creation of meaning can and should be a free exercise of the reader's "own productive energies" is to imply that we have reached that state of political perfection which explicitly Marvell intended to emphasize was not the case in 1672, and one can hardly suppose anyone would argue to be the case now. The question of who was behind the text was an absolutely central one in this debate. It is because Parker is Archdeacon of Canterbury, and not just any intolerant clergyman, that Marvell answers him and because Marvell is, among other things, a Member of Parliament for some of the "trading part of the Nation" whom Parker denounces as dangerous, that it falls suitably to him to answer Parker. It is because he is threatened for so doing that he prints the threat, which names Parker, with his own name on the title page of his second book.

Easthope's avoidance of analysing the concept of transcendent individuality seeming to merely transfer it from the author to the reader, not asking how it comes to be "supposed," leads to exactly the "abstracted and dehistoricised version of discourse and subject position" he assigns to "some," presumably other, modes of critical discourse.[9]

Marvell does not allow us, as readers, the free play of our productive energies upon his text, nor himself a free play upon Parker's. Marvell's text is characterized by playfulness and creativity, and he allows us and himself as much free play as is possible to his political end, but no more. The question of the status of the creative individual, the right to believe and to practise according to one's conscience, is central to that political end. The question of the proper behaviour of the subject as writer, reader and religious practitioner, is vital. The position of that subject is complex and constrained, neither the metasubject Easthope rightly finds so unnecessary, nor one whose creativity can reside in the production of infinite readings, the enjoyment of writability, itself an idea that seems closer to Parker's notion of Christian liberty of conscience as comprising the right to think what one liked but not to practise according to one's beliefs. Marvell's text can perhaps help us to discover the variety, the various versions of the historicized subject.

The two parts of Marvell's book, which are really two books, are both placed in absolutely precise historical situations. Their situations are not, of course, recoverable but to read them we must imaginatively reconstruct possibilities and probabilites, being always aware that we can only suggest how it may have been and how it seemed to him. We may begin with what he says he is attempting, in a passage early in his second book reflecting upon both, and then consider the situation, the "season," in which he is attempting it, as far as possible through his letters and comments and those of his contemporaries. There are also the pamphlets themselves: John Owen's *Truth and Innocence Vindicated* (1669), which answered Parker's first book on the issue of toleration, *A Discourse of Ecclesiastical Politie* (1670), the full title of which merits quotation, "Wherein the Authority of the Civil Magistrate over the Consciences of Subjects in Matters of Religion is Asserted: The Mischiefs and Inconveniences of Toleration are Represented, And All Pretences Pleaded in Behalf of Liberty of Conscience are Fully Answered"; Parker's answer to Owen, *A Defence and Continuation of the Ecclesiastical Politie* (1671); and his *Preface Shewing what grounds there are of Fears and Jealousies of Popery* (1672), which gave Marvell the occasion for his first book. I can only here deal with Owen and Parker very briefly. Marvell's editor, D. I. B. Smith finds "nothing could be objected to the orthodoxy of the doctrine behind the glittering façade" of his book;[10] I hope to show that, while Marvell did not want to evoke needless objections, his orthodoxy is a strategy and his concern with doctrine not central. If we consider his book in the political light that he indicates that we should, his position is both clearer and less orthodox than Smith finds it.

At the beginning of *The Rehearsal Transpros'd: The Second Part*, Marvell takes "leisure," confident in the success and generally beneficial effect of that book, to "deduce the order of my thoughts" upon the business of writing "upon that and this occasion":

> Those that take upon themselves to be Writers, are moved to it either by Ambition or Charity: imagining that they shall do therein something to make themselves famous, or that they can communicate something that may be delightful and profitable to mankind. But

therefore it is either way an envious and dangerous imployment. For, how well soever it may be intended, the World will have some pretence to suspect, that the Author hath both too good a conceit of his own sufficiency, and that by undertaking to teach them, he implicitly accuses their ignorance. So that not to Write at all is much the safer course of life: but if a mans Fate or *Genius* prompt him otherwise, 'tis necessary that he be copious in matter, solid in reason, methodical in the order of his work; and that the subject be well chosen, the season well fix'd, and, to be short, that his whole production be matur'd to see the light by a just course of time, and judicious deliberation. Otherwise, though with some of these conditions he may perhaps attain commendation; yet without them all he cannot deserve pardon. For indeed whosoever he be that comes in Print whereas he might have sate at home in quiet, does either make a Treat, or send a Chalenge to all Readers; in which cases, the first, it concerns him to have no scarcity of Provisions, and in the other to be completely Arm'd: for if any thing be amiss on either part, men are subject to scorn the weakness of the Attaque, or laugh at the meanness of the Entertainment. (159–160)

We notice that he means to have an effect, delight is also to be profitable. He excuses himself both explicitly and implicitly from seeking fame, modesty is his chosen role, and it would need to ring true. It becomes clear too that he means to offer rather the "treat" than the challenge, making no attempt to be completely armed and proving thereby that he considers the challenge the inferior mode. Parker chose most explicitly to send a challenge, beginning his preface to *A Discourse of Ecclesiastical Politie* "Reader, I cannot Imagine any thing, that our Dissenting Zealots will be able to object against this Ensuing Treatise, unless perhaps in some Places the Vehemence and Severity of its Style; for cavil I know they must."[11] Whether treat or challenge Marvell's six requirements of writing stand and he invites us to judge his work in the light of these "conditions." As he goes on to justify his proceedings against Parker (that even an "invective" is justified, even a second one, and that even against a clergyman if his "evil arts" merit it (163)), we must assume that Marvell is very far from asking pardon.

To the modern reader reason and method may seem at times somewhat to contradict the demands of copiousness, so we should perhaps first consider the function of this latter, less familiar quality. Walter Ong in his book *Orality and Literacy*, tells us that rhetoricians' demand for copiousness was a survival, "by a kind of oversight," in literary culture from a previous oral culture, when one could not pause to collect one's thoughts. However, as he notes that it survives at least into the nineteenth century, we must conclude that it has some function in entertaining and involving the audience in the writer's, as well as the speaker's, train of thought.[12] Marvell also uses a specifically conversational tone, with frequent asides, to establish an intimacy with his reader, but his requirement of copiousness in matter is a specifically literary one here. Like the authors of fat modern best-selling paperbacks, Marvell believes in offering a good read, a variety of entertainment which may include some pleasurable repetition. John Kenyon wrote confidently in 1978 that the "involuted" manner of *The Rehearsal Transpros'd* "is infinitely tedious and irritating to our tastes."[13] Michael Long, however, argues that the carnival laughter and flyting spirit of Marvell's book is immensely attractive. Long's distinction between the narrow purposes of satire and the superabundance of Marvell's attack upon Parker is a valuable one in helping us to describe how this book should be both understood and enjoyed.[14] Copiousness of matter comes more easily to Marvell's position than to Parker's, for Parker's position is that there is no alternative, and Marvell's that, in the real world, there are always, inevitably, alternatives. Marvell accuses Parker, who beat him in the matter of quantity, of being tediously repetitious, all his dishes being of "pork" insufficiently, and this his chief point, "disguised," or made palatable, "by good cookery" (142).

Modern critics agree that Marvell's subject is well chosen, even if they vary somewhat in their precise assessment of what it is, tending sometimes too much to the idea of freedom of speech when the freedom Owen and Marvell were concerned with was a freedom of action. Even Parker allowed thought was free, Marvell observed, "we are however obliged to him for that, seing by consequence we may think of him what we please" (52). Neither Parker nor his opponents considered a freedom of speech that disallowed action. As to the solidity of Marvell's reasoning, Raymond Anselment even suggests that Parker was the better at theory: one might allow that he is the more obvious, but not only had he really only one point to make, but also he could afford directness, since he had the Archbishop of Canterbury behind him.[15] Anthony Collins (an eighteenth-century critic whom Anselment opens his book by quoting, though he does not appear to have encountered this passage) remarks that "such authors as Rabelais, Saint Aldergonde, Blount, Marvel, Hickeringill, and many others, would never have run into that Excesse of Burlesque, for which they are all so famous, had not the Restraint from writing seriously been so great."[16] Marvell can be explicit enough when he chooses, once, that is, he has established an audience and a permission to be heard. The passage we are here examining is one example, the most notable being perhaps that in a later part of *The Second Part* when he explains his beliefs as to the authority of the magistrate in religion (232–343). But his position requires him not to engage in more theory than is necessary. At first therefore both Marvell's books may seem disorganized and confusing. Even when he has established a space from which to speak he can seem, as Anselment remarks, to be "unmethodical" and his "wit" of a kind that "strains conventional notions of relevance."[17] We must, however, ask why; accepting Marvell's own judgement that his work is the product of "judicious deliberation." His remaining rule of seasonableness is one he frequently accuses Parker of transgressing and is the one least considered by critics. I hope to suggest that it is a very important one, indeed the deciding factor in his writing the book at all, and shall begin therefore by considering the historical season of *The Rehearsal Transpros'd*. Relevance is a political as well as a literary category.

My final problem as a critic examining Marvell's book is that I am confronting a text that set out to prove the disadvantages of making challenges and the superior social virtues of offering a treat, but I have to do so in a form, the academic essay, which is itself far more readily identified with the challenge. I am attempting thus to describe a work in terms which that work itself has set out to invalidate. The critical platitude about reducing a text by describing it is, in the case of Marvell's books, given a particular sharpness. He makes one feel, in making the attempt, rather like Parker. Because of the effectiveness of Marvell's method in literary terms, however hard to describe, I am only able to see Parker's work as not merely a challenge but one inadequately armed. I am consoled, however, by the thought that Marvell would find such a critical dilemma not without amusement. These books are about humour and politics, and Marvell explicitly tells us that the aim of his first book was to show that both can and should be sustained.

In this essay I am only going to consider Marvell's first book, partly for reasons of space, but also because the books are significantly different. This is primarily because the first book was anonymous and the second was not, and therefore carried the name, not only of the MP for Hull but also of the author of the now famous book, *The Rehearsal Transpros'd*. Marvell's first book paves the way for what he says in the second where, although he still must keep Parker where he has put him, and uses broadly the same methods to do so, he is more concerned with presenting his own view. *The Second Part* is thus less concerned than the first with strategies as opposed to argument and beliefs, and is therefore less comfortably considered within the terms of this collection of essays. Strategies are not, of course, opposed to argument and beliefs in any other sense than emphasis of attention. Marvell's beliefs determine his strategies, but the emphasis in reading *The Second Part* must, I believe, be on the former.

Marvell's previous literary work does not lead us to expect *The Rehearsal Transpros'd*, though some lines in *The First Anniversary of the Government under His Highness the Lord Protector* in 1655, do indicate that he had some intention to write on the question of what might be loosely described as the politics of religion, and more specifically the need for continued reformation. Here he describes Cromwell's "pattern" of divinely inspired government and the "observing princes" who cannot conceive of the "great designs kept for the latter days" and "what they know not, hate."[18] He addresses them as

> Unhappy Princes, ignorantly bred,
> By Malice some, by Errour more misled;
> If gracious Heaven to my Life give length,
> Leisure to Time, and to my Weakness Strength,
> Then shall I once with graver Accents shake

> Your Regal sloth, and your long Slumbers wake:
> Like the shrill Huntsman that prevents the East,
> Winding his Horn to Kings that chase the Beast.
>
> (11.117–124)

The beast here is the Church of Rome, a "monster" Cromwell "pursues" towards "her Roman den impure" (11.128–130). It is to Marvell's political work and the circumstances in which that work was pursued that we must look for the season of *The Rehearsal Transpros'd* and the reasons why Marvell decided he should write it.

The Rehearsal Transpros'd has generally been placed in the context of the King's Declaration of Indulgence in 1672. The first book indeed does call directly upon the Declaration as part of its frame of reference and this has led to some confusion as to why Marvell should apparently be defending, in this respect, the King's prerogative in matters of religion, while arguing against the magistrate prescribing religious practice. In his *Reproof to The Rehearsal Transpros'd* Parker asserts that Marvell voted against the Declaration.

When the Commons rejected the Declaration, however, they proposed instead a Bill of Ease for Protestant dissenters. Wallace did refer briefly to the Bill and to Marvell's evident intention to "further the cause of toleration in Parliament" but other critics do not seem to have followed him.[19] If one looks in a little more detail at the progress of this Bill, Marvell's books fit well into the most probable strategy of those who were for toleration, but for toleration established lawfully through Parliament and not by royal edict. Marvell's letter to Edward Harley, of 3 May 1673, makes clear his writing is not solely a personal decision, and notes the forthcoming *Reproof*, some proofs of which he had seen:

> I must desire the advice of some few friends to tell me whether it will be proper for me and in what way to answer it. However I will for mine own private satisfaction forthwith draw up an answer that shall haue as much of spirit and solidity in it as my ability will afford & the age we liue in will endure.

He adds, "But I desire that all the discourse of my friends may run as if no answer ought to be expected to so scurrilous a book."[20] That is to say, there is a shared political strategy here also.

There is a series of Acts and attempted Acts of Parliament against Conventicles from the Restoration into the 1670s. The enforcement of these Acts depended considerably, however, upon the willingness of the local magistrates. The King, whose central concern was with Catholics rather than Nonconformists, though broadly in favour of religious toleration, was not consistent. When Charles prorogued Parliament in December 1669 until 14 February it was believed by some that it was to prevent the Act passing. "Blessed be God," Edward Harley remarked.[21] Marvell writes to Hull on 12 December 1669, "It is enough to tell you that prorogation makes all bills votes & proceedings of this session null & voyd as if nothing had bin don or said. God direct his M^{ty} further in so weighty resolutions'' (96). Charles proved quite ready to allow Nonconformists to be harried and run "upon precipices" during the summer of 1670,[22] perhaps to make them so grateful for the respite of an indulgence that they would not care if it was for Catholics also. Many magistrates still avoided enforcing the laws when they could.

In March 1670 Marvell describes to his nephew William Popple "a terrible Bill against Conventicles" again in progress, now sent to the Lords where "they are making mighty Alterations" in it "which, as we sent up, is the Quintessence of arbitrary Malice." He believes they "will, at the End, probably, affix a *Scotch* Clause of the King's Power in Externals. So the Fate of the Bill is uncertain, but must probably pass, being the Price of Money" (314–15). On 21 March Marvell plainly stated to Popple that it was his "Opinion that the King was never since his coming in, nay; all Things considered no King since the Conquest, so absolutely powerful at Home, as he is at present. Nor any Parliament, or Places, so certainly and constantly supplyed with Men of the same Temper. In such a Conjuncture, dear *Will*, what Probability is there of my doing any Thing to the Purpose?" (315). On April 14th he writes to him again, uncertain that his last letter had reached him in Bordeaux,

> the Lords sent down to Us a Proviso for the King, that would have restored Him to all civil or eccliastical Prerogatives which his Ancestors had enjoyed at any Time since the Conquest. There never was so compendious a Piece of absolute universal Tyranny. But the Commons made them ashamed of it, and retrenched it. The Parliament was never so embarassed, beyond Recovery. We are all venal Cowards, except some few. (317)

On 26 March 1670 Marvell reports to Hull Corporation on the progress of the Conventicle Bill and tells them that the clause added by the Lords leads some to suppose "that it is & will be in his M^{tys} power to dispense with the execution of the whole bill" (104). John Owen had been asked to submit his opinion of it to the Lords, and he pointed out its ill effect both on the trading corporations and upon the magistracy.[23] On 23 May Charles Whittington, the Collector of Customs at Hull, writes to Joseph Williamson in the Secretary of State's office that he had found Nonconformists very active on his return after a visit to Derby:

> It is the same here at Hull: they have their private meetings still and there was a great disturbance yesterday in the chief church occasioned by a Nonconformist who through a cunning contrivance of the Mayor got into the pulpit to preach, and was commanded down by Mr. Crowle, a justice of peace, which caused a great hubbub; had it not been for the soldiers from the garrison, it would not have so quietly ended . . . there is no question but the Presbyterians have some design in hand, it being impossible there should be so much smoke and no fire.[24]

Hull was important as a garrison town controlling the North.

On 29 May a letter from Gilby, Marvell's fellow MP, but more particularly here the Commander of the Garrison at Hull reports, "There have been great disturbances in the garrison, by the seditious meetings in Conventicles, during my 10 days absence, and though Capt. Bennet endeavoured to prevent them he was unable to do so, for want of help from the civil power."[25] The Government evidently pursued the matter and on 10 June Whittington writes again, "if you wish for affadavits, I would rather have the Governor put upon the business ... it would be much to my prejudice ... till accounts are received of what is done at London, nobody will prosecute the rigour of the law."[26]

On 14 June Marvell seems to be referring to this incident when he writes to Hull, "There hath been from some in your parts a misrepresentation hither of that late accident about M[r] Billingsly" (108). This warning may be the cause of Gilby's letter of 23 June which corrects a "mistake" in the government's "information". "Though it is true that most of the magistracy here are too much disaffected to the government of the Church and too backward in the prosecution of the law against Coventicles, yet there is a mistake in the information given to his Majesty, concerning words spoken upon the occasion of putting the Act in execution." He does not report the "words" but remarks, "It is apparent, however, that his [the minister's] coming was by consent of the Mayor, and with knowledge of most of the people," adding, "we do not know how to proceed against Alderman Acklam, as Crowle, to whom the words were spoken, is from home; but on his return I will send Lord Arlington a perfect account."[27] In Gilby's letter to Williamson of 12 June he reports, "Since my coming to Hull, I have prevented the meeting of the sectaries by placing spies in every street."[28] The Archbishop of York wrote to the Corporation on 8 June 1670 to remind them of their duty: "Though I have no power to put in execution the Act against Conventicles (for there may be Conventicles even in Churches;) yet I think it my duty to put you in mind of yours." He asks them to "give good example to the countrey about you" so "that there may be no cause of complayning to the higher powers for redresse" and signs himself, not entirely convincingly in the circumstances "Your very loving friend."[29] Acklam was elected Mayor in October. The business provides a useful gloss upon Marvell's remark that bad laws fall into disuse.[30]

On 1 July Whittington writes to Williamson, "The Presbyterians are so high at Hull that London cannot exceed them, and are so excited by private letters from London, – telling them how their party despise the law, and openly speak against the Government, – that they generally think the King cannot reign long." By August, however, he finds this encouragement to have ceased. In October 1670 he notes them encouraged again by the election of Acklam as mayor, though by 7 December "much discouraged" by "Hayes and Jekell's business." The Nonconformists "had hopes that the House would have been favourable towards them."[31] In London, Marvell writes to William Popple on 28 November 1670, "the Lieutenancy of *London*, chiefly *Sterlin*, the Mayor, and *Sir J Robinson*, alarmed the King continually with the Conventicles there. So the King sent them strict and large powers." He adds, "To say Truth they met in numerous open Assemblys, without any Dread of Government." Though "the Train Bands in the City, and Soldiery in *Southwark* and Suburbs, harrassed and abused them continually; they wounded many, and killed some Quakers, especially while they took all patiently. Hence arose two Things of great Remark," one being that "The Lieutenancy, having got Orders to their Mind, pick out *Hays* and *Jekill*, the innocentest of the whole Party, to shew their Power on" (317–18). Grey records Marvell speaking for Hays and Jekill, on 21 November attempting to get the matter considered by a Committee.[32] But the Commons merely endorsed Lord Mayor Sterling, who accused Hays of attempting to bribe him.

On 5 April the Bill against Conventicles was finally sent to the Lords whence it seems not to return, nor do the Commons, as they later did on the Bill of Ease, remind them about it. On 13 April 1671, however, Marvell writes to Hull, "We daily expect an Act of Grace from his M^{ty} for the Kingdome wch will come very welcome and is already prepared. We labour every day and night almost at the Committee to hinder the report from the Committee of the necessity of continuing that act & hitherto we have prevailed" (139). This seems likely to be the Act against Conventicles. Whittington's letters report Hull quiet and contented, their trade going well, through the summer of 1671. But by December Joseph Strangeways who appears to be a paid informant writes, "Agents from the fanatics are abroad. ... It is high time someone were sent to Hull to inspect, for the stream runs not as it did at the spaw, it is among the seamen and merchants. ... There are strange things in agitation."[33] Frank Bate notes that by December "it was taken for granted by those close to the king, that the issue of a declaration was merely a matter of time."[34] He quotes Williamson: "let the rule be as wide as maybe, and then a provision for liberty to all Dissenters under certain incapacities. ... This to be first framed by the King with all secrecy, upon feeling of the pulses of all parties" (44–6). Owen would certainly have been amongst those consulted, even Marvell himself might have been. Bate maintains that "secrecy" was well preserved, but those consulted would surely have discreetly spread the word. Marvell's letter of 13th April seems to refer to the Declaration and is unusually partisan. "We" cannot surely here be the whole House. We need not deduce from this that he considered the Declaration either in prospect or in the form in which it finally appeared to be the ideal solution, but it would give time for Nonconformists to build up a Parliamentary lobby and show their strength. It would put the issue of toleration firmly on the political agenda.

Thus Marvell's political life was not only much involved with questions of religious toleration but, because of the complex circumstances, his involvement was necessarily not a matter of merely proposing an ideal settlement but of working with whatever came to hand to further the purpose. The Declaration of Indulgence finally appeared on 12 March 1672. It offered protection for Marvell's book as it could appear to support the King.

Marvell himself relates the Church's efforts to suppress it, but the King liked it, as Burnet tells us, and after some few alterations the book was allowed.[35] Because Charles was standing for toleration it was possible to separate the issue of the magistrates' power from the King. The King was, in a sense, giving up his power to control religion, though actually by doing so claimed the right to control it if he chose. Additionally he was claiming the power to put aside legislation. Parliament objected firmly to this and a long series of Addresses was exchanged between King and Commons on this matter.[36] Marvell could only make very limited use of the Declaration and as Wallace pointed out, had much greater freedom in *The Second Part* of *The Rehearsal Transpros'd* when the Declaration had been withdrawn and only the Bill of Ease remained in question.[37]

The Declaration of Indulgence came out at the time of the declaration of war against Holland, Parliament being adjourned. It was aimed at keeping Dissenters at home on the Government side. Burnet observed, "great endeavours were used by the Court to persuade the Nonconformists to make addresses and compliments upon it. But few were so blind, as not to see what was aimed at by it."[38] Parliament was due to meet again in October 1672 and Marvell's book came out at about that time. Though Parliament was in fact adjourned again until February, this allowed Marvell's book even more time to be read.

The Declaration did put the question of toleration on the Parliamentary agenda. Marvell's object, as that of his "friends," was to ensure toleration established upon a proper legal basis. In the Debate on the Declaration on 14 February 1672 Sir Richard Temple proposed "to provide for relief of dissenting brethren."[39] It was duly decided that, as well as sending an Address against the Declaration, "this House will on Monday Morning next, at Ten of the Clock, resolve into a Committee of the whole House to consider of the subject Matter of the Bill [of Ease]."[40] The Address occasioned the House rather more concern than the Bill. *The Rehearsal Transpros'd* might be read as in part seeking to show their intimate connection. Nonetheless the Bill was submitted to the Lords who put it aside. The Commons sent Thomas Lee to remind them of it on 24 March, but they returned it only with a clause demanding the King's and his descendants' right "by his Proclamation under the Great Seal to take off the liberty granted by this Act to any Person or Persons whatsoever, as to him or them shall appear meet or convenient," which the Commons rejected.[41] The Lords appeared, as in March 1670, to be insisting upon the King's power in religion, though now attaching it to a Bill of opposite intention. Grey quotes Thomas Meres, 28 March 1673, that by the Lords' alteration the Bill was "the same in effect as the Declaration."[42]

There was much debate on the Lords' amendments when they returned the Bill. The Commons remarked on 29 March "that we conceive it will be for the advantage of the Church to invite as many to come in as may consist with its Safety; and to remove such unnecessary Scruples as may offend or hinder others from uniting with us."[43] They were about to vote on the Lords' amendments allowing the King's right to proclaim upon religion when the House was adjourned until 20 October 1673. One may suppose *The Rehearsal Transpros'd The Second Part* appeared in time for their return. When they did return, however, they occupied themselves with other matters and the Bill of Ease was not revived, as Marvell and his friends must have hoped it would be.

The book Marvell was defending was Owen's *Truth and Innocence Vindicated*. Owen was important as the chief spokesman of the Independents, as Baxter was of the Presbyterians. Marvell's defence is not of what he was saying but of his right to say it and to be considered seriously, for if he was not, then the opinions of a large minority were also being dismissed. Parker maintained that they were inconsiderable in every respect, Marvell that all the people must in some measure be considered. He argued this chiefly in terms of expediency, particularly in his first book, but also in terms of political morality.

Owen found Parker dramatic, an idea Marvell develops. Owen associates Parker with the author of *The Friendly Debates*, Simon Patrick, whose letter to Parker is included in the latter's *Defence*. The *Debates* were written as a dialogue between a conformist and a non-conformist, in which, Owen asserts, the author intended "to render the sentiments and Expressions of his Adversaries ridiculous, and thereby to expose their persons to contempt and scorn."[44] Patrick was not nearly so contemptuous as Parker but, like Marvell, Owen finds such disrespect for fellow citizens a central issue. The drama is not a fit model for social intercourse, or the discussion of theology. Owen's position requires that he deal seriously with Parker. He criticizes Parker's "new way" of arguing, instead of "a direct and particular debate of the matters specially in difference, carried on until their Conviction by evidence of Truth" (2): "In general a supposition is laid down, and it is so vehemently asserted as is evident that it is accompanied with a desire that it should be taken for granted" (153). Owen puts this down to Parker's youth and lack of "experience of the uncertainty of things in this world" (8). He observes that his language suggests that "he hath been some great Commander" and "has scattered all the legions of his Enemies" (13). Owen also observes that he will take note of "the character that in the entrance" of his book Parker "gives of himself; and such other Intimations of his principles as he is pleased to communicate" (7). In this too Marvell follows him. Owen also observes Parker's lack of "noble Generosity of Spirit" (44), and asks, "hath this Gentleman really considered what the meaning of that word Trade is, and what is the concernment of this nation in it?" or whether "the Vital Spirits and Blood of the Kingdom" must be "offered in Sacrifice" to Parker's "Notions and Apprehensions" (78–9).

After dealing at some length with the importance of trade Owen goes on to survey Parker's book chapter by chapter until the sixth, after which he declares himself "utterly wearied with the frequent occurances of the same things in different dresses" (281). Owen's book would seem a perfectly reasonable answer to Parker but Parker's answer to it required some other response.

The nature of Parker's reply to Owen, and a fair idea of his general argument can perhaps be best appreciated by taking a fairly random but substantial sample. In the opening of his third chapter we find in the contents "Various Instances of our Authors pitiful and disingenuous way of Cavilling," amongst which proves to be:

> How he has bestirred himself to raise Mists upon my clearest and most perspicious Expressions? And what clouds of Words has he pour'd forth to involve the Evidence of my Arguments, and the plainess of my Method? How dextrously does he cull out a single Proposition to oppose to the scope and plain meaning of the coherent Discourse? And when he has got the poor naked and defenceless Thing alone, how unmercifully does he turn and tease it into a thousand postures? and how wantonly does he tire himself with insulting over the feebleness of its supposed Escapes and Subterfuges?

The language serves to license Marvell to reflect upon Parker's sexual life. Parker continues:

> But to give you some particular Instances of this woful way of trifling.
> In the first place he quarrels my first Paragraph as obscure and ambiguous. Why! because it gives not any Definition of the Nature of Conscience, nor any Account of the Bounds of its liberty, nor determining divers other great and weighty Difficulties relating to the present Enquiry. What a monstrous fault is this! Not to couch the thought of three hundred pages into one single section.

He asks:

> Pray Sir, by what rules of Art am I bound to determine the Right of the Cause when I onely undertake to represent the Pleas and Pretences of the different Parties? If I have not accurately enough described the Competition between the liberties of Conscience, and the Prerogatives of Princes then let him cavil at that.[45]

Parker goes on to repeat his "first Proposition":

> viz. That 'tis absolutely necessary to the Peace and Government of the World, that the Supreme Magistrate of every Commonwealth should be vested with a Power to Govern and Conduct the Consciences of Subjects in Affairs of Religion. And though I have at large proved this Assertion from that Powerful Influence that Religion has upon the Peace of Kingdoms, and the Interests of Government; yet as for Proofs, he always scorns them. (217)

Parker seems almost to be writing to Owen's description of him. If he had not been Archdeacon of Canterbury he might have been ignored by those seriously concerned in the issue, but he was and so he could not be.

Owen's opening statement provided a marked contrast with Parker's approach: "Among the many Disadvantages which those who plead in any sense for Liberty of Conscience are exposed unto, it is not the least, that in their arguings and Pleas they are enforced to admit a Supposition, That those whom they plead for, are indeed really mistaken," otherwise "there remains no proper field for the Debate about Indulgence to be managed in" (1—2). This disadvantage is a theological one. By shifting the field of debate to politics Marvell, quite properly, avoids it. He asks why Parker and the clergy like him are making their assertions against Nonconformity and proves that it is they who are using religion as a cover for seeking political power, as Parker accuses the Nonconformists of doing. Marvell thus finds Parker's "pushpin divinity" a central concept in the explicitness of its connection of religion and the state and his reduction of "grace" to "morality" significant in its confining of religion, and hence individual liberty, to a realm controllable by the temporal power of church and state. Thus Parker, by extending the Church's proper spiritual realm into the realm of temporal power reduces it by as much as the temporal is beneath the spiritual. This point is not, however, Marvell's central concern.

Marvell begins with a character of Parker and his struggles with the "seditious meetings of Letters" (5) which keep him from that matter of "comfortable importance," which Marvell decides "must be ... a Female" (6). As "Never Man certainly was so unacquainted with himself" (7), it is necessary for Marvell to depict him to himself as well as the reader. He considers Parker's presentation of Bishop Bramhall to whose work his *Preface* was attached, deciding, like Owen, that it is theatrical (12), which allows him to characterize Parker as Mr. Bayes, who is Buckingham's caricature of Dryden. Marvell borrows the name, professing to find him like Parker "in their understandings, in their expressions, in their humour, in their contempt and quarreling of all others, though of their own Profession" (9). Marvell finds Parker's real skill to be in "railing" (20) and goes on to give for contrast an example of civil conversation, between himself and some "Critical People" (24), who object to Parker's having put Geneva on the south side of the lake. Here Marvell himself appears "upon the doubtful and excusing part" (25). This grew "almost as good as a Play among us." We are, of course, to see that it was a good deal better than Parker's play of "Poor Mr. *Calvin* and Bishop *Bramhal*" (23). Marvell has thus established a character for himself of an amusing and generous companion. He even wonders if Parker "do not rather innocently write things (as he professes pag. 4, of his *Preface*) so *exceeding all belief*, that he may make himself and the company merry" (27). "But he takes care that I shall never be long deceiv'd with that pleasing imagination" (28). Marvell demonstrates that Parker's "pushpin divinity" is his main point, everything else being "subordinate" to it. This is (quoting *Ecclesiastical Politie*, p. 166) that "Magistrates" or (as Marvell quotes it) "*Princes cannot pluck a pin out of the Church, but the State immediately shakes and totters*" (47). (Marvell rarely makes even that much alteration in the frequent passages he quotes from Parker, who is thus reduced to accusing him, rather feebly, of plagiary.)

Marvell presents Parker's "grand Thesis" in "his own words" and at some length before examining it (44—47). He apologises for breaking "decorum" and discoursing "of ridiculous things seriously" (49). The function of this concept of decorum, borrowed from the Marprelate controversy, is to enable Marvell to do much what Parker complains of in his *Reproof*, that is, as far as possible, apparently to present Parker's argument "as if it were notoriously evident without proof that it directly subverts all the Principles of Religion and Government."[46] With asides to the reader ("But now among friends, was there ever any thing so monstrous?" (61)) Marvell presents Parker's argument as "Mr Bayes, his six Playes," the titles being: The Unlimited Magistrate, The Public Conscience, Moral Grace, Debauchery Tolerated, Persecution Recommended and Pushpin-Divinity (48). Marvell appears to refuse to deal seriously with Parker's arguments but introduces his own serious points. For example, he picks up a parenthetical remark of Parker's that only small errors are disputable: "I cannot understand the truth of this reasoning," observing that "even the most important matters are subject to controversie: And besides, things are little or great according to the Eyes or Understandings of several men; and however, a man would suffer something rather than commit that little error against his Conscience, which must render him an Hypocrite to God, and a Knave amongst Men" (53). To allow this would actually subvert Parker's whole argument. Marvell gradually builds up to his final point, "and besides," "and however," making it appear self-evident. When he later returns to these points they seem already familiar and so accepted.

Marvell next turns to Parker's "second Book," the *Defence*, upon which he speaks Parker's thoughts; "in all matters of Argument I will so muddle my self in Ink, that there shall be no catching no finding me; and besides I will speak alwayes with so Magisterial a Confidence, that no modest man (and most ingenious persons are so) shall so much as quetch at me, but be beat out of Countenance: and plain men shall think that I durst not talk at such a rate but that I have a Commission" (72). This, as well as being amusing, makes the serious points that modest men, like Owen, cannot handle Parker, and that Parker has, in effect, a commission, from Archbishop Sheldon. Dismissing the *Defence* as "nothing but tail and feather" Marvell proceeds to consider "the Preface to Bishop *Bramhall*, and to what *Juncture of Affairs* it was reconciled." This was, of course, the King's "Gracious *Declaration of Indulgence*, of which I with [wish?] His Majesty and the Kingdom much joy, and as far as my slender judgment can divine, dare augurate and presage mutual Felicity, and that what ever humane Accident may happen (I fear not what *Bayes* foresees) they will, they can never have cause to repent this Action or its Consequences" (73). This is vague enough to allow the accident to be its rejection by Parliament and the consequence to be a Bill of Ease.

As Wallace noted, Marvell is on difficult ground here.[47] Though he can so conveniently find Parker to be the King's enemy, to protect his own book, even though Charles himself agreed with him, the juncture of affairs in which that was possible was a brief one. Marvell finds Parker's *Preface*, though he would "let it be judg'd by the Company," also "in my poor opinion" merely railing: "And therefore, till I meet with something more serious, I will take a walk in the Garden and gather some of Mr. *Bayes* his Flowers'' (76–77). He asserts that "there being no method at all in his wild rambling talk; I must either tread just on in his footsteps, or else I shall be in a perpetual maze" (74). He thus presents his own book as artless and impromptu, laying blame for any apparent lack in his own method upon Parker. This allows him some useful shifts in deliberately rambling sentences and such diversions as to a "little book" by John Hales, "which though I had read many years ago, was quite out of my mind till I occasionally light upon't at a Book-seller's stall" (79). He then uses Hales, "one of the Church of *England*, and most remarkable for his Sufferings in the late times," to defend conventicles. He is at some pains to appear an amateur in these matters, though his declared "opinion" that Hales's pamphlet can "shut" both Parker and Hooker "out of doors" (adding "though I have a great Reverence for Mr. *Hooker*, who in some things did answer himself") also emphasizes that he is actually very well informed.

He goes on to "reflect most seriously upon the differences of their two wayes of discoursing" (83) and finds Parker, by comparison with Hales, a "disgrace" to the Church, then immediately asks his pardon for treating him "against *Decorum* here, with so much gravity." Marvell thus continuously alternates the serious with the amusing. Discussing Parker's claim that all "the fruits of the Spirit are not more than Morality" (86) he must both question the claim and retain his own character of the detached, rather amused observer. "For, if indeed there be no Judgment," he remarks, "How frequent opportunities have I mist in my life of geniality and pleasure, and fulfilling Nature in all its ends!" (88–89). He then goes on to note Owen's gravity in dealing with the same question of divine judgement (90), and that "'Tis possible that the Nonconformists many of them may be too censorious of others, and too confident of their own Integrity. Others of them are more temperate, and perhaps destitute of all humane redress against their sufferings" (89). Finally he laughs at Parker "for having proved that Nonconformity is the Sin against the Holy Ghost" (91).

Marvell now proceeds to "The truth," which "is in short and let *Bayes* make more or less of it if he can; *Bayes* had at first built up such a stupendious Magistrate, as never was of God's making. He had put all Princes upon the Rack to stretch them to his dimension. And, as a streight line continued grows a Circle, he had given them so infinite a Power that it was extended unto Impotency" (92–3). This attractive piece of geometry serves, one cannot help but feel, to add authority more than enlightenment, and intellectual entertainment above either: "Whereas indeed the matter is that Princes have always found that uncontrolable Government over CONSCIENCE to be both unsafe and impracticable" (93). Having thus established the argument upon political grounds Marvell proceeds to broaden his attack to a general one upon ambitious clergy whose appropriation of temporal power he discovers to be the cause both of the present persecution of Nonconformists and the past civil wars:

> They cannot endure that Humility, that Meekness, that strictness
> of Manners and Conversation which is the true way of gaining
> Reputation and Authority to the Clergy; much less can they content
> themselves with the ordinary and comfortable provision that is made
> for the Ministry; But, having wholly calculated themselves for
> Preferment, and Grandeur, know or practise no other means to make
> themselves venerable but by Ceremony and Severity. (107)

He goes on to assert:

> That which astonishes me, and only raises my indignation is, that of
> all sorts of Men, this kind of Clergy should always be, and have been
> for the most precipitate, brutish, and sanguinary Counsels. The
> former Civil War cannot make them wise, nor his Majesties Happy
> Return, good natured; but they are still for running things up unto
> the same extreams.

Kings, he observes to Parker,

> are fain to condescend to many things for peace-sake, and the quiet
> of Mankind, that your proud heart would break before it would bend
> to. They do not think fit to require any thing that is impossible,
> unnecessary, or wanton, of their people; but are fain to consider the
> very temper of the Climate in which they live, the Constitution and
> Laws under which they have been formerly bred, and upon ill
> occasions to give them good words, and humour them like Children
> (108–9)

He surrounds this observation with references to rulers whose predecessors
were "murdered" or "assassinated" (105) and various stories of how
monarchs have had to "humour" their subjects. Parker, not unreasonably,
is ready in *The Reproof* to point out that Marvell has "not a syllable of
advice or exhortation to Subjects to perswade them" to obey kings.[48]
Marvell implies that kings are only superior to other people by virtue
of their "trade," as he refers to it in an aside to Parker: "'Tis a Trade,
that God be thanked neither you nor I are of, and therefore we are not so
competant Judges of their Actions" (108). Their function places even more
demands upon their good behaviour towards their subjects than their
subjects to them or to each other. Thus civil war can be deduced to be
the king's failure, or, as Marvell here argues, the fault of misleading
ecclesiastical advisers. Kings, he asserts,

> do not think fit to command things unnecessary, and where the profit
> cannot countervail the hazard. But above all they consider, that
> God has instated them in the Government of Mankind, with that
> incumbrance (if it may so be called) of Reason, and that incumbrance
> upon Reason of Conscience. That he might have given them as large
> an extent of ground and other kind of cattle for their Subjects: but
> it had been a melancholy Empire to have been only Supreme Grasiers
> and Sovereign Shepherds. And therefore, though the laziness of that

brutal magistracy might have been more secure, yet the difficulty of this does make it more honourable. (111)

In the interweaving style in which *The Rehearsal Transpros'd* is written there is no precise point at which Marvell's serious political concerns can be said to come more confidently to the fore, but from now on they command attention. He does not give up the detached stance he has so carefully established, which allows him to attempt such observations as: "I say next, that it's very seldom seen that in the same age, a Civil War, after such an interval, has been rais'd again upon the same pretences: But Men are all so weary, that he would be knock'd on the head that should raise the first disturbance of the same nature. A new War must have, like a Book that would sell, a new Title" (112). Parker, unsurprisingly, picks him up on this and asks what will happen when they have rested.[49] The Declaration allows Marvell to discount Parker's assertion that the Nonconformists are not "*friends to the present Government*" and declare, "I know of no enmity they have to the Church it self, but what it was in her power always to have remedied, and so it is still. But such as you it is that have always strove by your leasings to keep up a strangeness and misunderstanding betwixt the King and his people" (122).

Having made a number of fairly hazardous assertions Marvell now modestly confesses that "I grew hereupon much displeased with my own ignorance of the occasion of those Troubles so near our own times, and betook my self to get the best Information concerning them, to the end that I might, if it appear'd so, decline the dangerous acquaintance of the Nonconformists, some of whom I had taken for honest men nor therefore avoided their Company" (125). He tells Parker "because you are a dangerous person, I shall as little as possible, say any thing of my own, but speak too before good Witnesses. First of all therefore, I will without farther Ceremony, fall upon you with the but-end of another Arch-bishop," which is a confident revelation of his tactic so far. He further disarms Parker by confessing, with considerable bravura,

> a particular aversion, that I have upon good reason, against [the clergy] disposing of our Money. And Mr. *Bayes*, I will acquaint you with the Reason, which is this. 'Tis not very many years ago that I used to play at *Picket*; And there was a Gentleman of your robe a *Dignitary of Lincoln*, very well known and remembered in the Ordinaries but being not long since dead, I will save his name. Now I used to play *Pieces*, and this Gentleman would always go half a Crown with me, and so all the while he sat on my hand he very honestly *gave the Sign*, so that I was alwaies sure to lose. I afterwards discovered it, but of all the money that ever I was cheated of in my life, none vexed me so, as what I lost by his occasion. And ever since, I have born a great grudge against their fingring of any thing that belongs to me (126).

By insisting on not taking himself seriously, he deprives Parker of the tactic he himself has used against him, of disparaging an argument by disparaging the person who presents it. This is a benefit of anonymity; in his second book he must be more personally present. He goes on to observe,

> Nay I dare almost aver upon my best observation, that there never was, nor ever will be a Parliament in *England*, that could or can refuse the King supplies proportionable to his occasions, without any need of recourse to extraordinary wayes; but for the pick-thankness of the Clergy, who will alwaies presume to have the thanks and honour of it, nay, and are ready always to obstruct the Parliamentary Aids, unless they may be gratified with some new *Ecclesiastical Power*, or some new Law against the *Fanaticks*. This is the naked truth of the matter. Whereas *English* men always love to see how their money goes, and if there be any interest or profit to be got by it, to receive it themselves. Therefore Mr. *Bayes* I will go on with my business, not fearing all the mischief that you can make of it. (126–127)

Indeed, this mixture of mockery and solemnity proves quite beyond Parker's handling. He persists in characterizing Marvell as a gamester without seeing how well that serves Marvell's purpose, how much more useful that such a disinterested person should present these arguments than the MP for Hull and ex-civil servant of Oliver Cromwell.

Marvell now proceeds upon a history of the events leading up to the Civil War quoting Archbishop Abbot on the Sibthorpe and Manwaring cases, which concerned their recommending of illegal methods of raising supplies to the King. Of Laud he speaks himself: "I am confident the Bishop studies to do both God and his Majesty good service, but alas how utterly was he mistaken. Though so learned, so pious, so wise a Man, he seem'd to know nothing beyond *Ceremonies*, *Arminianism*, and *Manwaring*. With that he begun, and with that ended, and thereby deform'd the whole reign of the best Prince that ever wielded the *English* Scepter" (134). Parker objected to "leering and mannerly abuses that are suggested under the pretence of friendship" as "more impudent than downright railing."[50] That is, Marvell refuses to be the pure enemy that Parker is determined to make him. Marvell goes on:

> For now was come the last part of the *Archbishops* indiscretion; who having strained those strings so high here, and all at the same time, which no wise man ever did; he moreover had a mind to try the same dangerous Experiment in *Scotland*, and sent thither the Book of the *English Liturgy*, to be imposed upon them. What followed thereupon, is yet within the compass of most Mens memories. And how the War broke out, and then to be sure Hell's broke loose. Whether it were a War of Religion, or of Liberty, is not worth the labour to enquire. Which-soever was at the top, the other was at the bottom; but upon considering all, I think the Cause was too good to have been fought for. Men ought to have trusted God; they ought and might have

> trusted the King with that whole matter. The *Arms of the Church are Prayers and Tears*, the Arms of the Subjects are Patience and Petitions. The King himself being of so accurate and piercing a judgement, would soon have felt where it stuck. For men may spare their pains where Nature is at work, and the world will not go the faster for our driving. Even as his present Majesties happy Restauration did it self, so all things else happen in their best and proper time, without any need of our officiousness. (134–135)

We should recall that Hull closed its gates to the king on his way to Scotland to enforce the "English Liturgy."

This is quite the best known passage in any of Marvell's political writings, frequently quoted as his opinion in 1672 and not infrequently suggested to be his opinion in 1641 as well. Both Kenyon and Wallace, for example, suggest that this might be the case.[51] They both also believe that Marvell intended to say that Charles I could have been trusted to accomplish the necessary reform, in conjunction with the inevitable processes of history. Warren Chernaik also finds this passage "combines a recognition of the inevitability of historical processes with a sigh of regret that history took the path it did."[52] He also suggests that "the distance imparted by coupling the downfall of Charles I with the return of Charles II gives the events of contemporary history an inevitability that is as much comic as tragic" in its "view of human striving."[53] The comic element in Marvell's announcement might more properly be surmised to indicate that his faith in Charles I's judgement was less than, for reasons of policy, he felt able to suggest. The Restoration demanded some considerable officiousness for its accomplishment, as Marvell, being at the time in a government job, was probably very well aware. Further, as he has just described it, Charles was plainly very easily led astray by the Church in general and Laud in particular. Wallace notes that "there is perhaps a logical flaw in Marvell's famous declaration" but assumes it was not one he intended to be observed, only that "it captures like no other not only his recognition of a deformed nature through which God still works, but a rare regret that providence had not been more kind, and men more conscious of the slow, but generally even, tenor of its way."[54] It seems that critics are too ready to discover an olympian detachment here that is suitable to that "metasubject," the "poet" but rather odd in a political writer. Why is Marvell writing if not to drive things a little faster in the direction he believes they should go?

Marvell has by now made it quite clear that he regards it as a war of both liberty and religion, the two are not separable. The Church was imposing upon the people, and the King "being a Prince truly Pious and Religious, was thereby the more inclined to esteem and favour the Clergy" (134) while they "did for recompense assign him that imaginary absolute Government, upon which rock we are all ruined." And still, "It hath been observed, that whensoever his Majesty hath had the most urgent occasions for supply, others of [the clergy] have made it their business to trinkle with the *Members of Parliament*, for obstructing it, unless the King would buy it with a new Law against the Fanaticks" (138). Having granted Parker's argument by proving that he himself seeks political power under cover of religion, Marvell now grants it in asserting, with apparent casualness, that the civil war was, of course, about liberty as well as religion. Against Parker's narrow-minded and obsessional concern with law and order Marvell offers a broad and confident vision of the way things are and how to handle them. He presents himself as a disinterested gentleman, angered by Parker's arrogance, but able without anxiety to contemplate not only Owen's ideas but even Parker's. Marvell's requirement that "the season" be "well fix'd" is conveniently ambiguous. The seasonable can be both what is inevitable and what is chosen, the unseasonable, in Parker's case, being the mischosen.

Whilst writing a book intended to make an intervention upon political affairs Marvell evades appearing to be driving against the inevitability which he, for politic reasons, chooses to find to control those affairs, by finding Parker unseasonable. After he has "(which I think is due) given the Reader, and the Authour, a short account of how I came to write this Book, and in this manner," which is because of Parker's manner, his repetitiousness, and his handling of trading corporations, scripture and grace, Marvell concludes: "And now I have done. And shall think my self largely recompensed for this trouble, if any one that hath been formerly of another mind, shall learn by this Example, that it is not impossible to be merry and angry as long time as I have been writing, without profaning and violating those things which are and ought to be most sacred" (145). We give the more credit to the justice of his anger for having been so much more aware of his humour, which is of course exactly what he intended.

It is a mistake to require, as Warren Chernaik does, "an organising myth" of *The Rehearsal Transpros'd*, its "element of fictionality" is deliberately "intermittent," as Marvell himself pointed out, and it is so because Marvell is not intending to leave us with a memorable satirical figure of authoritarianism, but to persuade us to note and act upon his own serious political contribution to the debate about toleration.[55]

Marvell's problem was how to deal with Parker's outrageousness. His solution is to deal with him "betwixt jest and earnest" intermixing "things apparently fabulous, with others probably true" (187 and 170). It is mistaken, too, to suppose, as does Raymond Anselment, merely that "Marvell refuses to be drawn into remote theorizing, where Parker's temperament and philosophy hold the advantage."[56] Marvell's pragmatism avoids only the remoteness. His concern is with the realms of both political theory and social behaviour. To make his political points he had to win himself an audience. One of his last criticisms of Parker, and in these terms one of the most telling, is that "you will believe none but your self. This is that which hath seduced you, and because you preach'd over your notes of *Ecclesiastical Politie* in a private Congregation, without being interrupted, you imagined the whole world had been of that mind" (325). It is persuasive rhetoric, and not merely coherent polemic, that matters. Far from avoiding theory, Marvell's whole enterprise is to find a way to make his understood. To some modern critics – his editor, unfortunately included – he has failed, but he is writing within different conventions. Anselment describes him as "straining" relevance, but in the process of challenging the relevance, the seasonableness, of a political view, one must strain its conceptions of relevance, pushing through the boundaries of what has been said to say something else.[57] Marvell here suggests indeed that the monolithic view Parker asserts with its obsession with control, and its constraints upon relevance, is essentially incoherent, because it falls apart under the pressure of the diversity of reality. This he states most clearly in his critique of Parker's push-pin divinity (remove one pin from the Church and the whole state crumbles). To those to whom Parker's views appeal, who desire law and order above all, it is necessary to demonstrate and not merely to state an alternative. As Owen observed in the book whose right to speak Marvell defended, "Men therefore in such Discourses, speak not to the nature of the things themselves, but to the Apprehensions of them with which they have to do."[58] It matters who speaks and how believable they are.

Marvell dissolves Parker's reputation and establishes his own because he has something to "communicate" that is "delightful and profitable" to his readers, which is not only that his mind is a more pleasant habitation than Parker's but that to be tolerant is better and safer than to be fearful and intolerant, and that the state should be governed upon that principle. The range of his book encompasses both an argument and an example of the "noble generosity" with which politics might be conducted.

JENNIFER CHIBNALL

NOTES

1. See John S. Coolidge, "Martin Marprelate, Marvell and *Decorum Personae* as a satirical theme," *PMLA*, 74 (1959).
2. T. S. Eliot, "Andrew Marvell," first printed *TLS*, 31 March 1927; M. C. Bradbrook and M. G. Lloyd Thomas, *Andrew Marvell* (Cambridge, C.U.P., 1961); John M. Wallace, *Destiny His Choice: The Loyalism of Andrew Marvell* (Cambridge, C.U.P., 1968); Annabel M. Patterson, *Marvell and the Civic Crown* (Princeton, Princeton U.P., 1978); Warren L. Chernaik, *The Poet's Time* (Cambridge, C.U.P., 1983), p. 1.
3. David Norbrook, *Poetry and Politics in the English Renaissance* (London, Routledge and Kegan Paul, 1984), p. 1.
4. Andrew Marvell, *The Rehearsal Transpros'd and The Rehearsal Transpros'd The Second Part*, ed. D. I. B. Smith (Oxford, Clarendon P., 1971), p. 160. Further references by page to this edition.
5. Antony Easthope, "Towards the autonomous subject in poetry: Milton 'On his Blindness'" in *1642: Literature and Power in the Seventeenth Century*, ed. Francis Barker et al. (Colchester, Essex U.P., 1981), p. 301.
6. Bradbrook and Lloyd Thomas, *Andrew Marvell*, p. 104.

7. Norbrook, *Poetry and Politics*, p. 9.
8. Easthope, "Towards the autonomous subject in poetry," p. 301.
9. Easthope, "Towards the autonomous subject in poetry," p. 302.
10. *The Rehearsal Transpros'd*, ed. D. I. B. Smith, pp. xviii–xix.
11. Samuel Parker, *A Discourse of Ecclesiastical Politie* (1670), p. iii.
12. Walter C. Ong, *Orality and Literacy* (London, Methuen, New Accents, 1982), p. 41.
13. John Kenyon, "Andrew Marvell: Life and Times," in R. L. Brett ed., *Andrew Marvell: Essays on the tercentenary of his death* (Oxford, O.U.P. for the University of Hull, 1979), p. 41.
14. Michael Long, *Marvell, Nabokov, Childhood and Arcadia* (Oxford, Clarendon P., 1984), Chapter 22.
15. Raymond A. Anselment, *"Betwixt Jest and Earnest." Marprelate, Milton, Marvell, Swift and the Decorum of Religious Ridicule* (Toronto, Toronto U.P., 1979), p. 101.
16. Antony Collins, *A Discours Concerning Ridicule and Irony* (London, 1729), p. 71.
17. Anselment, *"Betwixt Jest and Earnest"*, p. 101.
18. *The Poems and Letters of Andrew Marvell*, ed. H. M. Margoliouth, 3rd edition revised by Pierre Legouis with the collaboration of E. E. Duncan-Jones (Oxford, Clarendon P., 1971), I, 111.
19. Wallace, *Destiny His Choice*, p. 189.
20. Marvell, *Poems and Letters*, II, 328. Further reference by page to this edition.
21. *Historical Manuscripts Commission Report xiv*, MSS of the Duke of Portland. Appendix II, vol. iii, 1894, p. 323.
22. Marvell, *Rehearsal Transpros'd*, p. 234.
23. John Owen, *Works*, ed. T. Russell with Memoirs of his life and writings by W. Orme, 28 vols. (London, 1826), vol. 21.
24. *Calendar of State Papers Domestic* 1670, X (London, 1895), 233.
25. *CSPD* 1670, X, 240.
26. *CSPD* 1670, X, 267.
27. *CSPD* 1670, X, 289.
28. *CSPD* 1670, X, 270.
29. Hull Corporation Ms (L.807).
30. Marvell, *Rehearsal Transpros'd*, p. 251.
31. *CSPD* 1670, X, 506.
32. Anchitell Grey, *Debates of the House of Commons, 1667–1694* (London, 1769), I, 294.
33. *Calendar of State Papers Domestic* 1671–1672, XII (1897), 104–5.
34. Frank Bate, *The Declaration of Indulgence 1672: a study in the rise of organised Dissent* (London, A. Constable and Co., 1908), pp. 74–5.
35. Gilbert Burnet, *History of his Own Time*, ed. M. J. Routh (London, 1833), I, 564–5.
36. *Journals of the House of Commons* (London, 1803), IX, 251–7.
37. Wallace, *Destiny His Choice*, pp. 189–91.
38. Burnet, *History*, p. 565.
39. Grey, *Debates*, II, 28.
40. *Journals of the House of Commons*, IX, 252.
41. *Journals of the House of Commons*, IX, 274, 280.
42. Grey, *Debates*, II, 30.
43. *Journals of the House of Commons*, IX, 281.
44. John Owen, *Truth and Innocence Vindicated* (London, 1669), p. 47.
45. Samuel Parker, *A Defence and Continuation of the Ecclesiastical Politie* (London, 1671), pp. 216–17.
46. Samuel Parker, *A Reproof to the Rehearsal Transpros'd* (London, 1673), p. 4.
47. Wallace, *His Destiny His Choice*, p. 189.
48. *Reproof*, p. 211.
49. *Reproof*, p. 431.
50. *Reproof*, p. 359.
51. Kenyon, *Andrew Marvell: Essays on the tercentenary of his death*, p. 24; Wallace, *Destiny His Choice*, p. 189.
52. Chernaik, *The Poet's Time*, p. 23.

53. Chernaik, *The Poet's Time*, p. 22.
54. Wallace, *Destiny His Choice*, p. 203.
55. Chernaik, *The Poet's Time*, p. 184.
56. Anselment, *Betwixt Jest and Earnest*, p. 101.
57. Anselment, *Betwixt Jest and Earnest*, p. 101.
58. *Truth and Innocence Vindicated*, p. 2.

The Autobiographer as Apologist:
Reliquiae Baxterianae (*1696*)

The Puritan divine Richard Baxter (1615−91) would not have been well pleased to find *Reliquiae Baxterianae* discussed in a book of essays devoted to English controversial prose. It is true that, as a young man caught up in the excitement of intellectual discovery and in the "vigour" of his "youthful Apprehensions," he was "very apt to start up Controversies ... and also ... desirous to acquaint the World with all that I took to be the Truth, and to assault those Books by Name which I thought did tend to deceive them, and did contain unsound and dangerous Doctrine."[1] It was consequently as a controversialist that he first appeared in print, challenging, in his *Aphorismes of Justification* (1649), what he took to be antinomian tendencies in Calvinism. It is also true that in the subsequent course of an extraordinarily prolific literary career extending over forty years, he was to be frequently embroiled in ecclesiastical and doctrinal disputes. This was, however, an activity of which he came to hold no very high opinion. Engagement in it soon taught him "how much in most of our Controversies is verbal, and upon mutual Mistakes ... how impatient Divines were of being contradicted ... how hardly Mens Minds are charged [*sic*] from their former Apprehensions be the Evidence never so plain." Controversy was not only laborious and often misguided: it was also counter-productive, for "nothing so much hindreth the Reception of the Truth, as urging it on Men with too harsh Importunity, and falling too heavily on their Errors: For hereby you engage their Honour in the business, and they defend their Errors as themselves ... In controversies it is fierce Opposition which is the Bellows to kindle a resisting Zeal; when if they be neglected, and their Opinions lie a while despised, they usually cool and come again to themselves" (I. 125−6, §213 (2)). Baxter had bitter experience of the calumny and vindictiveness of such "Opposition,"[2] and he recognised that he had himself been guilty of the unedifying belligerency and censorious vituperation which controversy so easily provoked (I. 137, §213 (2)). In later life, he concluded that it was a cast of mind and a literary genre far better avoided:

> In my youth I was quickly past my Fundamentals, and was running up into a multitude of Controversies, and greatly delighted with metaphysical and scholastick Writings ... But the elder I grew the smaller stress I layd upon these Controversies and Curiosities (though still my intellect abhorreth Confusion), as finding far greater

Uncertainties in them, than I at first discerned, and finding less
Usefulness comparatively, even where there is the greatest Certainty.
And now it is the fundamental Doctrines of the Catechism, which
I highliest value, and daily think of, and find most useful to my self
and others: The Creed, the Lord's Prayer, and the Ten Command-
ments, do find me now the most acceptable and plentiful matter, for
all my Meditations: They are to me as my daily *Bread* and *Drink*: And
as I can speak and write of them over and over again; so I had rather
read or hear of them, than of the School Niceties, which once so much
pleased me. (I. 126, §213 (3))

Hence, in the bibliography of his works which he himself annotated at
the end of his life, treatises of moral, devotional and homiletic divinity are
those which he singles out for especial recommendation.[3] When practical
works were refused a licence for publication, Baxter withheld also some
controversial pieces, which would have been authorized, lest their sole
appearance should suggest he willingly confined his literary endeavours to
controversy. He arranged for his practical works to be sold more cheaply
than the controversial; he excluded controversy from his sermons; and it was
to "Affectionate Practical *English* Writers" that he directed his readers.[4]
Above all, he insisted repeatedly that reconciliation and moderation were
to be preferred to contention and extremism:

At first I was greatly inclined to go with the *highest* in Controversies,
on one side or the other; as with Dr. [William] *Twisse*, and Mr.
[Samuel] *Rutherford*, and *Spanhemius de Providentia, & gratia*
[Friedrich Spanheim, *Disputatio de Gratia Universali* (Leiden,
1644–8)], &c. But now I can so easily see what to say against both
extreams that I am much more inclinable to reconciling Principles.
And whereas then I thought that Conciliators were but ignorant men,
that were willing to please all, and would pretend to reconcile the
World by Principles which they did not understand themselves; I have
since perceived that if the amiableness of Peace and Concord had no
hand in the business, yet greater Light and stronger Judgment usually
is with the Reconcilers, than with either of the contending Parties.
(I. 130, §213 (13))

This is the authentic Baxterian position. He described it as "the chief
study and labour" of his life "to promote Unity, Peace and Concord,"
and he has with justice been called the first exponent of Ecumenism in
England.[5] This he pursued in practical ways, through the Worcestershire
Association during the Interregnum, in ecclesiastical negotiations (particularly in 1660–1) and, as a nonconformist after 1662, by the practice
of occasional conformity.[6] It became also the great theme of his writings.
At the end of his life he calculated that he had devoted "above a hundred
Books" to the cause of church unity. When he did engage in controversy,
it was to take people off from controversies. His aim was, in the words
of one of his titles, *An End of Doctrinal Controversies* (1691). Works such

as *Richard Baxter's Catholick Theologie* (1675) sought to bring this about by arguing for a middle way between Calvinism and Arminianism based upon the "hypothetical universalism" of Möise Amyraut. Similarly, he endeavoured to reconcile the ecclesiastical differences between episcopalians, Presbyterians and Independents (or Congregationalists) by recommending the "modified episcopacy" of Archbishop James Ussher's *The Reduction of Episcopacie unto the Form of Synodical Government received in the Antient Church* (1656). Insisting, in book after book, that "True mediocrity is the only way that's safe," he presented himself not as a member of any party ("you could not," he wrote, "have trulier called me than an *Episcopal-Presbyterian-Independent*") but as "a CHRISTIAN, a MEER CHRISTIAN ... against all Sects and dividing Parties ... I am of that Party which is ... against Parties: If the Name CHRISTIAN be not enough, call me a CATHOLICK CHRISTIAN."[7]

This is the persona adopted in *Reliquiae Baxterianae*. The book comes before us as a history of "Pacificatory Endeavours" (I.106, §153), an autobiographical record of the "forty five years labour for Peace"[8] of one who could "as willingly be a Martyr for *Charity* as for *Faith*" (II.364, §236). This conciliatory narrator impresses himself upon us less by the assertion of his ecumenical principles than by his careful and considerate tone. His moderation is not produced by the lethargy of uninterestedness: the very length of the *Reliquiae* (900 folio pages) testifies to Baxter's sustained fascination with seventeenth-century affairs. Nor is it achieved by bland generalisation which glosses over awkward facts: Baxter's attention is keenly analytical and he looks as squarely at his own shortcomings as at the religious and political dissensions which so appalled him. On the contrary, it is created by the consistent openness and disinterestedness of a zealous commitment to the facts of the case, a commitment which has bite in it precisely because it does not prevaricate, but which is advanced always with due circumspection and regard for accuracy. "It must be acknowledged also impartially, that some of the Presbyterian Ministers frighted the Sectaries into this Fury by the unpeaceableness and impatiency of their Minds" (I.103, §148): the point is stern and to the disadvantage of those for whom Baxter had much sympathy, but it is restrained from an unjustified comprehensiveness, and so from partisan censoriousness and bigotry, by that indefinite pronoun "some." Although Baxter's gaze is steady and penetrating, his narrative is throughout tempered and moderated by such qualification.

The texture of the prose itself argues for the reliability and integrity of the narrator. It is plain in the obvious (and Puritan) sense of that word: syntactically straightforward and lexically unremarkable. It often has an ungainliness which suggests immediate composition. As in the narrative Baxter can insert out of order matters he had overlooked earlier (e.g. I.48, §70), introduce a new subject apparently on the spur of the moment (e.g. II.373, §244), repeat himself (e.g. I.44, §63), or promise, "If I remember," to provide what is later forgotten (e.g. II.379, §262), so within paragraphs and sentences additional points can be awkwardly intruded or the business in hand be lost as related or ancillary topics demand inclusion. The tenor may be resolute, but the tone is one of informality: the occasional rhetorical schemes are confined to the simpler forms of repetition and the relatively few images are never strikingly original or ingeniously developed. Baxter was unhappy about the intervention on his behalf of the nonconformist Edward Bagshaw in controversy with George Morley, then Bishop of Worcester, because "the Man hath no great disputing Faculty, but only a florid Epistolary Stile" (II. 378, §260).[9] The *Reliquiae*, by contrast, never appears to have been worked up for the reader: it speaks directly and openly.

This openness and reasonableness are most sustained and persuasive in the famous "self-review" which concludes Part I (I. 124–38, §213). This analysis of the changes which time and experience have "made upon my Mind and Heart since those unriper times, and [of] wherein I now differ in Judgment and Disposition from my self" (I. 124, §213) traces, with disarming honesty, a progress to ever greater catholicity. It is the fruit of prolonged meditation and introspection, but it is neither self-obsessed nor morbidly introverted. Indeed, one development Baxter notices is a decreasing preoccupation with self (I. 129, §213 (9)). He no longer sets much store by emotional displays of devotion or contrition (I. 129, §213 (7)), nor is his theology now predominantly soteriological (I. 129, §213 (8)). We read of a movement away from the individualistic and experiential which so horrified the later seventeenth century, but not of a denial of them. They are being placed in a larger context of rational enquiry and moral duty. Baxter is neither temporising nor compromising: he is comprehending (in both senses) the full nature of humankind and of Christian dedication. As his ideas cannot proceed beyond evidence (I. 128, §213 (5)), so his faith lies less in private introspection, and, equally, less in learning, and more in service and heavenly meditation (I. 129, §213 (11); I. 134, §213 (37)). The "self-review" charts a movement away from experiential, ecclesiastical and theological extremes (I. 130, §213 (15–18); I. 131, §213 (24–5); I. 133, §213 (29)), but not towards apostasy or latitudinarianism, for it involves a reaffirmation of evangelical concern (I. 130, §213 (20); I. 131, §213 (23)).

To many contemporaries, however, Baxter sounded far from moderate and the *Reliquiae* far from conciliatory. Thomas Long, a Prebendary of St. Peter's, Exeter, who had previously tangled with Baxter (III. 182, §19; III. 188, §60), denounced the entire *Reliquiae* as a pernicious sham in his *A Review of Mr. Richard Baxter's Life* (1697). Rather than a history of "Pacificatory Endeavours," Long saw in Baxter's autobiography "a virulent invective and grinning Satyr against all that live in conformity to the Ecclesiastical or Civil Laws" which represents Charles I as a Papist, the Cavalier Parliament as tyrannical, the established church as anti-Christian and its clergy as hypocritical time-servers. This was no surprise to Long: Baxter "was a great Incendiary of our Unnatural Wars ... [and] in our unchristian Divisions ... hath been the most forward Agent and Disputant." In the posthumous *Reliquiae* he is simply about his old business of sowing "Seeds of Division and Confusion."[10] The non-juror Charles Leslie was equally outraged by the impudent publication in 1702 of Edmund

Calamy's *Abridgment* of the *Reliquiae* with the names of no fewer than three stationers on its title-page. This work by the *"Arch-Rebel"* Baxter is among the most scandalous of "the many *Lewd* and *Poisonous Pamphlets* of Late spread Abroad to *Debauch* the *Nation*," particularly in its representation of Charles I "as the most *Unnatural* and *Bloody Monster*, and most Harden'd *Hypocrite* that ever the Earth bore."[11] In Isaac Sharpe's dialogistic *Animadversions* (1704) the character Orthodoxus finds the *Abridgment* "a crude, dull, insipid (tho' fly and cunning) History, and I was e'en fatigu'd by that time I got to the end on't ... an Infamous, Venemous, Falsifying piece of History, Publish'd with the greatest Effrontery against the Church and State".[12] And Benjamin Hoadly, who ended his career as Bishop of Winchester, felt obliged to defend *The Reasonableness of Conformity to the Church of England* (1703) against its misrepresentation in the *Abridgment* as *"a complication of the blackest and most unpardonable crimes."*[13]

That Baxter's irenic and pacificatory way proved this provocative we might put down simply to the animus and prejudice of his assailants, were it not for the fact that both his own editors, nonconformists entirely sympathetic to Baxterianism, were themselves sensitive to the controversial nature of Baxter's text. Matthew Sylvester, Baxter's literary executor and editor of the *Reliquiae*, prudently excised some too pointed passages, and, though in his preface he claimed that Baxter was a candid and impartial chronicler, he was yet aware that some readers "may possibly distaste his plainness" and "will judge him too impudent and unworthy in branding Persons with such ungrateful Characters, as do so evidently expose ... [them] to disgrace" (sigs. b1^V, b3, c1, c2^V).[14] Edmund Calamy, the third seventeenth-century divine of that name and grandson of the Smectymnuan, who had assisted Sylvester with the *Reliquiae*, took the precaution, before the publication of his own *Abridgment*, of securing sheets of Clarendon's *Historical Narrative of the Rebellion* (1702–4), then in the press, in order to satisfy himself that Baxter's account did not too directly challenge the former Chancellor's narrative.[15]

Reflection upon the fact that it was left to these men to publish the *Reliquiae* suggests, furthermore, that Baxter was himself fully aware of just how controversial his autobiography was. Calamy dated Part I of the work 1664 (sig. d2); Part II was written in 1665 (II. 448, §445); to Part III, begun on 16 November 1670 (III. 1), Baxter continued to make additions until January 1685 (III. 177, §1; III. 200, §90); and yet, in these twenty years, he never offered the manuscript for publication. The reason is not far to seek. Baxter had experience of Stuart censorship and press control quite sufficient to know that no such narrative would ever be licensed. The "two Say-masters of Orthodoxy," as Marvell called them, Thomas Tomkins and Samuel Parker, who, as chaplains to the Bishop of London, were among those who acted as censors, operated not an impartial licensing system but, in Marvell's words again, "a more authoriz'd way of libelling," while those libelled must keep silent.[16] Tomkins had, in *The Rebels Plea* (1660), attacked Baxter's *A Holy Commonwealth* (I. 119, §195), and in *A Discourse of Ecclesiastical Politie* (1670), the Parker who refused Baxter's irenic *Cure of Church-Divisions* a licence (III.61, §140; III.86, §186) declared himself an uncompromising defender of the monarch's absolute supremacy over private consciences and a remorseless advocate of persecution to enforce conformity. In his pamphlets and his paper *The Observator*, the Surveyor of the Press, Sir Roger L'Estrange, made Baxter a particular target and himself intervened directly on at least one occasion to prevent the printing of a Baxter title (III.102, §221). It may have been at L'Estrange's instigation that in 1685 Baxter was tried and convicted of publishing a seditious libel against the episcopal clergy in the glosses of his *Paraphrase on the New Testament* (1685).[17] When culpable topical comment could be inferred from Biblical exegesis, or from homiletic reflection upon the plight of the fallen world (I.120, §206 (50)), and when the censor's veto was exercised by men so hostile to nonconformity in general and to Baxter in particular, there was not the least likelihood that a licence would be granted to print a direct historical narrative of recent events by the man who had, in L'Estrange's view, taken upon himself "the *Patronage* of the *Non-Conformists* Cause."[18] The chaplain Thomas Grigg told Baxter plainly that even what was innocuous and admissible from an unexceptionable author would not be allowed if written by Baxter (I.123, §211 (2)).

A man who through many years works at an unpublishable manuscript can contemplate only one readership: posterity. Certainly, this was how Sylvester interpreted Baxter's intention: "The Author of the subsequent History (now with God) had an Eagle's Eye, an honest Heart, a thoughtful Soul, a searching and considerate Spirit, and a concerned frame of Mind to let the present and succeeding Generations duly know the real and true state and issues of the Occurrences and Transactions of his Age and Day" (sig. b1^v). In the text, Baxter himself addresses posterity directly (III.42, §96). He writes "lest the fable pass for truth when I am dead" (III.179, §8), that "Posterity may not be deluded by Credulity" (III.187, §51). He is setting the record straight.

To undertake to disclose the "real and true state" of recent history implies that quite another account of it was current. And so it was. That was why Calamy was apprehensive about the appearance of Clarendon's history and foresaw that the publication of his *Abridgment* was "not unlikely to draw some consequences after it."[19] Throughout the Restoration period, royalists and episcopalians of the stamp of Parker and L'Estrange hammered away at two points with what they claimed was historical evidence. The first of these was that nonconformists were, as the Puritans had been, hypocrites whose real intention was political subversion if not outright rebellion. 1642 showed what was really in their minds; Thomas Venner's 1661 Fifth Monarchist uprising what they were likely to perpetrate. This was the premiss of the "Clarendon Code" of penal religious legislation which was directed, in the words of what Marvell called "the Quintessence of arbitrary Malice," the Second Conventicle Act (1670), against "the growing and dangerous practices of seditious sectaries and other disloyal persons, who under pretence of tender consciences have or

may at their meetings contrive insurrections." "The maxim was," so
Halifax later recalled, "It is impossible for a Dissenter not to be a rebel."[20]
The second contention charged nonconformists with an irrational enthusiasm which was a barbarism with no place in reasonable and civil society:
"the State of *England*," wrote the royal tutor Edward Chamberlayne,
"doth account them no other Members then the *Pudenda* of the Nation,
and are ashamed of them."[21]

Despite the passing of the Toleration Act (1689), these opinions were
still prevalent at the end of the century in the polemics and sermons of such
as Leslie and the High Church Tory Henry Sacheverell. They were flatly
contradicted by the *Reliquiae*. It did so on the authority of personal
experience. Baxter is at pains to assure his reader that he confines himself
to matters of which he has first-hand knowledge: he prefaces a series of
exemplary character sketches of some of those ejected by the Act of
Uniformity on St Bartholomew's Day 1662 with the caveat: "I shall but
tell you what my own Neighbours were, not speaking by hearsay but by
personal acquaintance ... giving you nothing of any unknown Person by
bare report" (III.90, §202). Such reservation is characteristic: "if ever any
hereafter shall say, That at King *Charles* the Second's Restoration, the
Presbyterian Cause was pleaded ... I leave it here on Record to the Notice
of Posterity, *that to the best of my knowledge* the Presbyterian Cause was
never spoken for" (II.278, §113, my italics). It is a caution which increases
our confidence in the narrator's reliability and veracity: of the Interregnum
he writes,

> however Men that measure Godliness by their Gain and Interest and
> Domination, do go about to persuade the World that Godliness then
> went down, and was almost extinguished, I must bear this faithful
> Witness to those times, *that as far as I was acquainted*, where before
> there was one godly profitable Preacher, there was then six or ten;
> and taking one Place with another, *I conjecture* there is a proportion-
> able increase of truly godly People, not counting Hereticks or
> perfidious Rebels or Church-disturbers as such. (I.96−7, §139, my
> italics)

In this last example, Baxter excludes extremists from his estimate of the
godly and distances himself from those radicals with whom royalists and
episcopalians identified all nonconformists. We might expect one part of
Baxter's purpose to be to exonerate himself, and so it is: "I take it to be
my Duty to be so faithful to that stock of Reputation which God hath
intrusted me with, as to defend it at the rate of opening the Truth" (I.136).
Baxter, however, has a larger purpose. Personal history occupies an
unexpectedly subordinate place within the *Reliquiae*: Baxter is not primarily
telling his own story at all. He eschews that intense and myopic preoccupation with private spiritual experience characteristic of one seventeenth-
century autobiographical tradition. The experience of conversion, which
forms the major part of a work like *Grace Abounding*, is but a preliminary
episode in the *Reliquiae*, largely (if not entirely) without trauma and drama.

Baxter, unsure when his conversion occurred, regards justification as a
process rather than an event (I. 7, §6 (3)). The consequences of conversion
concern him far more than its experience, and those consequences are
conceived of not as intense moments of spiritual devotion or desolation,
devastating temptation or rapturous enlightenment, but as the continuing
practice of Christian duty in domestic, social, ecclesiastical and political
circumstances. Baxter heeds the world around him as Bunyan never does.
It is public affairs which occupy the bulk of the *Reliquiae*, and particularly
the events set in train by that Restoration which in George Fox's *Journal*
merits only a brief dismissive mention.[22] This bias is quite explicit:
although

> it is Soul-Experiments which those that urge me to this kind of
> Writing, do expect that I should especially communicate to others ...
> for any more particular Account of Heart-Occurrences, and God's
> Operations on me, I think it somewhat unsavory to recite them; see-
> ing God's Dealings are much what [sic] the same with all his Servants
> in the main, and the Points wherein he varieth are usually so small,
> that I think not such fit to be repeated: Nor have I any thing extra-
> ordinary to glory in, which is not common to the rest of my Brethren.
> (I. 124, §213; cf. I. 129, §213 (9); I. 136)

There is Baxter's characteristic moderation, his distaste for enthusiasm.
But there is something more: his claim to be representative delivers an
implicit retort to those for whom all nonconformists were fanatics wrapt
in absurd mysteries. Herein lies the key to Baxter's purpose and literary
strategy. His interest in his own personal history is an interest not in the
individual and unique but in the shared and common. His story matters
only so far as it illustrates a larger story: personal experience exemplifies
general experience. Consistently Baxter presents himself as a typical and
representative figure: he will not allow his reader the chance to dismiss his
cautiously phrased or persuasively advanced opinions as the exception,
merely one man's uncharacteristically singular interpretation of events. The
Baxterian position assumes authority and general applicability by becoming
merged with that of the Puritan tradition.

This identification begins early in Part I. As we read of Baxter's experiences in the 1640s and early 1650s, there is a growing sense of a band
of like-minded people comprising "The Ministers of *England* and *Scotland*,
and all the sober People who regarded them" (I. 65, §101). They shared the
pastoral commitment exemplified in Baxter's account of his Kidderminster
ministry (I. 83−96, §§135−7), and, like him, "went the middle way" in
the constitutional and religious debates of the Interregnum (I. 71, §114).
Baxter's determination to work for Christian unity (II. 144, §16) found a
ready response among them. And so, in 1653, there came together in the
Worcestershire Association of ministers "dis-engaged faithful Men"
(II. 148, §28), "meer Catholicks; Men of no Faction, nor siding with any
Party, but owning that which was good in all, as far as they could discern
it" (I. 97, §140). Though opposed by radicals on the one side and by

episcopalians on the other, the association movement spread to "most" other countries (II. 162, §34; II. 167, §§35–6). Baxter draws the inference emblematically: "The poor Church of Christ, the sober sound religious Part, are like Christ that was crucified between two Malefactors; the profane and formal Persecutors on one hand, and the Fanatick dividing Sectary on the other" (I. 103, §147). These "Reconcilers," as Baxter prefers to call them, "that were ruled by *prudent Charity* always called out to both the Parties, that the Churches must be united upon the Terms of primitive Simplicity" (I. 103, §148). Not only were these people of Baxter's mind: they were also in the majority:

> But the greatest Advantage which I found for Concord and Pacifi-cation, was among a great number of Ministers and People who had addicted themselves to no Sect or Party at all; though the Vulgar called them by the Name of *Presbyterians*: And the truth is, as far as I could discover, this was the Case of the greatest number of the godly Ministers and People throughout *England*. (II. 146, §23)

It is not Baxter who is singular nor the Puritans who are divisive: that is the import of the handling of the narrator in the *Reliquiae*.

The procedures of the *Reliquiae* are not, then, those of spiritual autobiography. Baxter has another model in mind. On the title-page of his *Church-History of the Government of Bishops* (1680) he described himself as a "hater of false history." In the prefatory essay "What History is Credible, and what not," he warns against trusting all histories and advises his reader to be on guard against bias and to look, above all, for convincing evidence in any historian's work. Amongst reliable early church historians he mentions Eusebius, and he particularly recommends Socrates and Sozomen; Jacques-Auguste de Thou, Francesco Guicciardini and Fra Paolo Sarpi are named from among continental writers; and amongst English historians we are directed to Matthew Paris, John Foxe, William Camden, John Rushworth, Thomas Fuller and Gilbert Burnet.[23]

The *Reliquiae* belongs in this tradition of the comprehensive chronicle.[24] In its manner, Baxter interrupts his narrative with large blocks of documen-tation. This does not make for easy reading, but it does establish that this history is factual and not opinionative. The printing of papers and letters exchanged during the Interregnum with Baptists, Independents and episcopalians puts beyond doubt the attempt of the Reconcilers to accom-modate all ecclesiastical persuasions (II. 150–62; II. 180–97, §§45–9). The inclusion of 1660 documents and of 1661 Savoy Conference papers similarly invites readers to assess for themselves the treatment meted out to moderate men by the episcopalians (II. 232–76, §§96–107; II. 308–33; II. 346–63, §§214–35; II. 366–72). As Joan Webber has remarked, Baxter challenges with the primary evidence, with facts: "the Reader ... may judge with what sort of Men we had to do" (II. 280, §116).[25] Baxter is not, however, always content to allow the historical record to speak for itself. We are, for example, reminded that the Thomas Warmestry, afterwards Dean of Worcester, who in 1653 signed a paper, duly reproduced, testifying that the Association conduces *"very much to the Glory of God, the Promotion of Holyness, the restraint of Sin, the removing of Scandal, and the setling of God's People in Christian Unity,"* is the same Warmestry who, after the Restoration, travelled "purposely" to Kidderminster to preach "vehement tedious Invectives" against Baxter's ministry there (II. 149, §30).

Setting the record straight is an important part of Baxter's business, but only as a means, not an end. He has, as passages quoted have incidentally shown, a case to argue. This is what made the *Reliquiae* so unpalatable: it irritated as autobiography and history, but it affronted as apologetic. The moderate persona, the generalising of personal experience, the marshalling of evidence, all are deployed in the service of an interpretation of events. Baxter discerns in the complexities of history a simple and fundamental opposition:

> There is an universal and radicated Enmity between the *Carnal* and the *Spiritual*, the *Serpent's* and the *Woman's* Seed, the *fleshly Mind*, and the *spiritual Law of God*, through all the World, in all Generations, *Gen.* 3.15. *Rom.* 8.6,7,8. Thus [*sic*] Enmity is found in *England*, as well as in other Countries, between the *Godly* and the *Worldly* Minds; as he that was born after the Flesh did persecute him that was born after the Spirit [Gal. iv. 29], even so was it here. (I. 31)

This *Cain and Abel Malignity*, as Baxter called it in one of his titles (1689), constitutes the shaping principle of, and the interpretative key to, historical processes. "If you ask" how the Civil War "came to pass," he says,

> it requireth a longer Answer than I think fit here to give: But briefly, Actions spring from *natural Dispositions* and *Interest*. There is somewhat in the *Nature* of all worldly Men which maketh them earnestly desirous of Riches and Honours in the World.... .
>
> On the other side, there is that in the new Nature of a spiritual Believer, which inclineth him to things above, and causeth him to look at worldly Grandeur and Riches, as things more dangerous than desirable.... And the Laws of Christ, to which they are so devoted, are of such a stream as cannot suit with carnal Interest ... every where serious, godly People, that would not run with others to excess of Ryot, were spoken against and derided by the Names of Precisians, Zealot, Over-Strict, the Holy Brethren, and other Terms of Scorn. (I. 31–2)

This was the fundamental distinction between Parliamentarians and Cavaliers (I. 33), but, though the Civil War is an unusually stark and dramatic case, it is not otherwise exceptional. Just such a holy war is discernible in every historical event. Indeed, in the fallen world, it is this conflict which constitutes history.[26]

Such typological exegesis demands evaluation and categorisation. Baxter adopts a variety of techniques to ensure that we are never in any doubt on which side to place each of the numerous historical figures mentioned in the *Reliquiae*. Individuals are, for example, often ranged in contrasting pairs or groups. Early in Part II, Baxter describes how in 1654, when he served on the sub-committee appointed to determine the limits of tolerable religious opinion under the Protectorate's *Instrument of Government*, his attempt to secure as broad a definition of orthodoxy as Reconcilers would favour was frustrated by "the tincture of Faction" (II.198, §53) in the "over-Orthodox Doctors, [John] *Owen* and [Francis] *Cheynell*" (II.199, §55). Upon this documented account (II.197−205, §§50−6), there follows immediately Baxter's recollection of his meetings in London with Ussher (II.206, §61), in whose view the terms of Baxter and the Reconcilers "might suffice for Peace and Unity among moderate Men" (II.206, §62). The juxtaposition makes the point, underlined later when Baxter remarks that the two of them "agreed in half an Hour" (II.217, §76). Implication may work to the same effect: Richard Sterne, then Bishop of Carlisle, who "look'd so honestly, and gravely, and soberly, that I scarce thought such a Face could have deceived me," is reported to have spoken only once at the Savoy Conference, to castigate Baxter's use of the word "nation" rather than "kingdom" as a veiled rejection of monarchy (II.338, §198). If episcopalian gravity issues in this, and episcopalian honesty can so mislead, what hope is there from those who made no pretence of sobriety? When, as in this example, individuals declare themselves, their inadvertent self-disclosures often anecdotally exemplify more general allegiances: at the Savoy, the Presbyterian William Bates pointed out to Peter Gunning, afterwards Bishop of Ely, that his line of argument would admit all the ceremonies of Rome; Gunning replied, "Yea, and so I think we ought to have more, and not fewer" (II.340, §205). It does not take many cases of this sort to establish the bias of episcopalianism.

The reader may be more directly prompted by tendentious epithets (the "more Politick Men of the Diocesan Way" understood very well that their chance had come in 1660 (II.229, §87)), by terse summary statements ("We spoke to the Deaf" is Baxter's conclusion on the Savoy Conference (II.336, §192)), and by pointed irony: when in a 1676 sermon William Jane, another censor and afterwards Regius Professor of Divinity at Oxford, takes exception to those saints who, in *The Saints Everlasting Rest* (1650), Baxter had hoped to meet in heaven, Baxter comments, "Which of these the Man knew to be in Hell, I cannot conjecture: It's like those that differed from him in Judgment" (III.177, §2). And the man who was bold enough to speak out against the dangers of Popery to Charles II (II.277, §110), even though his "plainness" and "freedom of speech" might jeopardize his cause (II.286, §130; cf. II.343, §209), does not shirk explicit comment: "whoever be the Sect-Masters, it is notorious, That the Prelates (tho' not they only) are the Sect-makers, by driving the Poor people by violence, and the viciousness of too many of their Instruments, into ... extreams" (III.43, §99).

Even there, however, the parenthesis preserves a judicious accuracy. Although he categorises and evaluates, Baxter is never reductive or simplistic. He is alive to the partisan and prejudicial nature of terminology and to the consequent inadequacy of party labels. He takes pains to distinguish the varieties of opinion and practice within both conformity and nonconformity (II. 386−429, §§284−416). Moral sobriquets are of no more service than ecclesiastical: Baxter does not need to be reminded that no one is simply good or evil (I. 129, §213 (11); I. 130, §213 (15)), that all inclinations to good are imperfect, or that the diversity of human nature invalidates any stereotype of either the saint or the sinner (I. 7, §6 (3−4)). However unqualified his assessments may be, they are reached only after sustained scrutiny of the words and behaviour of individuals. It is by analysis, not by assertion, that he would persuade the reader to accept his judgements. His view of Major-General James Berry as a man corrupted by success and diverted into radicalism by the pernicious influence of the New Model Army is advanced solely on the evidence of his actions (I. 57−8, §83). Baxter's similar assessment of Cromwell as one who did "begin low and rise higher in Resolutions as his Condition rose" (I. 100, §144) comes in a character sketch (I. 98−100, §144) which draws on the accumulated evidence of duplicity and growing ambition previously presented in a prolonged survey of his career (I. 59−72, §§87−115; I. 74−5, §118). Baxter's commemorative characters of the Presbyterians Simeon Ashe and James Nalton are entirely approving, but distinguish in them two very different dispositions (II. 430−1, §§420−1). Similarly, though the series of briefer vignettes of many of the Bartholomeans (III. 90−8, §§202−8) typify all these men as "of the Primitive sort of Christians for Humility, Love, Blamelessness, Meekness, doing good" (III. 17, §357), they are yet discriminatory, sometimes incisive, portraits of individuals.

It is this combination of percipience with evaluative stringency which distinguishes the *Reliquiae*. Though he is an autobiographer and historiographer, Baxter is no mere chronicler content but to observe either himself or the world around him. The *Reliquiae* contrives to present human affairs both realistically, as the consequence of secondary causes, and typologically, as manifestations of a single primary cause.[27] This is what makes it so effective as apologetic. It is an effectiveness which survives the work's great bulk and disorder. Certainly, the *Reliquiae* is no polished literary artefact: a sprawling "Rhapsody" Sylvester called it (sig. b4^v), and no one has ventured to gainsay him. This, however, is a structural, not a conceptual, confusion. It is the literary image of a comprehensive fidelity to the minutiae of arguments, the details of events and the complexities of experience, but not of a havering or indecisive narrative point of view.[28] Baxter may be bewildered by the "Torrent" of events through which the Popish Plot and Exclusion Crisis worked themselves out (III. 187, §51), but he is not at all perplexed about their significance. He knows where he stands, and throughout the *Reliquiae* he works to persuade the reader to stand upon the same ground, with him and with "the Primitive sort of Christians." He consistently deploys his material to place his reader in the position of "any sober Christian" whom "it would have grieved ... to observe how dangerously each party of the Extremes did tempt the other to impenitency and further Sin" (III. 40, §89). It is a vantage point from which seventeenth-century history no longer vindicates the witness of the martyred Archbishop

William Laud and Charles I in the rightful re-establishment of the Church of England and the defeat of rebellious enthusiasm. Those Restoration episcopalians who claim to be the legitimate heirs of the reformed English tradition are seen to have abandoned the moderate ways of Archbishops Thomas Cranmer, Edmund Grindal and George Abbot quite as divisively as radical "sectaries" (II. 149, §29). The Puritans and their nonconformist successors now appear as the true custodians of reformed religion, of the godly tradition of the Church of England. Theirs is the authentic *via media*, beset by the malignant enmity of ungodliness in the extremism of both radicals and Laudians.

And so, though rooted still in autobiographical and historical fact, Part III of the *Reliquiae* comes to have the quality of hagiography and of a martyrology as Baxter records "the great Inundation of Calamities, which in many Streams overwhelmed Thousands of godly Christians, together with their Pastors" (II. 385, §280). Baxter would have from his reader both recognition of the innocence of these "godly Christians" of the hypocrisy, fanaticism and subversion charged upon them, and sympathy for them in their sufferings (e.g. III. 3–4, §§8–13), but he would also have something more. It is not with the Restoration, the climactic event in royalist and episcopalian historiography, that he concludes Part II, but with a vision of judgement on the restored authorities in war, famine and plague (II. 448, §445). Providences are being re-interpreted. The Restoration is no longer the miraculous intervention Abraham Cowley exultingly celebrated as a divine rebuff to the Puritans:

> Where are the men who bragged that God did bless,
>   And with the marks of good success
> Sign his allowance of their wickedness?
> Vain men, who thought the divine power to find
> In the fierce thunder and the violent wind.
>   God came not till the storm was past,
> In the still voice of peace he came at last.
> The cruel business of destruction
> May by the claws of the great fiend be done.
> Here, here we see th'Almighty's hand indeed,
> Both by the beauty of the work we see't and by the speed.[29]

On the contrary, the disappointment of Puritan hopes in the debacle of 1658–60 and in the ecclesiastical negotiations of 1660–1, the splenetic partisanship of the Cavalier Parliament, the ejections on St Bartholomew's Day and the subsequent persecution of nonconformists, none of these is perceived as a Providential sign of divine displeasure: they are but that hostility from the carnal world which saints must expect in all ages. Indeed, suffering and worldly derision prove the integrity of their witness, for those "whom the Lord loveth he chasteneth" (Heb. xii. 6). The sorry tale of persecution in Part III, dark and distressing though it is, thus escapes from resignation and despair. It is resolutely, even absurdly (as this world goes) affirmative. In their defeat by the powers of the world lies the firmest assurance of victory to the Puritans, for "my kingdom is not of this world" (John xviii. 36; I. 132–3, §213 (28); II. 297, §150). No wonder Long and Leslie were outraged.

N. H. KEEBLE

NOTES

1. Richard Baxter, *Reliquiae Baxterianae* (1696), Part I, p. 125, §213 (2). Subsequent parenthetical references in the text are, unless otherwise indicated, to part, page and, where appropriate, numbered section of the *Reliquiae*.

2. For some account of the "Opposition" provoked by Baxter's early controversial writings, see N. H. Keeble, *Richard Baxter: Puritan Man of Letters* (Oxford: Clarendon, 1982), pp. 15–17, and Geoffrey F. Nuttall, "Richard Baxter's *Apology* (1654): its Occasion and Composition," *Journal of Ecclesiastical History* (hereafter *JEH*), 4 (1953), 69–76.

3. This "Compleat CATALOGUE of his Books" was appended to the second edition of Baxter's *Compassionate Counsel to all Young-Men* (1691), sigs. *1–*8^V. Its annotation is reproduced in the bibliography in Keeble, *Baxter*, pp. 157–69.

4. Keeble, *Baxter*, pp. 29–30, 37 (cf. pp. 69, 73).

5. *Richard Baxter's Penitent Confession* (1691), p. 41; Horton Davies, *The English Free Churches* (London: Oxford U.P., 1952), p. 79.

6. On the Worcestershire Association see Geoffrey F. Nuttall, *Richard Baxter* (London: Nelson, 1965), pp. 63–74, and "The Worcestershire Association: its Membership," *JEH*, 1 (1950), 197–206; Frederick J. Powicke, *A Life of the Reverend Richard Baxter 1615–1691* (London: Cape, 1924), pp. 163–76. On Baxter's part in Restoration ecclesiastical negotiations, see E. C. Ratcliff, "The Savoy Conference," and Roger Thomas, "Comprehension and Indulgence," in *From Uniformity to Unity*, ed. Geoffrey F. Nuttall and Owen Chadwick (London: S.P.C.K., 1962), pp. 89–148, 189–253. On the nature of Baxter's nonconformity, see Frederick J. Powicke, *The Reverend Richard Baxter Under the Cross (1662–1691)* (London: Cape, 1927), pp. 185–252.

7. Baxter, *Penitent Confession*, p. 75, *A Third Defence of the Cause of Peace* (1681), pt. I, p. 110, *Church-History of the Government of Bishops* (1680), sig. b1. "Mere Christianity" is discussed in Keeble, *Baxter*, pp. 22–8.

8. Baxter, *Of National Churches* (1691), p. 37; cf. his *Penitent Confession*, pp. 41, 44.

9. For Bagshaw and Morley see *DNB*, and for Bagshaw also A. G. Matthews, *Calamy Revised* (Oxford: Clarendon, 1934), s.v. This controversy is outlined in N. H. Keeble, "Richard Baxter's Preaching Ministry: its History and Texts," *JEH*, 35 (1984), 545–6.

10. Thomas Long, *A Review of Mr. Richard Baxter's Life* (1697), sigs. A3–A3^V, A5^V. For Long see *DNB*, and for his controversies with Baxter, N. H. Keeble, "Some Erroneous, Doubtful, and Misleading Baxterian Attributions in Wing and Halkett and Laing," *Notes and Queries*, 32 (1985), 190–1.

11. [Charles Leslie], *A Case of Present Concern* ([1703?]), pp. 1–2. The stationers were Thomas Parkhurst, John Laurence and Jonathan Robinson, who had, with John Dunton, jointly published the *Reliquiae*. For Leslie, see *DNB*.

12. [Isaac Sharpe], *Animadversions On some Passages of Mr. Edmund Calamy's Abridgment* (1704), p. 7.

13. Benjamin Hoadly, *The Reasonableness of Conformity* (1703), sig. A3. For Hoadly see *DNB*.

14. For Sylvester see *DNB* and Matthews, *Calamy Revised*, s.v. On his editing of the *Reliquiae* see Geoffrey F. Nuttall, "The Manuscript of *Reliquiae Baxterianae* (1696)," *JEH*, 6 (1955), 73–9; William Lamont, *Richard Baxter and the Millennium* (London: Croom Helm, 1979), pp. 79–88; and Keeble, *Baxter*, pp. 145–7.

15. Edmund Calamy, *An Historical Account of My Own Life*, ed. J. T. Rutt, 2 vols. (1829),

I, 376–80, 442–52, 456–9. On Calamy see *DNB*, and on his editorial work, Matthews, *Calamy Revised*, pp. xvi–xx.

16. Andrew Marvell, *The Rehearsal Transpros'd*, ed. D. I. B. Smith (Oxford: Clarendon, 1971), pp. 205, 166 (cf. pp. 196–8).

17. The charge of L'Estrange's instigation is in Baxter, *A Paraphrase on the New Testament*, 2nd ed. (1695), sig. 3E3^V, reprinted in Powicke, *Baxter Under the Cross*, p. 285. For Tomkins, Parker and L'Estrange see *DNB*, and for L'Estrange also George Kitchin, *Sir Roger L'Estrange* (London: Kegan Paul, 1913).

18. Roger L'Estrange, *The Casuist Uncas'd* (1681), sig. A2^V.

19. Calamy, *Own Life*, I, 442.

20. Andrew Marvell, *The Poems and Letters*, ed. H. M. Margoliouth, rev. Pierre Legouis and E. E. Duncan-Jones, 3rd ed., 2 vols (Oxford: Clarendon, 1971), II, 314; Andrew Browning, ed., *English Historical Documents 1660–1714* (London: Eyre & Spottiswoode, 1966), p. 384; George Savile, Marquess of Halifax, *A Letter to a Dissenter* (1687), in *Complete Works*, ed. J. P. Kenyon (Harmondsworth: Penguin, 1969), p. 116.

21. Edward Chamberlayne, *Angliae Notitia* (1669), in William Myers, ed., *Restoration and Revolution* (London: Croom Helm, 1986), p. 66. For Chamberlayne, see *DNB*.

22. *The Journal of George Fox*, ed. John L. Nickalls (London: Religious Society of Friends, 1975), pp. 361–2.

23. Baxter, *Church-History*, sigs. a2^V–a3.

24. Donald A. Stauffer, *English Biography before 1700* (Cambridge, Mass.: Harvard U.P., 1930), p. 192.

25. Joan Webber, *The Eloquent 'I': Style and Self in Seventeenth-Century Prose* (Madison: U. of Wisconsin P., 1968), p. 121.

26. This was, of course, an entirely traditional point of view: see C. A. Patrides, *The Grand Design of God* (London: Routledge & Kegan Paul, 1972), esp. pp. 70–122.

27. Owen Watkins, *The Puritan Experience* (London: Routledge & Kegan Paul, 1972), pp. 126–9, singles out "the interpenetration of the divine and the human in men's affairs" as a distinctive feature of the *Reliquiae*.

28. Webber, *Eloquent 'I'*, pp. 115, 118–20, argues the contrary case that "Baxter's autobiography is discontinuous and divided just because he was and his life was."

29. Abraham Cowley, "Upon his Majesty's Restoration and Return," 11. 134–44, in G. A. E. Parfitt, ed., *Silver Poets of the Seventeenth Century* (London: Dent, 1974), p. 228.

Defoe's Shortest Way with the Dissenters: *Irony, Intention and Reader-Response*

It can be frustrating for the critic when an author neglects to comment upon his artistic intentions in a particular work. When a writer is forced to rush into print to explain his meaning, however, we would be right to be chary of accepting his explanation uncritically. And if the same writer subsequently offers a different account of his original purpose, the critic has reason to be sceptical of statements of authorial intention. Moreover, when the author concerned is Daniel Defoe, there is surely serious cause for critical caution. While the debate over irony in Defoe's fiction continues unabated, largely because he failed to supply sufficiently unambiguous clues to his intentions in works like *Moll Flanders*, in the case of *The Shortest Way with the Dissenters* we have to choose between earlier and later interpretations of the pamphlet by its author. It is, therefore, scarcely surprising that there is a growing critical debate over the polemical strategy employed by Defoe in the work which resulted in his pillorying.

The appearance of the *Shortest Way* on 1 December 1702 caused an outcry. Ministers felt it to be "absolutely necessary to ye service of ye Government ... to discover who was the Author of it."[1] Apparently Defoe was picked up for questioning on this account, but he escaped by jumping out of a window.[2] He went into hiding. Meanwhile the Secretary of State, the Earl of Nottingham, issued a warrant on 3 January 1703 for Defoe's arrest, and *The London Gazette* carried advertisements in its issues for 11 and 14 January announcing a £50 reward for information leading to his capture. On 24 February he was indicted in his absence before the Justices of Oyer and Terminer at Justice Hall in the Old Bailey for writing and publishing a seditious libel. The next day the House of Commons ordered the offending pamphlet to be burnt by the common hangman.[3] The reason for the prosecution of the *Shortest Way* was never explicitly stated, but presumably it was on account of the inflammatory language used by Defoe, who had advocated harsh measures against the Dissenters:

> 'TIS vain to trifle in this matter, the light foolish handling of them by Mulcts, Fines, &c. 'tis their Glory and their Advantage; if the Gallows instead of the Counter, and the Gallies instead of the Fines, were the Reward of going to a Conventicle, to preach or hear, there wou'd not be so many Sufferers, the Spirit of Martyrdom is over; they that will go to Church to be chosen Sheriffs and Mayors, would go to forty Churches rather than be Hang'd.

> If one severe Law were made, and punctually executed, that who
> ever was found at a Conventicle, shou'd be Banished the Nation, and
> the Preacher be Hang'd, we shou'd soon see an end of the Tale, they
> wou'd all come to Church; and one Age wou'd make us all One
> again.[4]

It is not difficult to see why this was regarded as seditious. Contemporary
critics described the *Shortest Way* as "one of the most devilish Designs that
ever was heard of," an attempt to mobilise the Dissenters in order to "play
the Old Game of *Forty One* over again."[5] It was suggested that Defoe
"would by the villainous Insinuations of that pamphlet have frightened
the Dissenters into another Rebellion."[6]

Defoe felt obliged to justify himself in print. *A Brief Explanation of a
late Pamphlet, entitul'd, The Shortest Way with the Dissenters* was
published early in 1703 and appended to the second edition of the *Shortest
Way* itself. It opened in these words:

> The author professes, he thought, when he wrote the book, he should
> never need to come to an explication, and wonders to find there should
> be any reason for it.
>
> If any man take the pains seriously to reflect upon the contents, the
> nature of the thing, and the manner of the style, it seems impossible
> to imagine it should pass for anything but a banter upon the high-
> flying churchmen.
>
> That it is free from any seditious design, either of stirring up the
> Dissenters to any evil practice by way of prevention, much less of
> animating others to their destruction, will be plain, I think, to any
> man that understands the present constitution of England and the
> nature of our government.[7]

In this way, Defoe outlines two possible interpretations of the polemical
objective of the *Shortest Way*, both of which were put forward in all
seriousness by contemporaries. Not only was the pamphlet "an irony not
unusual" which was not to be taken at face-value as a genuine address of
a High Church bigot advocating the persecution and destruction of the
Dissenters, it was not an attempt to incite the Dissenters to violent action
either. Summarising the "meaning" of the *Shortest Way*, Defoe said it had
been written to tell High Church writers like Henry Sacheverell, Charles
Leslie and Philip Stubbs – "my More Direct Antagonists," as he called
them in private[8] –

> 1. That 'tis nonsense to go round about and tell us of the crimes of
> the Dissenters, to prepare the world to believe they are not fit to live
> in a humane society, that they are enemies to the government and law,
> to the queen and the public peace, and the like; the shortest way and
> the soonest would be to tell us plainly that they would have them all
> hanged, banished, and destroyed.
>
> 2. But withal to acquaint those gentlemen who fancy the time is
> come to bring it to pass, that they are mistaken; for that, when the

thing they mean is put into plain English, the whole nation replies
with the Assyrian captain, "Is thy servant a dog that he should do
these things?" The gentlemen are mistaken in every particular, it will
not go down; the queen, the council, the parliament are all offended
to have it so much as suggested that such a thing was possible to come
into their minds... .

Having explained his purpose in writing the *Shortest Way*, Defoe proceeded
to explain his objective in providing his *Brief Explanation*:

> From this declaration of his real design, he humbly hopes the lords
> of her majesty's council, or the House of Parliament, will be no longer
> offended, and that the poor people in trouble on this account shall
> be pardoned or excused.[10]

We would be justified in accepting at least the stated purpose of the *Brief
Explanation*. Defoe was making tremendous efforts to escape the consequences of the publication of the *Shortest Way*. There is also evidence to
support his contention that "the queen, the council, the parliament" were
all against the extermination of the Dissenters, and that that had been his
meaning in the original pamphlet. "Shall I Own to you," Defoe wrote to
William Paterson in April 1703, "That the Greatest Concern I have Upon
me is That the Govornment, whom I Profess I Did not foresee would be
Displeas'd, Should Resent This Matter."[11] However, contemporary critics
were unimpressed by Defoe's attempts to justify his conduct. The suggestion
"that he is free from any *seditious Design*," wrote the author of an answer
to the *Shortest Way*, "is such an *Irony*, that it must move Laughter more
than Attention or Belief, and make a Jest of himself and the Government
together."[12] Defoe, in 1703, claimed that he had written the *Shortest Way*
to expose the High Church controversialists, Sacheverell, Stubbs and Leslie,
and that "they are enrag'd to have all their designs, laid open in
Miniature."[13] He professed to be writing against these men, his "More
Direct Antagonists," rather than against the government, and that he was
"Perfectly Free From any Seditious Designs."[14] Strangely, this was not
how he subsequently described his purpose.

In *The Consolidator* (1705), Defoe offered an allegorical account of the
appearance of the *Shortest Way*, which, he stated, "had all the effect he
wish'd for."[15] Far from being disappointed that the Dissenters (and other
men of discernment) had failed to appreciate his irony, he was pleased that
they "themselves were surpriz'd at it, and so closely had the Author couch'd
his Design, that they never saw *the Irony of the Stile*, but began to look
about them, to see which way they should fly to save themselves." According
to this interpretation, Defoe *intended* that the Dissenters should be taken
in, otherwise the pamphlet could not have "had all the effect he wish'd
for," as he claimed. Further, the "*Men of Zeal* ... were so blinded with
the Notion" for eliminating the Dissenters suggested in the *Shortest Way*,
"which *suited so exactly with their real Design*, that they hugg'd the Book,
applauded the unknown Author, and plac'd the Book next their *Oraclar*

Writings [*sic*], or Laws of Religion.''[16] But it is Defoe's allegorical description of the ministry's attitude towards the *Shortest Way* which is the most interesting, in the light of his profession that his "Greatest Concern" was "That the Govornment," who he "Did not foresee would be Displeas'd, Should Resent This Matter." In *The Consolidator*, Defoe stated the case rather differently:

> The *Ministers of State*, tho' at that time *of the fiery Party*, yet seeing the general Detestation of such a Proposal, *and how ill it would go down with the Nation*, tho' they approv'd the thing, yet began to scent the Design, and were also oblig'd to declare against it, for fear of being thought of the same Mind.[17]

Now it appears that Defoe was trying to expose not only men like Sacheverell, Leslie and Stubbs, not merely the mass of the High Churchmen, but the government itself.

Which version are we to believe? The 1703 account of the "design" of the *Shortest Way*, or the later one which outlined a more subtle objective? In *The Consolidator*, Defoe claimed that the pamphlet "had all the effect he wish'd for," and in *The Present State of the Parties* (1712) he defended his strategy against those who argued that he should have drawn attention to the fact that he was parodying High Church writers:

> these Men do not see the Design of the Book at all, or the Effect it had, at the same Time, taken off the Edge of the Book, and that which now cut the Throat of a whole Party, would not then have given the least Wound. The Case the Book pointed at, was to speak in the first Person of the Party, and then, thereby, not only speak their language, but make them acknowledge it to be theirs, which they did so openly, that confounded all their Attempts afterwards to deny it, and to call it a Scandal thrown upon them by another.[18]

Hitherto critics have tended to ignore the differences between Defoe's own interpretations of the *Shortest Way*. Miriam Leranbaum, for instance, tried to explain why Defoe has not been taken "at his word," without noticing that there is considerable confusion about which particular word should be taken! "In most of his later references to the pamphlet and its reception," she asserted, "Defoe spoke more in sorrow than in anger."[19] This is not how I would describe the accounts offered in either *The Consolidator* or *The Present State of the Parties*, although in the aftermath of the publication of the *Shortest Way*, Defoe was sorrowful and fearful enough.

Similarly, critics have usually assumed that the contemporary reception of the *Shortest Way* was accurately described by a triumphant Defoe. Paul K. Alkon refers to "those who were later appalled at what they had been disposed to approve of before recognizing the hoax."[20] Where is the evidence for his change of heart? Defoe himself was fond of repeating the story which finally found its way into Oldmixon's *History of England*:

The wisest churchmen in the nation were deceived by the book. Those whose temper fell in with the times hugged and embraced it, applauded the proposal, filled their mouths with the arguments made use of therein; and an eminent churchman in the country wrote a letter to his friend in London, who had sent him the book, in the following words: "Sir, I received yours, and with it that pamphlet which makes so much noise, called *The Shortest Way with the Dissenters*, for which I thank you. I join with the author in all he says, and have such a value for the book, that, next to the Holy Bible and the Sacred Comments, I take it for the most valuable piece I have. I pray God put it into Her Majesty's heart to put what is there proposed in execution."[21]

But mere repetition does not confer authenticity, and the story itself might well have been another ploy on Defoe's part to embarrass the High Churchmen. Nor is there any indication of the reaction of such men on discovering that they had been the victims of a hoax. True, according to Charles Leslie, the *Shortest Way* was at first regarded as the genuine work of a High Churchman: "none of those," he wrote in the second part of the *New Association*, "that I could meet with, or hear of, did imagine it could be wrote by a *Whigg*; and I have heard one, and then another of the Church Party guessed at for the Author."[22] He also noted the pamphlet's "Effect all over the *Town*, among all sorts of People." As far as Leslie was concerned, the *Shortest Way* was written "to *Blacken* the *Church-Party*, as Men of a *Persecuting* Spirit."[23] Thus he offers his own interpretation of the pamphlet's polemical objective, and suggests that Defoe's polemical strategy lay strongly in the convincing impersonation of a High Churchman, rather than irony, or any other rhetorical technique. Yet there is no indication that readers "were appalled at what they had been disposed to approve of before recognizing the hoax," as Alkon suggests. If anything, the *Shortest Way* provoked anger.

Defoe, as I have remarked, explained that he was "speak[ing] in the first Person of the Party" so that, through using the same language, he would "make them acknowledge it to be theirs." And he claimed that this was indeed the effect of the *Shortest Way*. They embraced the pamphlet "so openly" that they could not "afterwards . . . deny it"; thus it had "all the effect he wish'd for." Ian Watt agrees that Defoe "very successfully imitated the style, the temper, and the basic strategy of the exasperated High Churchmen who at last saw an opportunity under Anne for crushing the Dissenters." But, because "many readers took the pamphlet as a genuine expression of extreme Tory churchmanship," the *Shortest Way* was "a masterpiece not of irony but of impersonation." "Defoe's vicarious identification with the supposed speaker was so complete that it obscured his original intention."[24] Watt's account raises starkly the critical issues of strategy, intention and reader-response, and shows the extent to which the *Shortest Way* causes interpretative problems. Is it or is it not ironic? What was the intention and how much should this be taken into consideration, given that Defoe was inconsistent in his explanation of the pamphlet's "design"? How can we assess contemporary audience-response to the rhetoric of the *Shortest Way*? What, indeed, was the pamphlet's audience?

In order to reach any valid conclusions about the techniques used by Defoe to manipulate the reader in this particular work, we need to know something about the audience (or audiences) at which it was aimed, and about its purpose. "While we can infer Defoe's general purposes from what he wrote in the pamphlet," Richard I. Cook asserts, "it is not easy to ascertain just what audience he hoped to reach and what effect he intended his tract to have."[25] Such statements indicate the extent to which an awareness of the concept of polemical strategy can assist in interpreting controversial prose. How can we "infer Defoe's general purpose" if we have no notion of his "target reader" or his polemical objective? Cook's uncertainty is revealed when he suggests that Defoe "almost certainly meant the public to make the mistake it did, and to swallow the pamphlet whole."[26] Yet, in the *Brief Explanation*, Defoe, writing of his "design" in the *Shortest Way*, remarked that "'Tis hard, after all, that this should not be perceived by all the town, that not one man can see it, either Churchman or Dissenter."[27]

Cook's sweeping generalisation gave way to Maximillian E. Novak's more subtle examination of Defoe's polemical strategy, which, in the first instance, enquired about the pamphlet's audience. "Surely Defoe wrote to deceive and convince," Novak argued, "to fool those who were secretly so committed to extremist arguments that they could not see the trick, and to inform his intelligent audience through irony."[28] Defoe consistently professed that the *Shortest Way* worked through irony. In the *Brief Explanation*, he called it "an *Irony not unusual*," and in 1710 he claimed that it was an "*Ironical Satyr*."[29] Although Novak pertinently points out that the *Shortest Way* was hardly "an *Irony not unusual*," Miriam Leranbaum argued for our acceptance of Defoe's own description of the pamphlet. She, too, distinguished between two audiences – one primary, the other secondary. Following the line taken by Watt, Leranbaum took Defoe's description of his polemical strategy at face-value. "If any man take the pains seriously to reflect upon the contents, the nature of the thing, and the manner of the style," he wrote in the *Brief Explanation*, "it seems impossible to imagine it should pass for anything but a banter upon the high-flying churchmen." Leranbaum agreed. "Defoe's banter strove for authenticity," she argued, "and sought to trap his primary audience into self-betrayal."[30] In this way, she offered a primary target reader, a polemical objective and a polemical strategy for the *Shortest Way*. However, although, according to Leranbaum, "the immediate audience of the speaker is composed not of his enemies but of his friends," he had a "secondary audience" composed of "those moderates whom he thought of as his allies." Thus he must also have had a secondary polemical objective and a secondary polemical strategy, even if they were interlinked. Leranbaum, like other critics, did not question Defoe's assertion that he achieved his first polemical objective – the exposure of High Church feelings towards the Dissenters. But she thought he failed to effect his other aim of gaining the support of the moderates.

Whether or not Leranbaum was right in her location of the "primary" and the "secondary" audiences of the *Shortest Way*, her analysis presents an immediate problem. She wanted to demonstrate why critics had been unable to take Defoe at his word when he described the pamphlet as "an *Irony not unusual*," a "banter upon the high-flying churchmen." But in *The Consolidator*, as I have already pointed out, Defoe argued that his "Paper had all the effect he wish'd for." He did not admit to having failed to win over the moderate men "whom he thought of as his allies." According to the account given in *The Consolidator*, the *Shortest Way* fully realised its polemical objective. Another consideration emerges. As well as the High Churchmen and the moderates – Leranbaum's primary and secondary audiences – we must not forget a third type of reader: the Dissenters themselves. Contemporaries regarded them as the target readers of Defoe's exercise in propaganda. "Were we not privy to the secret that *The Shortest Way with the Dissenters* is ironic," wrote Leranbaum, "we would be moved, depending upon our convictions, either to hasten into procession or dive behind the barricades."[31] This, of course, echoes what contemporary High Churchmen blamed Defoe for when they accused him of fomenting rebellion. We can hardly doubt that he had in mind what the reaction of his fellow Dissenters to his pamphlet's rhetoric would be. And, as I have suggested, it seems, despite the *Brief Explanation*, that he anticipated their dismay. He genuinely wanted or expected to scare them, before revealing that they, too, had been the victims of a hoax, as much as his High Chuch adversaries. Otherwise it would have "taken off the Edge of the Book."[32]

Novak makes a number of pertinent comments on this score. Citing Kierkegaard, who argued that irony "aims ideally at an audience of one" – the author himself – Novak observes that, nevertheless, "few writers of irony set out with the deliberate intention of deceiving the simple reader." Asserting that the *Shortest Way* "was extraordinarily clever, too clever in fact," Novak suggests that "Defoe probably underestimated the number of readers who would be fooled."[33] Once again, this seems to be following the 1703, rather than the post-1705, version of polemical objective given by Defoe. But it strongly indicates the complexity of Defoe's intentions, and offers clues to the understanding of his polemical strategy. Because Defoe appears to have set out to write in an ironic style which *was* intended to deceive *on first reading*, if not the whole, at least a great majority of his audience, High Churchman and Dissenter alike. He regarded it as ironic principally because he did not mean what the pamphlet said. The plan for the extermination of the Dissenters was not Defoe's, but the logical conclusion of the rhetoric of High Church writers. It was in this sense that the *Shortest Way* was "a Brat of" Sacheverell's "own begetting," and his exposure "by way of Irany [sic]" had made him "Scandaliz'd for contriving" Defoe's polemical strategy.[34]

Critics have been disturbed by the effect of Defoe's rhetoric because it deceived too well. His impersonation of a High Churchman was so effective that the fictional projection which has been recognised as the basis of the success of *Moll Flanders* has been seen also as his principal strategy in the *Shortest Way*. But that does not prevent the pamphlet from being an exercise in irony. Swift, too, creates a convincing character in *A Modest Proposal* by employing fictional techniques, yet no one questions his irony. Nor is it valid simply to object that, unlike Swift, Defoe failed to distance himself from his speaker if he originally *intended* to deceive both High Churchman and Dissenter. Novak notes the deception, but argues also that Defoe wrote to confirm the beliefs of "his intelligent audience through irony." This is nearer the truth. I shall consider the pamphlet's ironic pointers in due course. First it is necessary to stress that Defoe's polemical strategy was even more ambitious than envisaged by Novak and Leranbaum. He had more than one target reader, and some of them were meant to be fooled, as the High Churchmen and Dissenters evidently were. His ironic pointers were sufficiently subtle to escape the discernment of those who were not "Men of Tast" (to use Swift's phrase).[35] The effect of the *Shortest Way* consisted in not merely the exercise of reading. The recognition of irony was bound up with the spectacle of High Church reaction to the proposals apparently put forward in all sincerity. It was this conjunction which was intended to influence government policy:

> For as it caus'd *these first* Gentlemen [the *"Men of Zeal"*] to caress, applaud and approve it, and thereby discover'd their real Intention, so it met with Abhorrence and Detestation in all the Men of *Principles, Prudence* and *Moderation* in the Kingdom, who ... were not for Blood, Desolation and Persecution of their Brethren, but *with the Queen* were willing they should enjoy their Liberties and Estates, they behaving themselves *quietly and peaceably* to the Government.[36]

In this sense, even Defoe's protestation to Paterson that he "Did not foresee" that the government "would be Displeas'd" at the publication of the *Shortest Way*, could be justified. Before we can assess this, however, it is necessary to consider the context. And in this respect we must go further than simply recognising, as Watt does, that the High Churchmen "at last saw an opportunity under Anne for crushing the Dissenters."[37] It is important that the pamphlet was published within a year of the death of William III. But the precise timing of publication is crucial. Queen Anne succeeded William on 8 March 1702. Sacheverell's Oxford sermon, which is generally accepted as the principal work parodied by Defoe in the *Shortest Way* (later editions carried the caption, "Taken from Dr. Sach [evere]ll's Sermon, and others," on the title-page), was preached on 10 June 1702. Yet the *Shortest Way* did not appear until 1 December 1702. The next day the occasional conformity bill was due to be read for the first time in the House of Lords, having been introduced into the Commons the previous month.[38] It would seem reasonable to assume that Defoe was trying to influence the debate on the bill in parliament.

While *The Shortest Way with the Dissenters: Or Proposals For the Establishment Of The Church* should be viewed in the general context of Anglican reactions to the passing of the Toleration Act in 1689, then, its polemical objective is best analysed by keeping in focus the political situation during the winter session of 1702–3. This, in turn, sheds light on the pamphlet's polemical strategy. It may have been concerned with the growing High Church response to the accession of a "Church-of-England" queen, but its more immediate concern was perhaps much more specific: it sought to sabotage the occasional conformity bill. The author of *The Reformer Reform'd: or The Shortest Way with Daniel D'Fooe* recognised as much when he descanted on what Defoe would feel like "when the government has handled him a little." He thought it would teach him "not to endeavour again to set the Nation together by the Ears, and to instruct Her Majesty, and the Pillars of State, in the Administration of Affairs."[39] It was this audacity – the fact that a private man should presume to offer the queen's servants advice – which seems to have been behind the ministers' initial urgency to deal with the pamphlet. Lord Treasurer Godolphin wrote to the Earl of Nottingham, who, as Secretary of State, was responsible for the press:

> I had last night some talk with the speaker [Robert Harley], and he has had a mind to speak to you about a book lately Come out, called, a short way with the Dissenters. He seemed to think it absolutely necessary to the service of the government that your Lordship should endeavour to discover who was the author of it.[40]

As Speaker, of course, Harley was acutely aware of printed reflections on parliamentary affairs. But here he is talking of "the service of the government." That is why Defoe was being disingenuous when he said he "had it not in [his] Thoughts That the Ministers of State would Construe That [the *Shortest Way*] as Pointing at Them."

Defoe, then, was probably being truthful in *The Consolidator* when he claimed that the "*Ministers of State*, tho' at that time *of the fiery Party* ... were also oblig'd to declare against" the proposal made in the *Shortest Way*, "tho' they approv'd the thing." He was genuinely concerned about the attitude of at least some of the ministers, and had cause to be. They were in favour of the passage of the occasional conformity bill. Now Defoe himself was critical of the practice of occasional conformity, which he called "*playing Bopeep* with God Almighty,"[41] and he conceded that "if there was nothing else in the Bill, I believe no good Man would be against it."[42] There were, he felt, deeper designs of a political nature, however, which would lead to what he had suggested ironically in the *Shortest Way* – the total subjection of the Dissenters. As Charles Leslie put it in *The New Association*, one of the works named as a progenitor of the *Shortest Way*, "above all things, these Men are to be kept out of any Share in the *Legislature*. Neither to Sit in *Parliament* themselves, nor to have any *Voice* in the *Election* of *Parliament-Men*."[43] Whigs like Bishop Burnet were against the occasional conformity bill for political, as well as moral, reasons. After all, Dissenters were following the practice of occasional conformity − taking communion annually in the Church of England − so that they had the right to vote and the ability to stand for public office. Leslie might feel that "there is no Breach of Birth-right, if the Dissenters are *excluded* from their having any Part in the *Legislature*,"[44] but the Whigs thought otherwise. As Burnet put it, writing of the occasional conformity bill, "the intent of it was believed to be the modelling elections, and by consequence, of the house of commons."[45]

Critics have stressed the place of the *Shortest Way* in the debates over religious toleration after the Revolution of 1688. Some have even detailed the way in which it responds to the controversial pamphlets which appeared on the accession of Queen Anne, who promised, despite High Church pressure, "to preserve and maintain the Act of Toleration." But it is important, when questions of polemical strategy are to be confronted, to be aware of the threat posed by the occasional conformity bill to the position of the Dissenters in English society, and to recognise that Defoe saw that threat. Rather than simply trying to expose High Church rhetoric for what it was − a reading which reduces the *Shortest Way* largely to an exercise in demystification, with its polemical strategy merely, as Cook suggests, "the shock value of an outrageous or macabre suggestion ostensibly put forward in sincerity"[46] − Defoe perhaps had a more specific polemical objective: he wanted to make government support for the occasional conformity bill impossible in the debate in the House of Lords.

To this end, the *Shortest Way* had indeed to shock. It certainly seems to have shocked the Dissenters, who, according to Defoe, "plentifully loaded him with ill Language and Railing, and took a great deal of pains to let the World see their *own Ignorance and Ingratitude*."[47] Presumably it did not shock those High Churchmen who wanted the mock proposals put into practice. The large question is whether or not it produced the effect on the moderates described by Defoe. They, too, had to be shocked, both by the immoderate language used by the speaker of the pamphlet which Defoe wished to trap the extremists into accepting as their own, and by the apparent readiness of High Churchmen in and out of office to fall in with such proposals. Defoe claimed that the process of demystification was designed to show "that when the persecution and destruction of the Dissenters, the very thing they drive at, is put into plain English, the whole nation will start at the notion, and condemn the author to be hanged for his impudence."[48] And for once the account offered in the *Brief Explanation* tallies with that in *The Consolidator*. There Defoe asserted that the discovery of the "real Intention" of the High Churchmen led to "Abhorrence and Detestation in all the Men of *Principles*, *Prudence* and *Moderation* in the Kingdom."[49]

But this does not help us to know whether or not his rhetoric really worked. Nor is it easy to see how, in the short-term, arousing the indignation of the moderates would serve to head off the occasional conformity bill in the House of Lords. Defoe once again is throwing up a smokescreen. What mattered was the attitude of the government. Even the queen "was strongly in favour of the bill" in December 1702. Nottingham, the Secretary of State, was actually the bill's sponsor, although he had had it introduced into the Commons by his ally, William Bromley. True, Marlborough and Godolphin were lukewarm in their support for the measure, but, as Geoffrey Holmes puts it, the Whig peers themselves "did not venture to attack it frontally; for they were well aware that some of the moderates in their own party among the office-holders and pensioners would not support them in the Lords."[50] Yet it was in the Lords that the bill had to be blocked, as the massive Tory majority in the Commons had readily approved the bill.

How, then, did Defoe set about the difficult task of trying to influence the outcome of affairs in parliament? Novak notes that when Sacheverell "threatened reprisals against the Dissenters, he did it through implication, metaphor, and biblical allusion."[51] When Defoe parodied Sacheverell he removed the implication, and replaced it with a scheme which would have indeed got rid of the Dissenters the shortest way. Both writers referred to the practice of occasional conformity. But whereas Sacheverell had urged true Churchmen to "Watch against These Crafty, Faithless, and Insidious Persons, who can creep to our Altars, and partake of our Sacraments" in order to qualify for office, Defoe had advocated hanging: "they that will go to Church to be chosen Sheriffs and Mayors, would go to forty Churches, rather than be Hanged." "These Shuffling, Treacherous, *Latitudinarians*, ought to be Stigmatiz'd," Sacheverell had insisted, leaving the measures to be taken sufficiently vague. "If the Gallows instead of the Counter, and the Gallies instead of the Fines, were the Reward of going to a Conventicle," Defoe wrote, "there wou'd not be so many Sufferers, the Spirit of Martyrdom is over." In enunciating his "one severe Law," Defoe distanced himself from the rhetoric of Sacheverell.[52]

There was indeed a vast difference between what Sacheverell had actually put down in print and the proposals made in the *Shortest Way*. Interestingly, Defoe again offered conflicting statements about his *reductio ad absurdum* technique. In 1703 he emphasised the element of demystification. "The sermon preached at Oxford, the *New Association*, the *Poetical Observator*, with numberless others, have said the same thing in terms very little darker," he argued in the *Brief Explanation*, "but when the persecution and destruction of the Dissenters, the very thing they drive at, is put into plain English, the whole nation will start at the notion." However, in 1712 he claimed that Sacheverell, Leslie and their kind "had gone such a length already, as to say the same Thing in Print."[53] Now Leslie, in the *New Association*, had gone further than Sacheverell in formulating a scheme which would have resulted in the Dissenters being deprived of their civil rights. He called for them to be "*Dis-arm'd*, and not trusted in any *Office* or *Post* of the *Government*," whether or not they took the sacraments in the Church of England, because "there is no way but to *exclude* All who go to any other *Communion* than that *Established* in the *Nation*." This indeed would have destroyed the political power of the Dissenters, and could be said to have been the outline of a scheme to achieve this end. But there was no talk of the destruction of the Dissenters as a group, much less of their persecution. Leslie even asked "shall we *Persecute* them, and Reward them as they have served us?" "No, not even in that Case would I Persecute them," he answered, "but rather return *Good* for *Evil*."[54]

Clearly this was one of the passages parodied by Defoe in the *Shortest Way*. "I do not prescribe Fire and Faggot," rails his speaker, "but ... they are to be rooted out of this Nation, if ever we will live in Peace, serve God, or enjoy our own."[55] Leslie's wonted clemency is being mocked here. He does not want persecution, merely the disablement of the Dissenters. He would not even revenge himself upon them, although the power to do so is now in the hands of the friends of the Church of England. Defoe's speaker goes further than this, whilst recognisably considering the same point:

> THERE are some People in the World, who now they are *unpearcht*, and reduc'd to an Equality with other People, and under strong and very just Apprehensions of being further treated as they deserve, begin with *Aesop*'s Cock, to Preach up Peace and Union, and the Christian Duties of Moderation, forgetting, that when they had the Power in their Hands, those Graces were Strangers in their Gates.

Unlike Leslie, who advocates "return[ing] *Good* for *Evil*," Defoe satisfies the demands of his High Church audience: "*No Gentlemen*, the Time of Mercy is past, your *Day of Grace is over*; you shou'd have practis'd Peace, and Moderation, and Charity, if you expected any your selves."[56]

It has already been demonstrated that Defoe's "chief method of parody" in the *Shortest Way* "is to carry the arguments of his enemies to their furthest implications." The pamphlet's opening paragraphs provide examples of the parodic method at work. But Defoe chose to begin with a fable:

> Sir *Roger L'Estrange* tells us a Story in his Collection of Fables, of the Cock and the Horses. The Cock was gotten to Roost in the Stable, among the Horses, and there being no Racks, or other Conveniences for him, it seems, he was forc'd to roost upon the Ground; the Horses jostling about for room, and putting the Cock in danger of his Life, he gives them this grave Advice; *Pray Gentlefolks let us stand still, for fear we should tread upon one another.*[57]

Although Leranbaum tries to liken this introduction to Defoe's "prototypes,"[58] calling it "the exordium if we think of it as a sermon," it is a distinctive opening. And even if Sacheverell's *Political Union* was originally a sermon, Leslie's *New Association* and the obscure *Poetical Observator* − the "prototypes" acknowledged by Defoe himself − were obviously works of a different character. As Novak observes about Defoe's proposal, "since there is nothing in the writings of either Sacheverell or Leslie which resembles it, we ought to be surprised."[59] Seeing this is true also of the fable, it seems reasonable to enquire what it is doing at the beginning of the *Shortest Way*.

The reference to L'Estrange would put Defoe's High Church audience at its ease, as L'Estrange had been a High Church propagandist. Discerning High Church readers might also have remembered L'Estrange's own "reflexion" upon this fable: "So says many a Vain Fool in the World, as this Cock does in the Like Case, and Exposes himself to Scorn, as well as Destruction."[60] It might have seemed safe, to a High Church reader, to apply the fable as it was applied by Defoe's speaker — to the Dissenters. Thus the Dissenters, like the Cock, were vain fools, exposed to scorn and destruction in the new world of Queen Anne's reign. But the fable appears two-edged. Defoe consistently claimed he wrote to expose, not the Dissenters, but the High Churchmen. Could it be that they were deliberately being invited to apply the fable wrongly?

If the fable is intended to be applied specifically, then the Cock represents the Dissenters, and the Horses the High Churchmen. That in itself might be a pertinent description, given that horses were traditionally used as an example of stupidity, much as sheep would be today. The manuals of logic offered *equus* as one of "their most common examples of *animal irrationale*."[61] Perhaps this is being too ingenious, and the point need not be pressed. The way in which the Horses are described in Defoe's adaptation of L'Estrange's version of Aesop is enough. They are "jostling about for room." Why? Applied to the situation in 1702, the description is far from complimentary. If we "mythologize" further, we might wish to equate the "Racks, or other Conveniences" with the Toleration Act, or the special protection of William III. This is surely not being fanciful, for Defoe's speaker draws attention to it himself. The Dissenters, like the Cock, are now "*unpearcht*, and reduc'd to an Equality with other People." Even if we assume that this is the extent of Defoe's meaning in producing the fable, it is sufficiently suggestive.

Clearly the equation of the Cock and the Dissenters stresses their actual weakness. S. A. Black has already suggested that there is irony between this initial representation and the speaker's later insistence on their strength, and I think he is right to point to the pamphlet's frequent inconsistent statements of the Dissenters' numbers as potential ironic pointers.[62] However, the mere contrast between the single Cock, "in danger of his Life" because of the "jostling," and the Horses themselves, serves a number of ironic purposes. The disparity in size is ludicrous, and surely renders equally ludicrous the subsequent claims made by Defoe's speaker that the High Churchmen are in any danger from the Dissenters. This is pointed up by the absurdity of the Cock advising the Horses to "*stand still, for fear we should tread upon one another.*" The fear is all on the side of the Cock. These Horses are either easily scared, or they are being irrational, as it is in their nature to be. Only one person, or group of persons, is in danger of losing life: the Cock in the stable amongst the Horses, or, to apply the fable to the situation in 1702, the Dissenters now that they no longer have a nonconformist king on the throne. The Cock could not harm the Horses even if he wanted to; nor could he have harmed the Horses even when he was "pearcht."

If the *Shortest Way* is viewed in the light of the opening fable, then, the pamphlet's rhetoric is quite different in effect. The speaker's scheme is exposed for what it is, as the process of demystification is allowed to work against him. Take, for instance, the numerous references to the numbers of Dissenters, as remarked upon by Black, and how they might be regarded once the image of the Cock and the Horses is firmly imprinted in the reader's mind. The first reason given "why we should continue and tollerate [the Dissenters] among us" is the simple fact that "THEY are very Numerous." How does this correspond with the opening fable? The speaker answers this objection in three ways. He suggests that they are "not so Numerous as the Protestants in *France*," yet Louis XIV managed to root them out. Nor does he believe "they are so Numerous as is pretended." Second, "The more Numerous, the more Dangerous, and therefore the more need to suppress them." Finally, regardless of their numbers, the experiment of trying to get rid of them should be made. How is this passage likely to be read by the "Men of Tast" who understand irony? As if to point the discrepancy out more clearly, the speaker returns to the question of the strength of the Dissenters near the end of the pamphlet. "THEIR Numbers, and their Wealth, makes them Haughty," he argues, although "AT present, Heaven be prais'd, they are not so Formidable as they have been." Once more we have the ridiculous suggestion that a Cock in a stable amongst a number of Horses is, or has been, "Formidable!" How can such arguments be taken seriously?

Perhaps two ironic pointers are operating in conjunction here. If the import of the fable is allowed to colour the interpretation of the speaker's rhetoric, then, I imagine, that rhetoric is undercut. If not, then a careful reader should surely be disturbed at the inconsistencies of his argument, which goes something like this. If the Dissenters are dangerous because of their numbers, then they should be suppressed. If, on the other hand, their numbers have been exaggerated, then they should be suppressed. First they are powerful, then they are not so powerful. Either way, they should be destroyed. That, in essence, is the argument of the pamphlet. Leranbaum says that the speaker is "a good rhetorician, and therefore very dangerous."[63] This largely depends on what is meant by "a good rhetorician," for the rhetoric of the *Shortest Way* can be seen to be specious. In that sense it is very dangerous, and perhaps skilful enough to incite bigots into action, much as Sacheverell's call to the "*True Sons*" of the Church of England "to Hang out the *Bloody Flag*, and *Banner* of Defiance" was effective because of its resounding slogan. Defoe was showing how dangerous such rhetoric was on account of its effectiveness. Yet the arguments employed in the *Shortest Way* are not logical, but deeply flawed by inconsistency. In that sense, the speaker is a poor rhetorician.

Once the existence of genuine ironic pointers in the *Shortest Way* is granted, other nagging if comparatively trivial questions could be solved. Three principal types of potentially ironic statement are to be found in the pamphlet: simple error; the distortion or misrepresentation of facts; and apparent *suppressio veri*. Two examples of the first stand out and require interpretation. The speaker utilises a simile: "as *Scipio* said of *Carthage, Dlenda* [*sic*] *est Carthago*." Not only is this obviously inaccurate – a typo, conceivably – but Scipio thought Carthage should be preserved, Cato wanted it destroyed. Defoe's error? Critics are fond of comparing the *Shortest Way* with Swift's *Modest Proposal*. However, when Swift commits such inaccuracies they are usually taken as ironic pointers. Perhaps here Defoe is intent on unmasking his persona through revealing his sham learning: his determination to use a classical tag simply exposes his own ignorance. Similarly when the speaker tries to draw an analogy between the suggested behaviour of the Church of England and the reaction of Moses, "a merciful meek Man," to those who had fallen into idolatry, the reference is patently inaccurate. Exodus mentions a figure of 3,000, but the *Shortest Way* says that Moses "cut the Throats of Three and thirty thousand of his dear *Israelites*." Somehow an additional "3" has been added to the number, inflating it eleven times. This cannot be put down to a typo, because the figure is written in words, and inverted for rhetorical effect. Is this Defoe's mistake? Did he misread his Bible? Or is he ironically exposing his speaker? "Possibly a deliberate exaggeration," James T. Boulton tentatively suggests.[64] But to what end? The inversion, "Three and thirty thousand," indicates intention, with the true figure given in Exodus suddenly bumped by 1000% through the addition of a couple of words. Does this draw deliberate attention to the unreliability of the narrator? Is it Defoe's muddle, or his speaker's?

The representation of the history of the Dissenters in England in the *Shortest Way* provides examples of distortion. Inevitably, interpretation of such cases is more complex, as Defoe, presumably, is offering a version which will be acceptable to High Churchmen. Therefore it is to be expected that this will involve misrepresentation. The question is whether or not this was meant to be recognised by the reader, and raises once again the audience issue. "The first execution of the Laws against the Dissenters in *England*, was in the Days of King *James* the First," the speaker explains:

> and what did it amount to, truly, the worst they suffer'd, was at their own request, to let them go to *New-England*, and erect a new Collony, and give them great Privileges, Grants, and suitable Powers, keep them under the Protection, and defend them against all Invaders, and receive no Taxes or Revenue from them. This was the cruelty of the Church of *England*, fatal Lenity!

According to this version of the events of the reign of James I, the Dissenters were better off as a result of the demand that Puritan clergy conform by 30 November 1604 on pain of expulsion. All the advantage was on their side. But the sailing of the *Mayflower* for New England on 6 September 1620 was hardly a direct result of the Hampton Court conference of 1604. Nor was the foundation of a new colony "the worst" the Puritans "suffer'd" by the penal laws. True, James I's ecclesiastical policy "drove out only a small minority of the more extreme Puritans."[65] Around ninety clergymen were deposed after failing to accept the provisions of Article 36 of the Canons of 1604. The main point is that the speaker of the *Shortest Way* is fudging the issue. His account of James I's reign obfuscates. Defoe clearly is showing how High Church writers employ such techniques to confuse. But his imitation, once recognised for what it is, serves to demystify.

Such distortion borders on *suppressio veri*, but there are better instances of this. Take the brief account offered of James II's reign:

> KING *James*, as if Mercy was the inherent Quality of the Family, began his Reign with unusual Favour to them: Nor could their joining with the Duke of *Monmouth* against him, move him to do himself Justice upon them; but that mistaken Prince thought to win them by Gentleness and Love, proclaim'd an universal Liberty to them, and rather discountenanc'd the Church of *England* than them; how they requited him all the World knows.

James II's Declarations of Indulgence are mentioned, but it is as if Judge Jeffrey's Bloody Assizes had never taken place. Talk of the king trying to "win" the Dissenters "by Gentleness and Love," and refraining from "do[ing] himself Justice upon them," is perverse. No doubt this is what High Church bigots wanted to hear, in the same way that present-day right-wing groups offer obscene interpretations of the holocaust, but surely it cannot have been glossed over by more moderate readers? Here, if anywhere in the *Shortest Way*, the rules of simple irony seem to be operating. Impartial readers would sense that the truth of James II's reign was the opposite of the version given by Defoe. He may not have unmasked his speaker at this point as Swift does in the *Modest Proposal*, but the ironic pointers are there to be seen.

Imagery, too, contributes to the overall ironic effect of the *Shortest Way*. The famous comparison of Dissenters and "Serpents, Toads, Vipers, &c." suggests that something akin to double irony is often at work in this pamphlet, as Defoe at once imitates High Church tactics in order to demystify, and pursues his own polemical objective independently. His speaker tries to influence his target reader – the High Church supporter whose views of the Dissenters he wishes to confirm – by a spurious analogy which identifies the Dissenters with poisonous animals:

> 'TIS Cruelty to kill a Snake or a Toad in cold Blood, but the Poyson of their Nature makes it a Charity to our Neighbours, to destroy those Creatures, not for any personal Injury receiv'd, but for prevention; not for the Evil they have done, but the Evil they may do.

Such imagery serves to dehumanise the Dissenters, and fudges the question of cruelty by misrepresenting their destruction as an act of charity: "Serpents, Toads, Vipers, &c. are noxious to the Body, and poison the sensative Life; these poyson the Soul, corrupt our Posterity, ensnare our Children, destroy the Vitals of our Happyness, our future Felicity, and contaminate the whole Mass.'' The use of bestial imagery is thus linked with spiritual well-being, the contrast between Dissenters and the ordinary run of humanity emphasised by the insistence on their ability to affect not only the sensitive soul, but the rational as well: "Shall any Law be given to such wild Creatures: Some Beasts are for Sport, and the Huntsmen give them advantages of Ground; but some are knock'd on Head by all possible ways of Violence and Surprize.'' Suddenly the comparison between Dissenters and poisonous animals has hardened so that it is difficult to separate the two: "such wild Creatures" has become a phrase equally applicable to the Dissenters as to vipers, and bestial imagery is the ploy which has allowed this to happen. Dissenters are beyond the pale. It is absurd, Defoe's speaker implies, to imagine that they are protected by laws such as the Toleration Act. They are to be "knock'd on Head by all possible ways of Violence and Surprize.'' And the justification offered for this is that, somehow, they are less than human.

In impersonating a High Church rhetorician, Defoe has satisfied the demands of his High Church audience. To an uncommitted moderate who does not share the prejudices of this audience, however, the speciousness of such rhetoric is exposed. The analogy offered by Defoe's speaker is no answer to the objection that the extermination of the Dissenters will "be Cruelty in its Nature, and Barbarous to all the World.'' The reaction of this secondary reader will be different. Defoe's reference to law is an important further consideration. Novak mentions contemporary annotations on a copy of the *Shortest Way* which draw attention to those laws that these "Proposals for the Establishment of the Church" would have transgressed.[66] That is why the government had to take notice of this "seditious libel.'' And Defoe has taken care that the government is implicated in his speaker's plans. "I doubt not but the Government will find effectual Methods for the rooting the Contagion from the Face of this Land,'' he writes, and anticipates how the eyes of the moderate Churchmen will be opened "when the Government shall set heartily about the work.'' We are at the heart of Defoe's polemical strategy. Such statements could not be ignored, for they hinted at government involvement in plans for the destruction of the Dissenters, contrary to the laws of the land. His *reductio ad absurdum* method may have fooled the High Churchmen, but, more importantly, it forced the government to repudiate measures which could be interpreted as unnecessarily oppressive. Ministers were "oblig'd to declare against it, for fear of being thought of the same Mind,'' because "when the persecution and destruction of the Dissenters, the very thing they drive at, is put into plain English, the whole nation will start at the notion, and condemn the author to be hanged for his impudence.''

It is one thing to suggest the polemical objective of *The Shortest Way with the Dissenters* and to outline the strategies Defoe employed to achieve his aims, quite another to assess the success of his pamphlet. True, the first occasional conformity bill foundered after a dispute between the two houses of parliament, as the Lords inserted amendments "which they knew the Tory commoners would never accept.'' But it is impossible to say how much this outcome was influenced by the *Shortest Way*. Defoe's retrospective account of the efficacy of his rhetoric sounds exaggerated. However, by the start of the parliamentary session of 1703–04, attitudes to occasional conformity had perceptibly altered. The ranks of committed High Churchmen did not withdraw their support for a second occasional conformity bill, but "the enthusiasm of some Tory M.P.s for a second bill had noticeably cooled." As Geoffrey Holmes remarks, "when the Queen was rather less ardent, and when the duumvirs [Marlborough and Godolphin] were thoroughly averse to controversial legislation which endangered supply and threatened a head-on collision between Lords and Commons, some Tory peers were persuaded to abstain from voting by the Court."[67] Government policy had changed. In December 1702 it had been, if anything, in favour of an occasional conformity bill: eleven months later it was against it. Could it be that Defoe's pamphlet had played its part in convincing the men in power that it was not politically advisable to press legislation against the Dissenters?

The concept of polemical strategy insists that the immediate context of controversial prose be a primary consideration in any critical analysis. Otherwise, attempts to establish meaning and intention can be misinformed. *The Shortest Way with the Dissenters* is a prime example of this, as critics have argued over form rather than rhetorical technique. Novak's listing in his title, "Hoax, Parody, Paradox, Fiction, Irony, and Satire," indicates the extent of the problem, and others have continued to insist that the pamphlet is "a deception rather than a satire,"[68] or "characteristic Defoe fiction."[69] Concentration on strategies rather than the categorisation of types of controversial prose liberates discussions from stultifying exercises in generalisation. Instead, it draws attention to the individuality of each piece because of its overriding polemical concerns. In the case of *The Shortest Way with the Dissenters*, the recognition that it was written to meet a specific contingency – the debate in the House of Lords on the occasional conformity bill – together with a consideration of audience, leads to a different assessment of polemical objective and, in turn, of polemical strategy which markedly alters our perception of the pamphlet which changed Defoe's life.

J.A. DOWNIE

NOTES

1. British Library, Add. MS 29589, f. 400: the Earl of Godolphin to the Earl of Nottingham [14 Dec. 1702].
2. *The Shortest-Way with the Dissenters ... consider'd; his name expos'd, his practices detected, and his hellish designs set in a true light* (London, 1703), p. 14: "if he does not provide himself with Ways and Means to Jump out of the Window as he did, he may keep Company with his Printer."
3. City of London Records Office, Oyer and Terminer Sessions Files for 22 and 24 Feb. 1702–3; *Journals of the House of Commons*, XIV, 207.

4. *Selected Writings of Daniel Defoe*, ed. James T. Boulton (Cambridge: Cambridge U.P., 1975), p. 96. All references to the *Shortest Way* are to this edition.
5. *The Review and the Observator Review'd, with Some Observations thereon* (London, 1706), p. 6.
6. British Library, Add. MS 28094, ff. 165–6: "A Character of Daniell de Foe writer of the Pamphlett calld the Review."
7. *The Works of Daniel Defoe Carefully Selected from the Most Authentic Sources. With Chalmer's Life of the Author, Annotated*, ed. John S. Keltie (Edinburgh: William P. Nimmo, 1872), p. 538. Subsequently referred to as *Works*.
8. *The Letters of Daniel Defoe*, ed. George Harris Healey (Oxford: Clarendon Press, 1955, repr. corr., 1969), pp. 4–5: D[e] F[oe] to William Paterson, April 1703. Subsequently referred to as *Letters*.
9. *Works*, p. 538.
10. *Works*, p. 539.
11. *Letters*, p. 4.
12. *The Fox with his Fire-brand Unkennell'd and Insnar'd: Or, a Short Answer to Mr. Daniel Foe's Shortest Way with the Dissenters* (London, 1703), p. 3.
13. [Daniel Defoe], *A Dialogue between a Dissenter and the Observator* (London, 1703), pp. 25–6.
14. *Letters*, p. 2: De Foe to the Earl of Nottingham, 9 Jan. 1702[– 3].
15. [Daniel Defoe], *The Consolidator: Or, Memoirs of Sundry Transactions from the World in the Moon* (London, 1705), p. 208.
16. *The Consolidator*, p. 108.
17. *The Consolidator*, pp. 209–10.
18. [Daniel Defoe], *The Present State of the Parties in Great Britain* (London, 1712), p. 24 (quoted in Maximillian E. Novak, "Defoe's *Shortest Way with the Dissenters*[:] Hoax, Parody, Paradox, Fiction, Irony, and Satire," *MLQ*, 27 (1966), 406–7).
19. Miriam Leranbaum, "'An *Irony Not Unusual*': Defoe's *Shortest Way with the Dissenters*," *HLQ*, 37 (1974), 235.
20. Paul K. Alkon, "Defoe's Argument in *The Shortest Way with the Dissenters*," *MP*, 73 (1976), S12 [*sic*].
21. *Works*, p. 533, quoting from *The Dissenters Answer to the High-Church Challenge*. For Oldmixon's version, see *The History of England during the Reigns of King William and Queen Mary, Queen Anne, King George I* (London, 1735), p. 301.
22. [Charles Leslie], *The New Association, Part II* (London, 1703), p. 6.
23. Ibid. See also *Mercurius Politicus*, I, 3: 16–19 June 1705.
24. Ian Watt, *The Rise of the Novel: Studies in Defoe, Richardson and Fielding* (Harmondsworth: Pelican Books, 1972), p. 142.
25. Richard I. Cook, "Defoe and Swift: Contrasts in Satire," *Dalhousie Review*, 43 (1963), 30.
26. Cook, p. 30.
27. *Works*, p. 539.
28. Novak, p. 411.
29. Novak, p. 407.
30. Leranbaum, p. 231.
31. Leranbaum, p. 235.
32. [Defoe], *Present State*, p. 24.
33. Novak, pp. 402, 415.
34. *Review*, II, 277; *To the Honourable The C[ommon]s of England Assembled in P[arliamen]t. The Humble Petition and Representation of the True Loyal and always Obedient Church of England, Relating to the Bill for Restraining the Press* in J. A. Downie, "An Unknown Defoe Broadsheet on the Regulation of the Press?", *The Library*, fifth series, 33 (1978), 56.
35. *The Prose Writings of Jonathan Swift*, ed. Herbert Davis (Oxford: Basil Blackwell, 1939–62), I, 4: "Another Thing to be observed is, that there generally runs an Irony through the Thread of the whole Book, which the Men of Tast will observe and distinguish." Swift was writing about *A Tale of a Tub*.
36. *The Consolidator*, p. 209.

37. Watt, p. 142.
38. Narcissus Luttrell, *A Brief Historical Relation of State Affairs from September 1678 to April 1714* (Oxford, 1857), V, 242.
39. *The Reformer Reform'd: or The Shortest Way with Daniel D'Fooe* (London, 1703), pp. 2–3 (quoted in Novak, p. 403).
40. British Library, Add. MS 29589, f. 400.
41. *An Enquiry into the Occasional Conformity of Dissenters, in Cases of Preferment* in *A True Collection of the Writings of the Author of the True Born English-man* (London, 1703), p. 305.
42. *A Dialogue between a Dissenter and the Observator*, p. 21.
43. *The New Association of those Called, Moderate-Church-Men, with the Modern-Whigs and Fanaticks, to Under-Mine and Blow-Up the present Church and Government* (London, 1702), p. 9.
44. *New Association*, p. 10.
45. Gilbert Burnet, *A History of My Own Time* (Oxford, 1833), V, 50.
46. Cook, p. 28.
47. *The Consolidator*, p. 209.
48. *Works*, p. 538.
49. *The Consolidator*, p. 209.
50. Geoffrey Holmes, *British Politics in the Age of Anne* (London: Macmillan, 1967), p. 102.
51. Novak, p. 404.
52. Henry Sacheverell, *The Political Union: A Discourse Shewing the Dependence of Government on Religion* (London, 1702), pp. 61, 49; *Selected Writings*, ed. Boulton, p. 96.
53. *Works*, p. 538; *Present State*, p. 21.
54. *New Association*, pp. 8, 11.
55. *Selected Writings*, p. 95.
56. *Selected Writings*, p. 88.
57. *Selected Writings*, p. 88.
58. Leranbaum, pp. 231*n.*, 232.
59. Novak, pp. 409–10.
60. *Fables of Aesop and Other Eminent Mythologists* (London, 1694), p. 412 (quoted in Leranbaum, p. 232*n.*).
61. Irvin Ehrenpreis, "The Meaning of Gulliver's Last Voyage," *Review of English Literature*, 3 (1962), 23.
62. S. A. Black, "Defoe's *Shortest Way*," *American Notes and Queries*, 5 (1966), 51–2. Cf. Leranbaum, p. 232*n*.
63. Leranbaum, p. 229.
64. *Selected Writings*, p. 268.
65. *The Reign of James VI and I*, ed. Alan G. R. Smith (London: Macmillan, 1973), p. 13.
66. Novak, p. 411.
67. Holmes, p. 102.
68. Leranbaum, p. 250. Leranbaum argues that it is a deception because "there is no ... unmasking of the persona" (ibid., p. 229).
69. Benjamin Boyce, "*The Shortest Way*: Characteristic Defoe Fiction," *Quick Springs of Sense: Studies in the Eighteenth Century*, ed. Larry S. Champion (Athens, Ga: University of Georgia Press, 1974), pp. 1–13. This is not the view taken by the most recent commentator on Defoe's fiction, who returns to the position that "Defoe chose a fundamentally ironic strategy, and sought to ridicule the high Tory position by exaggerating it slightly." Ian Bell is right to point out that the "inflation of Sachervell's [*sic*] case was meant as a devastating satire, revealing the intellectual paucity of its speaker, and the inhumane severity of his arguments," but his reading is similarly divorced from a consideration of context except in the most general sense, and assumes that "Defoe had wholly misjudged the temper of the debate" (Ian A. Bell, *Defoe's Fiction* (London: Croom Helm, 1985), p. 22.

"In the case of David":
Swift's Drapier's Letters

Works of political persuasion are particularly vulnerable to misinterpretation unless we take into account the specific context in which the author
wrote. This sense of context is also required in order to appreciate the
emotional force of political writing fully. The impact of *The Drapier's
Letters* was to a large extent owing to Swift's exploitation of the feeling
of the time. The way in which the *Letters* were printed and distributed –
pseudonymously and cheaply by the thousand – contributed to that
impact. Today, first-time readers find Swift's polemic largely unmeaning-
ful. Isolated passages have the power to impress, but it is hard to understand how these letters could have had an unprecedented influence on Irish
politics. It may even strike modern readers as odd that Swift chose to
combat a serious threat to the Irish economy by publishing a series of
letters apparently written by a draper. If, however, we are able to obtain
information about the historical context, see the author responding to the
pressure of events, and gain an insight into the force of contemporary
rhetoric then *The Drapier's Letters* can produce something of the excitement
they originally created. If we also examine Swift's rhetorical strategy to
discover how he manipulates the reader then the subtlety of his work is
better appreciated. The first part of this essay outlines the historical situation
that gave rise to the *Letters*. The second part examines Swift's rhetoric in
more detail.

I

Swift wrote *The Drapier's Letters* between 1724 and 1725 in an effort to
unite Irish opposition to the copper halfpence coined in England for Irish
use. For the most part, the controversy was based on economic arguments.
However, the dispute also revived discussion about the question of
Ireland's political status and threatened to disrupt the stability of Walpole's
government.

In Ireland, during this period, there was a shortage of copper coins.
The problem was not an uncommon one in England. Copper money was
coined on an *ad hoc* basis and smaller currency was often scarce. But
Ireland's shortage was particularly severe and counterfeit coins or *raps* were
openly used out of necessity.[1] Ireland had no national mint. English
governments had repeatedly brushed aside Irish requests that the country

might be permitted to issue its own currency – a circumstance that irked the Irish greatly. Ireland, therefore, depended for gold and silver currency on the circulation of these coins as a result of European trade. The country was provided with copper money by the English monarch authorising a private citizen to mint copper currency exclusively for Irish use.

The Earl of Sunderland, first Lord of the Treasury, had given the disposal of a patent to issue copper coins in Ireland to the Duchess of Kendal. The Duchess was George I's mistress and Sunderland hoped to augment his standing with the King by granting the Duchess this favour. The Duchess was prepared to grant the patent to the person who could offer her the largest bribe. This man was William Wood, an iron merchant from Wolverhampton. Sunderland was forced to resign in 1721 and Walpole, who succeeded him, was faced with the question of Ireland's proposed copper coinage. He was unwilling to offend the influential Duchess and therefore lent his support to the project. On 12 July 1722, William Wood was granted a patent to coin 360 tons of copper for Ireland to the value of £100,800. It was reputed that he had agreed to pay the Duchess £10,000 for the privilege.

Rumours of the project reached Ireland in 1722 and caused angry complaint even before the English government sent over official notification of the patent. For one thing, it was extremely humiliating for the Irish to discover that a measure significantly affecting their economy had been ratified without any prior consultation with the Irish parliament or Irish officials. This neglect was a reminder to the Irish that they were a dependent nation, and an untimely reminder because the Irish were then especially sensitive on this point. Only two years earlier, in March 1720, the English parliament had passed the Declaratory Act which had affirmed the political dependency of Ireland on England.

However, the terms of the patent were sufficient in themselves to cause the Irish concern. Doubtless, Ireland suffered from a shortage of small change, but she needed nowhere near the amount of copper money that Wood was empowered to coin. £100,800 amounted to a quarter of the money already in circulation in Ireland. A more realistic estimate of the country's needs was £10,000 or £20,000 in copper money, and actually it was silver currency that Ireland chiefly wanted. The Irish tended to pay English debts in silver owing to the different rate of exchange between gold and silver in England and Ireland which allowed the Irish to save threepence in every guinea. Over the years this practice had depleted the nation's stock of silver money.[2]

Another criticism of the patent was that Wood's copper coins were not required to have the same intrinsic value as those coined for England. This would further weaken Ireland's currency. Her gold and silver coins were being drained away in payments for foreign goods and if she was provided with copper coin of low intrinsic value this would aggravate the problem. Moreover, there were opportunities for fraud. Wood was permitted to mint his coins at Bristol rather than in London as was usual. He would not, therefore, be subjected to rigorous supervision. James Maculla, in a pamphlet entitled *Ireland's Consternation*, warned that Wood's coins were of unequal weight with "edges snagled, and bulg'd."[3] Poor workmanship meant that counterfeiters were more likely to flood the market with base imitations. Nor had the English government established any safeguards to prevent Wood coining more than £100,800 of copper. Once his coins were current in Ireland it would be easy for him to ship over more money than had been specified in his patent. In addition, Wood was not required to pay the bearer of his coins legal tender on demand – although this safeguard had been a condition of former patents.

II

It is no wonder then that Irish officials were seriously alarmed when they learnt the terms of Wood's patent. Initially, they had been irritated by the high-handed manner in which the patent had been issued. On reflection they saw that the more pressing cause for concern was the threat that Wood's copper presented to the Irish economy. The Archbishop of Dublin, William King, and Ireland's Commissioners of Revenue wrote letters of protest but these were ignored by the English government. In September 1723, when the Irish parliament was convened, an investigation of the patent was ordered. Both houses sent an address to George I asking for the patent to be revoked. But English ministers reckoned that Irish objections to the patent rested, as at first, on the lack of consultation before it was passed. They failed to do justice to the economic arguments – partly, it must be said, because the Irish had not presented their case in a convincing manner.

Swift became actively involved in the conflict at a later stage when it was clear that the Irish would obtain no satisfaction by voicing their protest through official channels. Irish patriots considered that a national boycott of Wood's coins was the only route left open to them. An extensive publicity campaign would be required in order to get the message across to the common people and Swift was asked to initiate it. Swift had no great faith in the capacity of the Irish people to act in their own interest. In 1720 he had published *A Proposal for the Universal Use of Irish Manufactures* in which he advised the Irish to boycott foreign goods in order to support their country's economy. His advice was not taken. Indeed, his printer was jailed for making it public. Nevertheless, Swift agreed to act in the affair of Wood's halfpence. Probably he saw more reason to be optimistic about the outcome of this undertaking because Irish officials were united in opposition to the scheme.

Swift was, to use his own phrase, "a Whig in politics and a High Churchman in religion" – a notoriously difficult statement made more problematic by the Whigs and Tories themselves, who seemed to change places with regard to policies and political ideals in the years following the 1688 Revolution. When Swift termed himself a "Whig in politics" he meant that he adhered to "Old Whig" principles.[4] These were affirmed by the Revolution of 1688 which instituted a limited monarchy in England whereby the ruler governs with the people's consent. Later Whigs seemed to adopt increasingly dictatorial methods when pushing their measures through parliament. Civil liberties were eroded and liberal thinkers feared that the quality of life was in jeopardy. Swift may also have been attracted to the campaign against Wood's halfpence because it presented an opportunity for him to strike a blow against England's demonstrable tyranny towards Ireland. He did not disagree with the prevalent mercantilist theory which declared that dependent nations should contribute to the wealth of the mother country and be prevented from competing in trade.[5] However, he strongly objected to England's callous exploitation of Ireland. Swift saw the effects of this exploitation at first hand and both English greed and Irish apathy filled him with frustration and anger. Nevertheless, when Swift sat down to write against Wood's halfpence, he had specific aims more narrowly related to the task in hand. And as circumstances changed in the course of the dispute so Swift was required to tailor his arguments to fit modified and equally specific objectives.

III

Initially, the most pressing need was to convince the ordinary people of Ireland that Wood's money posed a threat to their livelihoods and that consequently they should utterly refuse to accept the coins as tender. The upper levels of Irish society were determined against the patent but their opposition would have been totally ineffectual if ordinary tradesmen accepted Wood's halfpence in their daily transactions.[6] It would have been impossible to reverse England's policy once the coins were in circulation.

Swift chose to publish his message to the common people in letter form — a perspicacious choice since this enabled him to adopt a familiar, even personal tone although addressing thousands of people. The epistolatory form also invited him to create an identity for himself, a persona to which his audience could relate. It was necessary that Swift conceal his identity in order to avoid possible prosecution. But an author who is practised in strategies of indirection provides himself with more opportunity for manoeuvre by creating a distinct persona than if he simply writes anonymously.

Swift adopted the persona of a draper. His *Proposal* of 1720 had been written in defence of the Irish cloth trade and he may have felt an affinity for the drapers who traded in the vicinity of his deanery. Also the clothing metaphor was commonly used to denote the hypocrisy that masks sin and if one takes an oblique view the Drapier is an appropriate persona for a writer engaged in polemics to expose sharp practice. Swift's choice of persona may also have been a tactical move.[7] Irish drapers had a reputation for opportunism at the expense of their country's true interest but Swift's Drapier, however mindful of his own well-being, is manifestly a true patriot.

Swift's choice of persona has obvious advantages in the first *Letter* when the Drapier addresses petty traders and the common people. It legitimises the use of concrete advice that such readers would find immediately forceful:

> For my own part, I am already resolved what to do; I have a pretty good Shop of *Irish Stuffs and Silks*, and instead of taking Mr. *WOOD's* bad Copper, I intend to Truck with my neighbours the *Butchers*, and *Bakers*, and *Brewers*, and the rest, *Goods* for *Goods*, and the little *Gold* and *Silver* I have, I will keep by me like my *Heart's Blood* till better Times. (X, 7)

In this and in similar passages, Swift presents the Drapier as an upright, plain-thinking man; without false modesty yet having a keen sense of community spirit. The Drapier gives the impression that he has turned the issue carefully over in his own mind before deciding on the best and most practical action for someone in his position. As he insists that an infiltration of Wood's copper coins will spell disaster for every person in Ireland, his resolutions are, by implication, those which other men should act upon.

At the outset, Swift probably did not foresee the need for a series of letters addressed to different categories of persons. Certainly, his persona works less well in subsequent letters when the argument requires a display of legal or constitutional knowledge. At such moments the Drapier's tone becomes uncomfortably self-conscious. In later letters Swift occasionally drops the persona altogether and apparently speaks in his own voice: "As to disputing the King's *Prerogative*, give me Leave to explain to those who are ignorant, what the Meaning of that Word *Prerogative* is" (X, 54). But in fact, the impetus of Swift's writing is such that the reader might not register the incongruity of a draper having such specialised knowledge if Swift did not himself draw attention to it: "Having thus given you some Notion of what is meant by the King's *Prerogative*, as far as a *Tradesman* can be thought capable of explaining it, I will only add the Opinion of the great Lord *Bacon* ..." (X, 55; cf. X, 28). The awkwardness of tone is an indication of Swift's difficulty here, but in the main he manages his persona with considerable skill. It must be remembered that Swift was not trying to create a rounded or consistent character. He could not have intended his readers to believe that the Drapier really existed. If naive readers believed so at first, they could not have been fooled for long.[8] Moreover, when reading *The Drapier's Letters* it is unhelpful to think of Swift's persona even as a consistent mask. Swift equips his persona with several tones of voice and the Drapier performs different rhetorical functions as different audiences are addressed. To think of the Drapier as a uniform disguise is to miss any subtleties.

One difference between the Drapier and Swift's earlier personae is that the Drapier's opinions are not treated ironically. They impress the reader as being Swift's own views although Swift removes himself from direct confrontation by voicing them indirectly. Unlike the Hack in Swift's *A Tale of a Tub*, for example, the Drapier is almost never ridiculed. On the contrary, it is essential to the rhetorical strategy of the *Letters* that Swift's mouthpiece is regarded as a man of sound principle and reason whom the reader can trust. And the fact that contemporary readers detected a real presence behind the persona, a clergyman known to be disinterested, surely contributed to the success of the *Letters*. Thus in some instances, what may appear to be lack of control or wilful exuberance – a broad hint at the author's identity that apparently results from pride in performance – may in fact be deliberate and part of Swift's technique. Nevertheless, Swift's playfulness with respect to his persona in the later letters is less purposeful. It conveys the pleasure to be derived from a skill in manipulating a disguised identity – little else.

IV

In the first *Letter*, the Drapier's preliminary remarks are uttered in a tone reminiscent of a preacher addressing his congregation. The tone may not be ideally suited to a draper but it has a reassuring effect:

> What I intend now to say to you, is, next your Duty to God, and the Care of your Salvation, of the greatest Concern to your selves, and your Children, your *Bread* and *Cloathing*, and every common Necessity of Life entirely depend upon it. (X, 3)

The Drapier exhorts the people "to read this paper with the utmost attention, or get it read to you by others" and doubtless, the pastor-like tone would be especially effective if the letter was read aloud to an illiterate audience whose experience of literature was largely confined to the Scriptures as they were read and explained in church. The tone of this passage helps to ensure that the Drapier's words obtain authority, whatever the circumstances in which the letter is read.

Elsewhere, the tone of *The Drapier's Letters* is contingent and often equivocal. For example, the third *Letter*, addressed to "the Nobility and Gentry of the Kingdom of Ireland" is more cultivated and the arguments more subtly reasoned than previously. Wood is once more permitted to be "Mr. Wood," although his title was contemptuously dropped in earlier letters. The Drapier reasons that the English Privy Council, asked to inquire into Wood's patent, have in fact prejudged the whole issue since the protests of the Irish parliament are referred to as a "universal clamour" in the Council's report. The point made here is one that a polemicist, keenly aware of the opposition's rhetoric, would pick up. It focuses on an affront to the pride of Irish gentlemen in order to fuel their opposition to the patent.

In general, the Drapier adopts a haughty attitude towards Wood. This may appear incompatible with their social positions but when reading the *Letters* the Drapier's tone seems justified since he clearly holds the superior moral position. Paradoxically, his haughty tone even supports his assumption of ethical superiority.[9] If the effect is occasionally one of incongruity then this is not without humour for those among Swift's audience able to perceive the wit resulting from his use of a persona.

Nor is this wit essentially detrimental to Swift's argument. The gap between what the Drapier says and what a common tradesman might be expected to utter in no way affects the author's right to say these things. The authority of the Drapier is also based on his assumed practical experience. The reader is satisfied that, as a successful tradesman, he has a shrewd understanding of basic economic facts. All the Drapier's allusions to his personal circumstances help to substantiate his claim to be heard on account of his practical experience as well as native common sense. Swift may have been influenced in this matter by Defoe's political tracts. Defoe habitually introduced personal details into his political journalism to win the confidence of his audience of London tradesmen. Swift preferred to distance himself from his readers in the manner of a more gentlemanly writer.[10] Nevertheless, Defoe had some success in winning over his target audience and since, at the outset of the campaign, Swift was trying to reach a comparable sector of society, he may have decided to employ similar tactics. The Drapier is a suitable agent to employ in order to simplify the economic and constitutional arguments in a form that an uneducated audience would find persuasive. If he had occupied a higher station in life, his tone might have seemed more condescending. Thus, by Swift's deft handling of the persona, the Drapier commands a hearing on a number of accounts: cultural, moral, and experiential.

V

Swift's chosen persona had yet another advantage in that it helped him to fictionalise Wood in a manner that suited his purposes. Swift not only had to overcome his readers' apathy. He also needed to allay their fears. It is for this reason, perhaps, that he repeatedly stresses that the Irish cannot be compelled to accept Wood's coin: George I can insist only that his subjects receive coins made of gold or silver. By setting up a Draper as Ireland's champion, Swift implies that Wood is an opponent so obscure and unremarkable that he can be thwarted by a Dublin shopkeeper.

One of the few advantages of poor communications between England and Ireland to the propagandist was that it permitted easy distortion of circumstance. It is not known whether Swift had an accurate knowledge of Wood's background when he began to write *The Drapier's Letters*. Since he misspells Wood's name in the first two letters it seems unlikely that his knowledge was extensive. Anyway, it suited Swift's purpose to distort his presentation of the antagonist, although as it happened certain of his allegations were not wide from the mark.[11] Swift consistently emphasises Wood's mean origins and low social station. Wood becomes lodged in the reader's memory as a "little impudent hard-ware man" (X, 18). This phrase, with variations, is often repeated – especially in those letters addressed to the common people. Swift was adept at judging the level of his audience and crude abuse of this sort can acquire something of the status of a witty remark by being often repeated. Certainly, it helps to render Wood all the more contemptible.

In order to write *The Drapier's Letters* Swift interrupted work on *Gulliver's Travels*, in which political insinuations are conveyed by the manipulation of physical dimensions. A similar technique is used in the *Letters*. Wood is isolated by Swift's rhetoric to become "one single, diminutive, insignificant, Mechanick" (X, 19). This is most apparent in the second *Letter*, written when the Committee of Inquiry, led by Sir Isaac Newton, had examined Wood's coins and presented a favourable report of their quality to the public. The report undermined economic objections to Wood's coin and consequently Swift alters the emphasis of his argument and attacks from a new angle. The Drapier now affects to believe that Wood has taken on the whole Irish nation: the Irish reject Wood's coin, "upon which he grows angry, goes to Law, and will impose his Goods upon us by Force" (X, 16). Swift presents the quarrel as if it is essentially a dispute between Wood and Ireland. As he has made Wood appear an obscure, insignificant creature, the patentee's attempt to impose his will on a nation seems utterly ridiculous and no cause for alarm. Many Irish feared that George I would exert his prerogative beyond strictly constitutional bounds and force the Irish to accept Wood's money. Swift allays these fears by having the Drapier accuse Wood of treason: "daring to prescribe what no King of *England* ever attempted, how far a whole Nation shall be obliged to take his Brass Coin" (X, 19). In this way, Swift contrives to ridicule Wood, "this little Arbitrary Mock-Monarch," while reassuring the people that legally the monarch had no power to compel receipt of Wood's coins. As the Drapier has become a symbol of Irish resistance, so Wood in similar metonymic fashion has come to symbolise English tyranny: but whereas the one is aggrandised, the other is belittled. Wood is made a target as English ministers could not be without fear of reprisal.

VI

The more reflective of Swift's audience would nevertheless have realised that no single person of Wood's low social status could exert the power that the Drapier claims for him. Since Wood has been reduced to a mere "creature" the enormity of his imputed ambition is beyond credibility. Greater, if more shadowy, powers seem involved in the dispute. To sharpen this impression, Swift exploits the apparent naivety of his persona in order to insinuate accusations he dare not state openly. In the second *Letter* Swift also prepares to raise the level of the debate by proceeding from economic arguments to those concerned with justice and human rights. From the outset, the Drapier's case had an implied ethical justification. He appeals to the reader at the level of common decency and fairness. And because the Drapier is presented as a bluff, honest tradesman outraged at Wood's underhand dealing – he terms the patent "a WICKED CHEAT from the *Bottom* to the *Top*" (X, 5) – so he allows Swift to make oblique accusations by seeming naively unaware of the logical deductions from his comments: "GOOD GOD!", the Drapier exclaims, "Who are this Wretch's *Advisors*?

Who are his *Supporters, Abetters, Encouragers,* or *Sharers*?'' (X, 19). The answer can only be: interested members of the Whig ministry. The Drapier's indignation apparently prompts him to continue,

> If the famous Mr *Hambden* rather chose to go to Prison, than pay a few Shillings to King *Charles* I without Authority of Parliament; I will rather chuse to be *Hanged* than have all my Substance Taxed ... at the Arbitary Will and pleasure of the venerable Mr. *Wood.* (X, 20)

Sarcasm, rare in the *Letters*, marks the Drapier's anger and the revolutionary allusion seems a calculated one on Swift's part. Hampden's defiance is a significant precedent and the allusion also contributes to the character of the Drapier who appears now as a champion of liberty. Nevertheless, when the Drapier makes his famous declaration: "Am I a *Free-man* in *England*, and do I become a *Slave* in six Hours by crossing the Channel?''[12] the passion of the speaker only partly disguises the fact that these words are less appropriate to a shopkeeper than to a man such as Swift with long experience of both countries. It is noticeable in this passage that the rhetoric is directed not only at the Irish but also at the English, who prided themselves on a constitution that safeguarded civil liberties. The use of the first person singular (admittedly a consequence of Swift's adoption of a persona), the heavy stresses, and the sequence of rhetorical questions make this outburst a particularly emotive one. The reader is placed, as it were, in the role of judge, and an appeal is made to the reader's sense of fundamental human rights. At the same time, Swift makes an insinuation calculated to evoke insecurity in an English reader as it would excite indignation in an Irish reader. If a subject of England can be deprived of basic rights by crossing a stretch of water, what safeguards exist to prevent these rights giving way to expediency even on English soil? The passage is effective because the author is not carried away by the force of his own rhetoric. Despite the use of the emotive word ''slave,'' he gives the impression that his outburst is pronounced from a considered political position. (In the fifth *Letter*, the Drapier implies that Ireland's relationship with England approximates to a condition of slavery since the Irish are governed by laws made without their consent.)

The word ''slave'' also reminds the reader of England's distant colonies and the Drapier's question implies that Ireland should not be regarded in the light of a colony. Moreover, by once again raising the level of the argument to the political sphere Swift side-steps the economic issue of the contribution Ireland should make as a dependent nation to the English economy. Yet he cannot be accused of neglecting this point altogether. Later the Drapier refers to the £800 a year which Wood was obliged to pay the crown during the term of his patent and wonders that this should be thought equivalent to the ruin of a kingdom worth far more to George I in terms of revenue. Typically, he raises the question in a manner calculated to impress English readers with how much they stand to lose if Wood succeeds and Ireland is ruined.

On the whole, Swift consolidates his case in the third *Letter*, setting out his arguments more dispassionately and logically for a more educated reader. Such a reader would also appreciate the irony in the Drapier's line of reasoning — for he is, in effect, confronting a Whig government with "Old Whig" principles that they were pledged to uphold, and answering those who adhered to mercantilist theory with arguments that seem only to take that theory one logical step further. Thus he points out that England stands to gain more by continuing to exploit Ireland than by bankrupting the kingdom.

VII

In *The Drapier's Letters* Swift accommodates himself to his audience: different letters are addressed to different readers and important arguments may be expressed so that they appeal to different sets of readers on different levels. Whenever the Drapier reflects on the absurdity of sacrificing a kingdom that yields a fortune in revenues he speaks to English greed as well as to Irish fears of economic ruin.[13] When he compares Wood's project to the practice of the French government who debased the currency only to call it in and recoin it at a higher rate, he appeals to English patriotism as well as to Irish anger. (The English liked to believe that their government was more "democratic" than that of the French and anti-French feeling ran high.) The Drapier appeals to the upper classes in addition to those who were less wealthy. In the second *Letter* he encourages estate owners to get up a petition against Wood's patent and to direct their tenants to refuse the copper money. When the English Privy Council advised that all officers in Ireland should be ordered to receive Wood's coin, the Drapier pointedly warned those in office not to agree to be paid in Wood's money. He declared that the bulk of the Irish people would never receive this coin and that consequently officers would "be Losers of Two Thirds in their *Salaries* or Pay" (X, 47). Similarly, when Ireland was in a state of apprehension at the premature arrival of Lord Carteret, the new Lieutenant General, lest it signified the introduction of measures to enforce Irish obedience, the Drapier warned place-seekers against complying with English demands in return for a bribe or a position. He believed that

> a Gentleman would rather chuse to live upon his *own Estate* which brings him *Gold* and *Silver*, than with the Addition of an *Employment*; when his *Rents* and *Salary* must both be paid in *Wood's* Brass, at above eighty *per cent*. Discount. (X, 59)

Such arguments are chiefly aimed at the rich but lesser people may have found them reassuring. The Drapier's reasoning is based on the logic of the market-place, is easily assimilated, and suggests that all classes in Ireland have good cause to stand together against Wood.

In those letters where Swift is able to specify his audience more precisely, it is an easier matter to select arguments that will be persuasive. In general, because Swift's audience was so heterogeneous, both in social and religious terms, it must have been difficult to present strong arguments without offending one party or another. For example, Swift addressed his fourth *Letter*, the most controversial, to "the whole People of Ireland" but it is doubtful whether in 1724 this phrase would have signified all Irishmen or only the Protestants.[14] Moreover, despite his efforts to simplify legal and constitutional matters for the less educated, such people must have found some passages in the *Letters* difficult to follow. Perhaps for this reason, Swift circulated ballads and songs among street singers so that the poorest classes would be turned against Wood's money. He presented the issue of Wood's patent as a rare instance of self-interest coinciding with public duty. It is an indication of Swift's opinion of mankind that he never neglects this point entirely, even when he also gives moral and political reasons for opposing Wood's patent.

VIII

The Drapier's Letters were designed to take advantage of popular feeling and it is evident that Swift distorted facts and exploited prejudice to produce the reactions he desired. However, his considerable skill in suiting his material to his audience and to the task in hand is not always so easily appreciated. He perverts the truth with such plausibility that misrepresentation rarely draws attention to itself. Thus the modern reader is faced with particular difficulties.

One aspect of the Drapier's arguments that does excite suspicion is his use of statistical information. Yet not all the figures given in the *Letters* are untrustworthy. The Drapier calculates that Ireland needs about £25,000 of copper money and this figure is in line with impartial estimations. In contrast, the Drapier grossly underestimates the population of Ireland at that time. He claims that there were about 1.5 million people in the kingdom when in fact there were at least one million more. It has been argued that in the 1720s and 1730s a number of Irish patriots deliberately falsified the figures because received opinion held that the wealth of a nation was directly related to its populousness. As Ireland was in a wretched condition, a significant proportion of the people made no positive contribution to the economy. Swift was therefore anxious to claim that Ireland's population was increasing at a slower rate than the rest of Europe. The implication is that once again England was acting against her true interest by placing such heavy burdens on Ireland that the country was unable to realise its economic potential.[15]

Swift's manipulation of the figures regarding Wood's halfpence is exceptionally subtle. He leads the reader into a maze of calculation and at any one moment the arithmetic appears to be sound. The difficulty arises when the reader considers how he or she entered a particular sequence of sums. Where did the Drapier obtain his figures? Can his confessed estimations be trusted? Why did he choose to demonstrate one set of comparative figures rather than another? Invariably, supposition and insinuation are compounded with correct arithmetic to the extent that readers cannot easily detect any fraud. In any case, original readers were probably disposed to credit exaggeration and to think the worst of Wood. Ultimately, the Drapier's spiralling figures reach such large numbers that it is difficult to conceive of the amounts of money in question. Readers are led to think that Wood is about to make vast profits. In fact, considering that Wood had to find a bribe of £10,000, it does not appear that his profits would have been great.[16]

In the *Letter to Shopkeepers*, Swift uses another technique. Apparently, the Drapier conducts his calculations with absurd literalness but in fact he builds up a fictional picture of the situation that involves much imagination. Having stated that a shilling of Wood's money is worth a penny of good money and that twenty shillings of Wood's money will weigh *"Six pounds Butter Weight,"* he estimates that a typical farmer's annual rent "will be at least Six hundred Pound weight, which is Three Horse Load" (X, 6). The absurdity of the notion is not so much cause for laughter as occasion for bitter mockery of Wood's scheme. Swift does much to ensure that this reaction is produced by judiciously mentioning causes of popular bad feeling. For example, the Drapier mentions William Conolly, Speaker of the Irish House of Commons, whose income was legendary and who also supported Wood's patent:

> They say SQUIRE CONOLLY Has *Sixteen Thousand Pounds a Year*, now if he sends for his *Rent* to Town, *as it is likely he does*, he must have *Two Hundred and Fifty Horses* to bring up his *Half Year's Rent*, and two or three great *Cellars* in his house for Stowage. (X, 7)

In the next paragraph, the Drapier alludes to the hardship James II caused during his unsuccessful Irish campaign when he debased the coinage to pay his soldiers. As this was within living memory for many, the allusion would have been a forceful one.[17] Swift also makes use of Ireland's grudge against the Dutch. They had previously counterfeited Ireland's debased coinage and used worthless coin to pay for Irish goods. The Drapier prophesies that Wood's money is so base, if it is accepted for general use, Dutch counterfeiters will soon be at work again. Finally, the Drapier warns that the kingdom will be ruined if Wood's copper is accepted. Estate owners will evict their tenants (bound by the terms of their lease to pay rents in sterling) and farm the land themselves, "run *all* into *Sheep* where they can, keeping only such other *Cattle* as are necessary" (X, 7). The enclosure of land for sheep farming was particularly resented. It depressed the population by depriving people of steady labour and was therefore thought to contribute to Ireland's poverty. The increase of sheep farming could be interpreted as another indication of England's tyranny and the Drapier's reference to it is strategically placed.

When Swift distorts information he may disguise the fact by using emotive rhetoric. He does so in the second *Letter* when the Drapier contemptuously dismisses a report that Ireland's lack of small currency had been confirmed by Irish merchants:

> But who are these *Merchants and Traders of Ireland* that make this report of *"the utmost Necessity we are under for Copper Money"*? They are only a few Betrayers of their Country, Confederates with *Wood*, from whom they are to purchase a great Quantity of his Coin, perhaps at half the Price that we are to take it, and vend it among us to the Ruin of the Public, and their own private Advantage. (X, 15–16)

The merchants are denigrated as "betrayers," "confederates" – a loaded word that suggests evil design. They are vilified profiteers who would put their own interest above that of their countrymen. It does not appear that the Drapier has tangible proof that these men are to purchase Wood's coin in bulk. He merely guesses that they will obtain a fifty per cent discount. But the vehement language and breathless punctuation temporarily remove any desire the reader might have to examine the logic of the passage.

IX

In the Drapier's concluding letter, "An Honourable Address to both Houses of Parliament," the reader is told, "I never had the least Intention to *reflect on His Majesty's Ministers*, nor on any other Person, except *William Wood*" (X, 123). But whatever the intention, the *Letters* cast many such aspersions. Indeed, the Drapier very soon proceeds to make another. Can it be denied or doubted, he asks, that the King and his ministers intended the patent as a benefit to Ireland and the Irish? Can Wood be otherwise regarded than as "the *Instrument*, the Mechanick, the *Head-Workman*, to prepare his Furnace, his Fuel, his Metal, and his Stamps?" But even allowing that the King's intent was a gracious one, the people of Ireland are united in thinking the project ruinous. Should the kingdom be *"wholly undone* ... for the Sake of *William Wood*?" In this passage the Drapier protests the King's benevolence to excess. The employment of Wood therefore seems inconsistent with the King's benevolent intention. Also, if Wood is to be thought of as a mere instrument of convenience, his wicked project must be countenanced by those in power. The Drapier combines this line of suggestion with less subtle hints of ministerial corruption: "I mention the Person of *William Wood* alone; because *no other* appears, and we are not to reason upon Surmises; neither would it avail, if they had a real foundation" (X, 126). Elsewhere, Swift misrepresents the situation by omitting facts that do not assist his argument. For example, he asserts that the Irish population has suffered owing to active discouragement of agriculture. He does not mention the Anti-Catholic laws passed in Queen Anne's reign which caused thousands of Catholics to emigrate. Such information would not have united Protestant and Catholic against Wood but instead would have fuelled old animosities. In the *Letters* Swift had to omit names of English ministers for fear of prosecution but he turns this to advantage. One glaring omission is that the Drapier himself never directly mentions Walpole.[18] Yet once the level of the argument has been raised to include principles of human justice, it is evident that Walpole is the Drapier's true opponent. Wood does not have the political power needed to impose his will on the Irish. Swift gains much by refusing to name Walpole. He can make the patent appear more evil by hinting at shadowy, malignant powers master-minding the project from a distance. He is also able to enhance the Drapier's position because it appears that the Drapier is not the kind of person directly to abuse social superiors. Finally, he avoids reprisals.

At every opportunity, Swift deliberately misrepresents the intention of his opponents. When Wood tried to conciliate the Irish by proposing that no one should be obliged to receive more than fivepence halfpenny of his coin in any one payment, the Drapier accused him of "daring to prescribe what no King of *England* ever attempted, how far a whole Nation shall be obliged to take his Brass Coin" (X, 19). When the report of the English Privy Council of Inquiry on Wood's patent was published in the *London Journal*, the Drapier pretended to believe that Wood was responsible for printing it. In the third *Letter* he writes,

> The whole is indeed written with the Turn and Air of a Pamphlet, as if it were a Dispute between *William Wood* on the one Part, and the *Lords Justices, Privy Council and Both Houses of Parliament* on the other. (X, 27)

Having ridiculed the whole tenor of the report, the Drapier can proceed to dismiss or undermine specific points with greater arrogance and contempt without seeming to criticise the English Privy Council directly. The tendency of his argument is always to polarise the issue. If the Irish parliament agreed to a compromise at this stage, an opportunity for Ireland to assert its rights would be lost. The polemical need of the moment fortunately accorded with Swift's typical rhetorical practice. He commonly polarised viewpoints and attitudes in order to exploit possibilities for irony and incongruity. In *The Drapier's Letters* polarisation is one way in which he falsifies Wood's case while still appearing to base his arguments on facts and thus persuading the reader that what he is saying is common sense.

X

On a casual reading, the *Letters* do not strike the reader as being "literary." In general, they are not well structured. Some bear the marks of having been written in haste; others are restricted because written to answer points made in specific documents. Nor are the *Letters* strikingly metaphorical. However, Swift does make effective use of imagery and this helps to unify the *Letters*. In addition, his allusions are carefully selected and he employs anecdote with an excellent sense of timing.

The imagery used in the *Letters* is generally undistinguished. Striking imagery would conflict both with the character of Swift's persona and with his desire to reach a wide audience. Instead, the Drapier tends to reinforce his case by employing imagery that was readily understood and clearly appropriate. When discussing the question of Ireland's dependency on England he makes use of the accepted image of the King as physician whose duty it was to ensure the well-being of the kingdom he ruled. When the Drapier describes how Ireland has reacted to news of Wood's patent, he writes: "And, as we are apt to *sink* too *much* under *unreasonable* Fears, so we are too soon inclined to be *raised* by groundless Hopes (according to the nature of all *consumptive* bodies like ours)" (X, 63). This passage connects with the disease imagery used to describe the consequences of allowing Wood's coin to enter the country:

> If it once enters, it can be no more confined to a small or moderate Quantity, than the *Plague* can be confined to a few Families; and that no *Equivalent* can be given by any earthly Power, any more than a dead Carcass can be recovered to Life by a Cordial. (X, 60–61)

This warning in turn picks up an earlier reference to illness and medicine, made when the Drapier angrily refuted Wood's claim that Ireland was so short of copper money it stood in need of his halfpence. The Drapier asks, "If a Physician prescibe to a Patient a *Dram* of Physick, shall a Rascal pothecary cram him with a *Pound*, and mix it up with *Poyson*?" (X, 15). The cumulative effect of this train of reference is to suggest the severity of the English government towards Ireland, particularly since Wood emerges as a tool of the Whig ministry. George I ought to be concerned about the welfare of Ireland and behave as a good physician to his patient, but apparently his neglect is contributing to the nation's destruction.[19]

Swift is later able to build upon the reference to a rascal apothecary cramming his patient with poison when the Drapier alludes to the threat, reported in a newspaper, that "*Mr. Walpole will cram his Brass down our Throats*" (X, 67). A less fortuitous occurrence of cumulative imagery and allusion is to be found in the Drapier's references to thieves and robbery. Wood is more than once described as a robber. In the following example the homiletic turn of phrase lends authority to the Drapier's words:

> Will a Man, who hears Midnight Robbers at his Door, get out of Bed, and raise his Family for a common Defence? and shall a whole Kingdom lie in a Lethargy, while Mr. *Wood* comes at the head of his *Confederates* to rob them of all they have, to ruin us and our Posterity for ever? (X, 22–23)

Ironically, Wood's dishonesty is potentially a means of keeping habitual thieves honest and the Drapier is able to enliven his argument with sour humour:

> Let *Wood* and his *Accomplices* Travel about the Country with Cart-Loads of their *Ware*, and see who will take it off their Hands: There will be no Fear of his being robbed: for a *Highway-Man* would scorn to touch it. (X, 46)

This string of references is more particularly effective because Swift can tap the resource of common experience, or at least common agreement: "For, if one single Thief forces the Door, it is in vain to talk of keeping out the whole Crew behind" (X, 105). This is a form of words easily remembered if readers needed to justify their opposition to Wood's coin. Later Swift employs the allusion to robbery when the Drapier apologises for his prose style: "But when a House is attempted to be robbed it often happens that the weakest in the Family runs to stop the Door" (X, 48). In this instance, Swift combines apparent humility with a sentimental appeal to Irish patriotism, however obliquely stated. Elsewhere he evokes sympathy for Ireland's plight with more subtlety by creating an analogy between the nation's relations with England and that of a maiden, seduced and abandoned by her ravisher:

> *Is it, was it, can it*, or will it ever be a Question, not whether such a Kingdom, or *William Wood*, should be a Gainer; but whether such a Kingdom should be *wholly undone, destroyed, sunk, depopulated*, made a Scene of *Misery* and *Desolation*, for the Sake of *William Wood*? (X, 126)

The semantic range of the verbs "undone," "destroyed," "sunk," is significant here, especially when it is remembered that in 1707 Swift wrote *The Story of the Injured Lady* in which the injured lady is Ireland, whom England took advantage of and then jilted in favour of her less worthy rival, Scotland.[20]

Swift kept literary references to a minimum in the *Letters* and instead provided biblical allusions which an uneducated but churchgoing audience could appreciate. He demonstrates an inventiveness in his use of the Bible that partly compensates for this self-imposed restriction. One use is to quote the Scriptures in order to endorse the Drapier's arguments: "St. *Paul* says, *All Things are* lawful, *but all Things are not* expedient. We are answered, that this Patent is *lawful*; but is it *expedient*?" (X, 41). He finds significant parallels in the Bible, as when the Drapier compares Wood to Goliath, armed from head to foot in brass, and he himself to David, attacking with puny weapons, a sling and a stone (X, 48). Paradoxically, as Wood has already been pared down to insignificance, this comparison with a giant dwarfs him further. In contrast, the Drapier is magnified because David is known to be the victor against Goliath and because David has christological significance. Swift's biblical allusions have oblique political import. When the Drapier prepares to raise the question of Irish independence in the fourth *Letter*, he alludes pointedly to Esau, who sold his birthright for a mess of pottage.[21]

Swift's use of the Bible helps to suggest that Wood's scheme is iniquitous and that the Irish who oppose it have God on their side. The Drapier concludes the first *Letter* by comparing Wood's halfpence to "the *accursed Thing*, which, as the *Scripture* tells us, the *Children of Israel* were forbidden to touch" (X, 12). His biblical references indirectly remind readers that they are subject to a higher law than that of the English courts. This helps a number of the Drapier's comments to work on two levels. When he alludes to the report that Ireland needed copper money, he writes, "Who were the Witnesses to prove it, hath been shown already: But in the Name of God, who are to be *Judges*? Does not the Nation best know its own wants?" (X, 43). The passage is reminiscent of Matthew 7, 1: "Judge not, that ye be not judged" and augments Irish indignation by its implicit as well as by its overt meaning. It reminds readers that all men are equal while questioning merely whether England is a best judge of Ireland's monetary needs. In the Drapier's final letter, the accumulated weight of biblical references and homiletic turns of phrase permit him to imply with greater credibility that when the Irish rejected Wood's halfpence the Irish were doing God's will (X, 126).

XI

Many of the Drapier's arguments appear to be pragmatic and dictated by reason. Readers of polemic, however predisposed to agree with the author, need to be persuaded that the arguments are grounded in reason. Yet the appeal of the *Letters* is not wholly reasonable: the Drapier makes an emotional appeal to religion and patriotism. This tells us something of Swift's conception of his audience. The Drapier complains that some English think "we have neither *common Sense*, nor *common Senses*" (X, 55). Nevertheless, he seems himself to have little confidence that the Irish will act in their own interest and he presents Ireland's economic distress as partly the result of the nation's irrational folly. He places his trust in the middle ranks of society who stood to gain most from an improvement in Ireland's economy but implies, finally, that he is the victim of naive optimism. In his last *Letter* he compares his endeavours to those of a crazy projector – a comparison all the more bitter since he earlier condemned Wood as a projector.[22] It might be thought that Swift thereby avoids the charge of distorting facts: his speaker dissociates himself from comments made earlier when he might often have been accused of "saying the Thing which was not." Swift is self-conscious enough to submit his own position to analysis and seems aware that writing is of dubious efficacy in a political world governed by power. A final ironical twist in this instance is that Swift's tractarian rhetoric, a manipulation of fiction and reality, helped to rectify what he presented as a gross abuse of reason by the English government.

Swift was proud of the *Letters*: although dependent upon events they helped to make history. He also found himself in the satisfying position of being given credit for a work to which he had never publicly set his name.

Yet the success of the *Letters* was temporary. Swift appealed to *"Law* and *Liberty,* and *the Common Rights of Mankind"* (X, 93) but succeeded largely because he identified self-interest with patriotism. The Irish were sufficiently motivated to ensure Wood's defeat, but the economic exploitation of Ireland by England continued because Irish protests had less effect against the broader interests of the Whig oligarchy, and Swift made no attempt to encourage insurrection.[23]

The literary aspect of the *Letters* is of more enduring interest: they constitute a remarkable example of persuasive writing. Swift's satirical works are ambivalent — notoriously so. But the Drapier's message admits of no doubt: Swift's polemic contains no exploitation of a disjunction of form and meaning. The *Letters* are distinctive in that although the Drapier addresses different audiences — sometimes managing to achieve this simultaneously in a single passage — the text offers one meaning for all readers. The power of the *Letters* results from this control, all the more remarkable since the presence of the author is distinctly problematic. A subtext is perhaps available to modern readers who might quibble that, although the Drapier gives priority to natural rights, his literary form conveys a reminder of inequality since his writing is inaccessible to the illiterate. However, Swift does take the needs of the unlettered into account.

Swift was sensitive to the differences between writing and speaking, and in the *Letters* he attempts to combine the effects of both. Several of the *Letters* were written to be read aloud to the illiterate, and many passages lend themselves to declamation. The Drapier's arguments also seem to draw upon an oral culture. He often destroys the opposition's case by a humorous anecdote that supplies a commonsense, pragmatic viewpoint to place events in a different light and show how the English have misjudged matters. This occurs when the Drapier cites a newspaper report that Walpole *"hath sworn to make us swallow his Coin in Fire-Balls"* (X, 67) and comments:

> This brings to my Mind the known story of a Scotch Man, who receiving Sentence of Death, with all the Circumstance of *Hanging, Beheading, Quartering, Embowelling,* and the like; cried out, *What need all this cookery?* (X, 67)

Swift, an experienced political pamphleteer, knew the importance of undercutting his opponent's rhetoric. But whereas Swift draws attention to a debased use of language by Wood and his supporters, he by no means encourages readers to suspect that the Drapier's language might be similarly specious and divorced from reality. This is unlikely to be an unconscious omission: Swift's view of language was hardly naive. In *Gulliver's Travels* he mocks those who attempt to purify their discourse and communicate by holding up physical objects in order to avoid semantic confusion.[24] It has been argued also that for Swift, fine writing was not simply "proper words in proper places": "Correct writing for him did not merely conform to reality. It was reality, better still, it was an event necessitated by other events, and leading to still other events."[25] Swift's view of correct writing necessarily ties his work to a particular time and place. *The Drapier's*

Letters remain of interest partly because they disclose the power of writing reacting with other kinds of power that operate in society. Rhetorical skill of the kind Swift demonstrates in the *Letters* can be a tool of good or evil, and when it suits his purpose he alerts the reader to the force of rhetoric. Swift also shows that language is a means of defence. The Drapier claimed that he could not express his arguments in the language of the elite: "I was in the case of *David*, who *could not move in the Armour of Saul*" (X, 48). In fact, he employs several kinds of political discourse. By decoding Swift's polemic readers are more likely to be properly armed against those who employ language to mislead.

MARGARETTE SMITH

NOTES

1. See *The Prose Works of Jonathan Swift*, edited by Herbert Davis et al, 16 vols (Oxford: Blackwell, 1939–1974), vol X (1941), 4. All subsequent references to *The Drapier's Letters* are taken from this edition and are given in the text.
2. For this account of Ireland's financial situation I am indebted to Irvin Ehrenpreis, *Swift: the Man, his Works, and the Age*, 3 vols (London: Methuen, 1962–83), III, 187ff.; Oliver W. Ferguson, *Jonathan Swift and Ireland* (Urbana: U. of Illinois P., 1962), pp. 83–138; A. Goodwin, "Wood's Halfpence," *English Historical Review*, 51 (1936), 647–74.
3. James Maculla, *Ireland's Consternation* (Dublin, 1723), p. 4. Quoted by Ferguson, p. 87.
4. Davis VIII, 120. See J. A. Downie, *Jonathan Swift: Political Writer* (London: Routledge & Kegan Paul, 1984), p. 26.
5. See Louis A. Landa, "Swift's Economic Views and Mercantilism," *ELH*, 10 (1943), 310–35.
6. See Davis, X, 110–11.
7. See C. J. Rawson, "The Injured Lady and the Drapier: A Reading of Swift's Irish Tracts," *Prose Studies*, 3 (1980), 17 and Davis, X, 136.
8. It is easy to find inconsistencies in Swift's portrayal of the Drapier. E.g. in *Letter* I the Drapier seems ignorant of Latin (Davis, IX, 9); in *Letter* II he translates Latin (Davis, IX, 20); in *Letter* V he says he learnt Latin at school (Davis, IX, 82). See Ferguson, p. 97, and David Nokes, "The Radical Conservatism of Swift's Irish Pamphlets," *British Journal for Eighteenth-Century Studies*, 7 (1984), 172.
9. See Rawson, "The Injured Lady and the Drapier," pp. 32ff.
10. See R. I. Cook, *Jonathan Swift as a Tory Pamphleteer* (Seattle: U. of Washington P., 1967), pp. 100–1.
11. See J. M. Treadwell, "Swift, William Wood, and the Factual Basis of Satire," *Journal of British Studies*, 15 (1976), 76–91.
12. Davis, X, 31. Swift's debt to Locke and Molyneux has been noted. See Downie, p. 246, and Clive T. Probyn, *Jonathan Swift: The Contemporary Background*, Literature in Context series (Manchester: Manchester U.P., 1978), pp. 135–6.
13. See Davis, X, 8 and 22.
14. See Rawson, "The Injured Lady and the Drapier," p. 38, and p. 43 n. 59.
15. See Clayton D. Lein, "Jonathan Swift and the Population of Ireland," *Eighteenth-Century Studies*, 8 (1975), 431–53.
16. See Goodwin, p. 650.
17. It has been argued that this allusion indicates Swift had a Protestant audience in mind. See J. C. Beckett, "Swift and the Anglo-Irish Tradition," in *The Character of Swift's Satire: A Revised Focus*, edited by C. J. Rawson (London and Toronto: Associated U.Ps.), p. 158.

18. Walpole is mentioned in *Letter* VI (to Midleton), unpublished until 1735. In *Letter* IV, the Drapier rebukes Wood for mentioning Walpole by name (Davis, X, 63).

19. Swift's use of imagery suggests that he sees himself in this role. See the opening of *Letter* IV: "I conceived my task was at an end: But I find, that cordials must be frequently applied to weak constitutions, political as well as natural" (Davis, X, 53).

20. See also *The Story of the Injured Lady*, Davis, IX (1945), 5. England has ruined Ireland by "the common Arts practised upon all easy credulous Virgins, half by Force, and half by Consent, after solemn Vows and Protestations of Marriage."

21. This was the traditional explanation for the ascendency of one nation over another. See Ehrenpreis, III, 262.

22. See Rawson, "The Injured lady and the Drapier," p. 26.

23. See David Nokes, *Jonathan Swift, A Hypocrite Reversed* (London: Oxford U.P., 1985), p. 296.

24. See *Gulliver's Travels*, Davis XI, 166–70.

25. Edward W. Said, "Swift's Tory Anarchy" in *The World, the Text, and the Critic* (London: Faber & Faber, 1983), p. 60.

Junius and the Grafton Administration
1768 – 1770

On 29 July 1766, when the 25-year-old Philip Francis was a Clerk in the War Office, George III wrote from Richmond Lodge to William Pitt:

> I have this day signed the warrant for creating you an Earl, and shall with pleasure receive you in that capacity to-morrow, as well as entrust you with my privy seal; as I know the Earl of Chatham will zealously give his aid towards destroying all party distinctions, and restoring that subordination to Government, which can alone preserve that inestimable blessing, Liberty, from degenerating into Licentiousness.[1]

The Chatham administration was conceived as a non-party administration whose ministers would be individually responsible to the Crown. The position of First Lord of the Treasury, having been declined by Earl Temple, was given to the Duke of Grafton; but Chatham as Lord Privy Seal was to exercise prime-ministerial authority. The Secretaries of State were the Earl of Shelburne, who shared Chatham's hostility to "parties banding together," and General Conway, whose loyalties were divided between Chatham and the Marquess of Rockingham. Places were found for some ministers from the previous administrations, including the Earl of Northington and the Marquis of Granby; but most members of the Bedford, Grenville and Rockingham connections went into opposition. Eight years later, in a speech on American taxation, Edmund Burke passed metaphoric judgment on Chatham's cabinet-making of 1766:

> He made an administration, so checkered and speckled; he put together a piece of joinery, so crossly indented and whimsically dovetailed; a cabinet so variously inlaid; such a piece of diversified Mosaic; such a tesselated pavement without cement; here a bit of black stone, and there a bit of white; patriots and courtiers, king's friends and republicans; whigs and tories; treacherous friends and open enemies: that it was indeed a very curious show; but utterly unsafe to touch, and unsure to stand on.[2]

Chatham, whose status was less dependent than Burke's on membership of a party, believed himself to be rescuing the constitution from the stranglehold of oligarchical management; but Burke's metaphor naturally commends itself to those who see the importance of this decade in its contribution to the growth of a party system.

In December 1766 Chatham went to Bath for the sake of his health; and

in February 1767 he suffered an attack of gout which was to exclude him
from active politics for more than two years. The administration was further
weakened by Grafton's lack of authority, Conway's indecision, and the
boldness with which Charles Townshend as Chancellor of the Exchequer
developed his own plans for taxing the colonies. The Bedford, Grenville
and Rockingham connections achieved sufficient unity of purpose to form
a strong opposition; but in July 1767 the King, by inviting Rockingham
to draw up plans for a new administration, forced them to reveal that they
could not agree on terms for accepting office. When the opposition had
been thus divided, the way was open for negotiations between the administration and the Bedfords. These negotiations took some months, during
which Townshend died and was succeeded by Lord North; but they were
completed in December 1767, when Earl Gower replaced Northington as
Lord President and Viscount Weymouth replaced Conway as Secretary of
State. James West reported despondently to the Duke of Newcastle:

> The Court are sanguine, applauding the Duke of Grafton's abilities
> in dividing the opposition and getting this vast acquisition, and
> declaring nothing can be done now but Lord Rockingham's shaking
> hands with Mr. Grenville and shewing their joint feeble efforts for
> another two or three years.[3]

In January 1768 the Earl of Hillsborough, another member of the Bedford
group, became Secretary of State for the Colonies; and Chatham received
an anonymous letter, which encouraged him to distrust his colleagues:

> During your absence from administration, it is well known that not
> one of the ministers has either adhered to you with firmness, or
> supported, with any degree of steadiness, those principles, on which
> you engaged in the King's service.... Mr. Conway, as your Lord-
> ship knows by experience, is every thing to every body, as long as by
> such conduct he can maintain his ground.... Lord Hertford is a little
> more explicit than his brother, & has taken every opportunity of
> treating your Lordship's name with indignity.... It is understood
> by the publick that the plan of introducing the Duke of Bedford's
> Friends entirely belongs to the Duke of Grafton, with the secret con-
> currence, perhaps, of Lord Bute, but certainly without your Lord-
> ship's consent.... My Lord [, the] man, who presumes to give your
> Lordship these hints, admires your Character without servility, and
> is convinced that, if this Country can be saved, it must be saved by
> Lord Chatham's spirit, by Lord Chatham's abilities.[4]

The author of this insidious letter, which plays cunningly on Chatham's
known defects of character, has sometimes been identified with Junius; and
so has the author of an anonymous letter received in February by George
Grenville, which caters for a different taste by offering detailed and very
tedious advice on taxation policy.

The general election of March 1768, in which boroughs were sold for
prices of between £3,000 and £5,000, initiated a new controversy by

returning John Wilkes as M.P. for Middlesex; but it did not significantly alter the balance of parliamentary forces. The Bedford influence, however, promoted a new severity in colonial policy, which left Shelburne at odds with his colleagues; and in October 1768, when Grafton agreed to the dismissal of Shelburne, Chatham resigned the Privy Seal. Chatham's resignation created the possibility of a new alliance embracing the followers of Chatham, Grenville and Rockingham; and this plan was actively promoted by Francis' patron John Calcraft, who was in communication with both Chatham and Temple. Such an alliance was as yet a distant prospect, since Chatham was still incapacitated and Grenville and Rockingham held opposite views on colonial policy. The issue that might be expected to unite the three, however, was the Middlesex election; and it was on this issue that Junius appeared to concentrate in his letter to the *Public Advertiser* on 21 November 1768. Though it was not included in the collected edition, this letter is wholly characteristic in its union of magniloquence and venom. The constitutional issues raised by the Wilkes case are quickly dismissed, on the ground that "the highest Authority" will deal with them; and attention is focused on the image of a man who has been betrayed by his friend and therefore deserves "the generous Sympathy of Mankind." The final sentences, however, convert this expression of humane concern into a threat to the supposed traitor's power: "In the present Instance the Duke of Grafton may possibly find that he has played a foolish Game. He rose by Mr. Wilkes's Popularity, and it is not improbable that he may fall by it."[5] Without presenting any argument on the political issue or any evidence on the personal one, the letter contrives to suggest that the administration has violated the constitution and that Grafton is an inhuman monster unfit for public office.

This attack on the First Lord of the Treasury was followed on 21 January 1769 by the more comprehensive denunciation which Junius later placed in the forefront of his book. Once again he begins with a resonant assertion of constitutional idealism: "The submission of a free people to the executive authority of government is no more than a compliance with laws, which they themselves have enacted."[6] The elevated tone is skilfully maintained through the opening paragraphs, the harmony of a well-governed state being contrasted with the "distrust and dissatisfaction" which prevail where the government is "weak, distracted, and corrupt." In lamenting the transformation "which the misconduct of ministers has, within these few years, produced in Great Britain," Junius pays suitably unconvincing tribute to the king's "unbounded goodness of heart"; and then in the fifth paragraph he swoops down with sudden ferocity on his first victim: "The finances of a nation, sinking under its debts and expences, are committed to a young nobleman already ruined by play."[7] The contemptuous portrait of Grafton is followed by similarly magisterial condemnations of the Chancellor and the Secretaries of State; and then Junius turns to the service ministers, the Marquis of Granby and Sir Edward Hawke. The portrait of Granby is a *tour de force* in the manipulation of tone recalling the satiric characters of Dryden and Pope:

It has lately been a fashion to pay a compliment to the bravery and generosity of the commander in chief, at the expence of his understanding.... Nature has been sparing of her gifts to this noble lord; but where birth and fortune are united, we expect the noble pride and independence of a man of spirit, not the servile, humiliating complaisance of a courtier.... What thanks are due to a man, whose cares, notoriously confined to filling up vacancies, have degraded the office of commander in chief into a broker of commissions?[8]

The heroic commander is transmuted first into an aristocratic nonentity, then into a parasitic courtier, and finally into a sordid emblem of avarice. Against Hawke, Junius has no arguments at all; and so he devises a rhetorically-effective variation of his method, and passes judgment in a single sentence: "With respect to the navy, I shall only say, that this country is so highly indebted to Sir Edward Hawke, that no expence should be spared to secure him an honourable and affluent retreat."[9]

These dismissive character-sketches serve as a foil for the solemn assessment of an unnamed judge, whose abilities are treated with deliberate respect so that his alleged subservience to government may be represented as a dangerous evil. With this portrait Junius regains his elevation of tone; and he can therefore advance, with no sense of incongruity, to the panoramic gloom and resonant periods of his peroration. Professing horror at the desperate condition of the nation, he tries to imagine Posterity's attitude to a time when "a Duke of Grafton was Prime Minister, a Lord North Chancellor of the Exchequer, a Weymouth and a Hillsborough Secretaries of State, a Granby Commander in Chief, and a Mansfield chief criminal judge of the kingdom."[10] This catalogue of incongruities might seem a too-obvious way of summarising the letter's argument; but it gathers strength from the dehumanising use of indefinite articles, the long-delayed naming of the Lord Chief Justice, the ambiguity of the words "criminal judge," and the indignant, stammering prolongation of the final phrase.

This letter established the persona of Junius and the style which helped to define it. The tyrannicidal purpose suggested by the name's Roman associations authorised both the assertion of high constitutional principle and the ruthless destruction of individual reputations. Skilful modulations of tone made entertainingly slanderous accusations seem part of a fearless defence of liberty; and the carefully-varied manner of the portraits identified the unknown writer as a man who challenged Mansfield as a social equal and regarded Granby *de haut en bas*. Between 26 January and 3 March 1769 this persona was developed through a public controversy with Sir William Draper, an "honest soldier" who rashly undertook to defend his commander-in-chief. The letters to Draper differ from the attack on the ministry rather as Dryden's *MacFlecknoe* differs from *Absalom and Achitophel*: the note of condescending ridicule identifies the addressee as an insignificant parasite of the public enemy, a bungling controversialist whose arguments evoke laughter rather than anger. The opening sentences of these letters convey Augustan contempt in the false accents of paternal benevolence, unconstrained mercy and literary admiration:

Your defence of Lord Granby does honour to the goodness of your heart.[11]

I should justly be suspected of acting upon motives of more than common enmity to Lord Granby, if I continued to give you fresh materials or occasion for writing in his defence.[12]

An academical education has given you an unlimited command over the most beautiful figures of speech. Masks, hatchets, racks, and vipers dance through your letters in all the mazes of metaphorical confusion.[13]

In what follows, Junius bewilders his opponent with a pyrotechnic display of false compliments and loaded questions, feigned reluctance and plausible misinterpretation; and, having left the reputations of both Granby and Draper severely damaged, he takes his leave in tones of Olympian superiority: "In truth, you have some reason to hold yourself indebted to me. From the lessons I have given you, you may collect a profitable instruction for your future life."[14] The victory is sealed, in the collected edition, with a footnote which attributes the end of hostilities to Granby's request that Draper "should desist from writing in his Lordship's defence"; and this explanation is made more plausible by the omission of Draper's fourth letter, which Junius had not bothered to answer.[15]

The controversy with Draper gave Junius some useful publicity; but it was a mere interlude in his campaign to discredit the Grafton administration. A new opportunity presented itself in March 1769, when a royal pardon was granted to Edward MacQuirk, an Irish chairman who had been found guilty of murder after an election riot at Brentford. Since MacQuirk had been in the service of a ministerial candidate, his pardon could plausibly be attributed to Grafton's sympathy for his own agent:

> The honourable service for which he was hired, and the spirit with which he performed it, made common cause between your grace and him. The minister, who by secret corruption invades the freedom of elections, and the ruffian, who by open violence destroys that freedom, are embarked in the same bottom.[16]

Junius' main interest, however, was in the contrast between the administration's treatment of MacQuirk and its treatment of Wilkes:

> Has it never occurred to your Grace ... that there is another man, who is the favourite of his country, whose pardon ... would have healed all our divisions? Have you quite forgotten that this man was once your Grace's friend? Or is it to murderers only that you will extend the mercy of the crown?[17]

There was in fact substantial justification for the pardoning of MacQuirk, and the ministry's case was soon presented at length in *A Vindication of the Duke of Grafton*. This pamphlet was anonymous; but Junius affected to believe that it had been written by Edward Weston, a 66-year-old civil servant. He accused Grafton of provoking an "unhappy gentleman to play the fool ... in public life, in spite of his years and infirmities"; [18] and he informed Weston that he could not "descend to an altercation ... with the impotence of [his] age, or the peevishness of [his] diseases." [19] The *Vindication* had not circulated widely; and Junius, having exploited the MacQuirk case for its propaganda value, moved on to more important tasks.

What the opposition needed was a major popular issue on which they could unite against the administration; and that issue presented itself in the Middlesex election of 13 April 1769. Having been three times elected and expelled, Wilkes stood again and polled 1,143 votes to his opponent's 296; but on 15 April, despite the protests of Grenville and Burke, the House of Commons voted by 197 to 143 "that Henry Lawes Luttrell Esq. ought to have been returned a Member for Middlesex and not John Wilkes Esq." While a committee of Middlesex freeholders prepared to submit a petition to Parliament, Junius composed a letter to Grafton in his most elevated and insulting manner. Recalling the government's failure to enforce the law in March 1768, this letter mocks not only the Prime Minister and his mistress but also the hesitant General Conway and the hotheaded Viscount Weymouth:

> The security of the Royal residence from insult was then sufficiently provided for in Mr. Conway's firmness and Lord Weymouth's discretion; while the prime minister of Great Britain, in a rural retirement, and in the arms of faded beauty, had lost all memory of his Sovereign, his country and himself. [20]

With this indolence Junius contrasts the "uncommon exertion of vigour" which has now chosen Luttrell as representative of an electorate which voted for Wilkes: "With this precedent ... and with a future house of commons, perhaps less virtuous than the present, every county in England, under the auspices of the treasury, may be represented as completely as the county of Middlesex." [21] He argues, with fitting solemnity, that this decision is an attack not merely on Wilkes but on the rights of electors:

> You have united this country against you on one grand constitutional point, on the decision of which our existence, as a free people, absolutely depends. You have asserted, not in words but in fact, that the representation in parliament does not depend upon the choice of the freeholders. [22]

The magniloquent passage through which this point is developed offers a plausible statement of constitutional idealism, with suitable references to past conflicts and to "the birth-right of Englishmen." Such rhetoric contributes to the image of Junius as heir to the heroic Romans who defied Tarquin and Caesar; but it is complemented, in the final paragraph, by a rhetoric more fitted to the idle and treacherous agent of modern tyranny who is the letter's fictional addressee:

> Return, my Lord, before it be too late, to that easy insipid system, which you first set out with. Take back your mistress; — the name of friend may be fatal to her, for it leads to treachery and persecution.

Indulge the people. Attend Newmarket. Mr. Luttrell may again vacate
his seat; and Mr. Wilkes, if not persecuted, will soon be forgotten.[23]

The cause promoted in this letter is not political reform but conciliation
on the basis of a change of ministry; but the letter's populist aggressiveness
must have commended it to the metropolitan radicals.

The creator of Junius had many styles at his command; and one of these
can be seen in a private letter of 5 May 1769 to the printer of the *Public
Advertiser*:

> Sir,
>   it is essentially necessary that the inclosed should be published to
> morrow, as the great Question comes on on monday, & Lord Granby
> is already staggered.
>   if you shd receive any answer to it, You will oblige me by not
> publishing it, till after Monday.
>
>   C[24]

The letter thus recommended, which presents yet another persona, was a
flattering appeal to Granby signed "Your Real Friend"; and its object was
to persuade the Commander-in-Chief that he could recover "the public
Esteem" by voting against the administration on the petition of the
Middlesex freeholders. On 8 May, when that petition was considered, the
Commons decided by 221 votes to 152 that Luttrell had been "duly elected";
but this defeat led to a closer association among the main opposition groups.
On 25 November 1768 Chatham had been reconciled with Temple and
Grenville "through the medium of their mutual friend, Mr. Calcraft";[25]
and on 11 May 1769 the unity of the opposition was further advanced when
Grenville dined with the Rockingham Whigs at the Thatched House Tavern.
On 30 May, no doubt encouraged by this development, Junius launched
his fiercest attack so far on the morale and reputation of the Duke of
Grafton. Pretending to despair of influencing events when the constitution
is being openly violated, he professes to review Grafton's career "merely
as a subject of curious speculation." In the fastidious prose of an impartial
historian, he notes with surprise that even "the wildest spirit of inconsistency" has not once betrayed Grafton "into a wise or honourable
action." Alluding to the Duke's descent from an illegitimate child of
Charles II, he identifies "hereditary strokes of character" which identify
him as a true Stuart. Recalling his treacherous behaviour to Chatham,
Rockingham and his friend Wilkes, he admires the political wisdom of
Grafton's marriage-alliance with Bedford; and he suggests that such connections may in time enable him to control George III as the Pelhams
controlled George II. After cataloguing the changes in his colonial policy
and giving him credit for the French conquest of Corsica, Junius sum-
marises Grafton's contribution to the well-being of the nation:

> An amiable, accomplished prince ascends the throne under the
> happiest of all auspices, the acclamations and united affections of

his subjects. The first measures of his reign, and even the odium of a favourite, were not able to shake their attachment. *Your* services, my Lord, have been more successful. Since you were permitted to take the lead, we have seen the natural effects of a system of government, at once both odious and contemptible. We have seen the laws sometimes scandalously relaxed, sometimes violently stretched beyond their tone. We have seen the person of the Sovereign insulted; and in profound peace, and with an undisputed title, the fidelity of his subjects brought by his own servants into public question. Without abilities, resolution, or interest, you have done more than Lord Bute could accomplish with all Scotland at his heels.[26]

This pseudo-historical account might be interpreted as a demand for Grafton's resignation; but in the final paragraph Junius offers it simply as negative guidance for later generations. Like Pope's *Epistle to Augustus*, the letter has used the style and intellectual structure of a panegyric to serve the purposes of personal and political satire; and its attack on the Prime Minister has discreetly prepared the ground for an attack on the King.

The numerous replies to this letter created a problem for its author, since he could not easily maintain the dignity of his persona while responding to multiple conjectures about his identity and motives. His solution was to create a new character named Philo Junius, whose concise and factual manner would complement the expansive eloquence of his principal. In the *Public Advertiser* of 12 June 1769, Philo Junius re-directed attention to the case against Grafton with a series of blunt questions:

1. Have not the first rights of the people, and the first principles of the constitution been openly invaded, and the very name of an election made ridiculous by the arbitrary appointment of Mr. Luttrell?

2. Did not the Duke of Grafton frequently lead his mistress into public, and even place her at the head of his table? ...

6. Was he not the bosom friend of Mr. Wilkes, whom he now pursues to destruction? ...

10. Is there any one mode of thinking or acting with respect to America, which the Duke of Grafton has not successively adopted and abandoned?[27]

Similar aphorisms appeared in Philo Junius' next letter, which was printed on 22 June: "Doctor Blackstone ... recollected that he had a place to preserve, though he forgot he had a reputation to lose."[28] "The Duke of Grafton has always some excellent reason for deserting his friends."[29] The creator of Junius found it hard to maintain this laconic manner, however; and in responding to the arguments of Old Noll, Philo Junius engaged in some very Junian games with his opponent's signature, Grafton's Stuart ancestry, and the surname of the Treasury secretary Thomas Bradshaw.[30] The concept of regicide was never very far from Junius' mind; and some of his supporters at this time employed the pseudonym Brutus, which Junius himself had discreetly avoided.[31]

The Commons decision of 8 May had aroused widespread indignation, which was expressed not only through popular demonstrations but also through petitions. The petition campaign began in Middlesex and London, but between May 1769 and January 1770 it was taken up in counties and boroughs from Cornwall to Northumberland. An ode by Gray for Grafton's installation as Chancellor of Cambridge University on 1 July 1769 sought to banish "Mad Sedition's cry profane" by tracing the Duke's ancestry to the Tudors;[32] but on 5 July the Lord Mayor and four Members of Parliament presented the King with the petition of the London livery, a strongly-worded document which he "received with the utmost coldness and neglect."[33] Horace Walpole attached more importance to Chatham's unexpected appearance on 7 July at the King's levée:

> He was twenty minutes alone with the King; but what passed, neither of their Majesties has been pleased to tell .... That the moment of his appearance, *i.e.* so immediately after the petition of the Livery of London, set on foot and presented by his friend Alderman Beckford, has a hostile look, cannot be doubted.[34]

It was in this atmosphere of anger and expectation that Junius, on 8 July 1769, brought out his fifth letter to Grafton. Since the multiplying of grievances by the London radicals was alienating support among the gentry, he now focused like Grenville and Rockingham on the "grand constitutional point." While continuing to insult his victim with vituperation disguised as panegyric, he shows less interest in Grafton's personal vices than in those qualities which have made him a willing agent of the Favourite:

> Lord Bute found no resource of dependence or security in the proud, imposing superiority of Lord Chatham's abilities, the shrewd inflexible judgment of Mr. Grenville, nor in the mild but determined integrity of Lord Rockingham. His views and situation required a creature void of all these properties; and he was forced to go through every division, resolution, composition, and refinement of political chemistry, before he happily arrived at the caput mortuum of vitriol in your Grace.[35]

The charge that Grafton took orders from Bute was quite unfounded; but in making it Junius pays expedient tribute to the current opposition leaders, and shows some originality in the use of metaphor.

The opposition's purpose during the summer recess of 1769 was to organise petitions in as many counties and boroughs as possible; and in this context they wanted backing that was both numerically impressive and socially respectable. While the Supporters of the Bill of Rights sought to make petitions more forceful by listing numerous grievances, the Rockingham Whigs dissociated themselves from Wilkite rioters by confining attention to the Commons' acceptance of Luttrell. The objective now was not to frighten the administration but to persuade the country gentlemen; and Junius therefore addressed his letter of 19 July not to the Prime Minister but to the *Public Advertiser*. Eschewing personalities and satiric irony, he offered a suitably prosaic definition of the point at issue:

I take the question to be strictly this: "Whether or no it be the known, established law of parliament, that the expulsion of a member of the house of commons of itself creates in him such an incapacity to be re-elected, that, at a subsequent election, any votes given to him are null and void, and that any other candidate, who, except the person expelled, has the greatest number of votes, ought to be the sitting member".[36]

He then proceeded, without further reference to Wilkes or Middlesex, to explain that the affirmative case had no basis either in law or in precedent; and he ended by declaring that the "fund of good sense" in the country would not allow the ministry to "alter the constitution of the house of commons."[37] The conspicuous dullness of this letter may have served a strategic purpose; but it also suggests that the author was becoming tired of his persona and discouraged about the opposition's prospects. Some confirmation of these points is afforded by a private letter to Woodfall written on 21 July:

I really doubt whether I shall write any more under this Signature. I am weary of attacking a Set of Brutes, whose writings are too dull to furnish me even with the materials of Contention, & whose measures are too gross & direct to be the subject of Argument or require Illustration.[38]

These sentences indicate that the writer has been overpersuaded by his own eloquence; but it seems likely, nonetheless, that they reflect some aspects of his real state of mind.

The opposition's campaign was continued, during the summer of 1769, both in the newspapers and in separate publications: the latter ranged from the sobriety of *The Question stated: Whether the Freeholders of Middlesex lost their Right, by voting for Mr. Wilkes at the last Election* to the extravagance of *Harlequin Premier, a Farce as it is daily acted* and the vehemence of *The Fate of Tyrants, or the Road from the Palace to the Scaffold.*[39] Between 29 July and 4 September the creator of Junius made at least six contributions to this campaign, three of them as Junius and three as Philo Junius. In particular he engaged in a debate with Sir William Blackstone, contending (as Grenville had done in the Commons) that Blackstone's pro-ministerial arguments could be disproved on the evidence of his own *Commentaries*. The interplay of personae was managed here with some skill, the high manner being used to answer Blackstone's pamphlet and the low manner to record his discomfiture in the House; but Junius was unable, in this examination of legal precedents and distinctions, to generate that verbal energy which had characterised his attacks on Grafton. In a private letter to Woodfall, which may perhaps have been written on 9 August, he reverted to the problem of finding material appropriate to his role: "As to Junius, I must wait for fresh Matter, as this is a Character, which must be kept up with credit."[40] His next letter as Junius, the bawdy reply to Junia which appeared on 7 September, was by no means calculated to "keep up" its signatory's character; but it was equivocally disavowed four days later, in accordance with its author's instructions.[41]

Re-publication of the earlier letters in pamphlet form evoked a challenge from Draper, which Junius answered by justifying his anonymity:

> As to me, it is by no means necessary that I should be exposed to the resentment of the worst and the most powerful men in this country, though I may be indifferent about yours. Though *you* would fight, there are others who would assassinate.[42]

Neither opponents nor associates would allow him to remain silent, and so his desire to "wait for fresh Matter" was forcing him into a defensive posture. Junia had celebrated him, however, as "Calumniator-general to the opposition";[43] and he now sought to regain the initiative by tackling a new subject within the terms of that office. The Duke of Bedford was not a member of the administration, but he was the acknowledged head of its most powerful faction. Though old and almost blind, he had visited Devon in July to use his influence against the petition campaign; and in Exeter and Honiton he had been attacked by mobs, who "pelted him with stones, and set bulldogs at him."[44] On 19 September 1769 Junius launched an attack on Bedford in the high-vituperative manner of his earlier attacks on Grafton:

> You are so little accustomed to receive any marks of respect or esteem from the public, that if, in the following lines, a compliment or expression of applause should escape me, I fear you would consider it as a mockery of your established character, and perhaps an insult to your understanding. You have nice feelings, my Lord, if we may judge from your resentments. Cautious therefore of giving offence, where you have so little deserved it, I shall leave the illustration of your virtues to other hands.[45]

In ironically elevated prose, Junius contrasts what "the richest peer in England" might have been with what in reality he is; and he proceeds to a selective history of Bedford's career, in which the significant events include a horsewhipping at Lichfield races, the acceptance of French bribes over the Treaty of Paris, and insulting behaviour towards the King at a ministerial audience. The image created is that of a power-hungry and mercenary politican, so universally hated that in his old age he can find no secure place of retirement. The techniques of pseudo-panegyric and malicious innuendo are used no less ruthlessly than in the letters to Grafton; but although the manner is still authoritative, the false reasoning is never inventive enough to divert attention from the obvious cruelty. The savage injustice of this attack invoked a convincing reprimand from Draper; and when Junius in a thinly-argued reponse challenged Bedford's defenders to provide evidence of his generosity, the evidence proved embarrassingly real.

On 16 October Junius' much-vaunted elegance was questioned by Modestus, who despite his pseudonym may have been the author of *Fanny Hill*. Modestus claimed to have found many absurdities and linguistic errors in Junius' most recent letter; and on that basis he affirmed that it was the work of "the muddiest head from the muddiest bog in Ireland."[46] Francis, who had left Dublin at the age of ten, attached great importance to "polish"; and when he read Burke's *Reflections on the Revolution in France*, he offered to teach its author how to write English. It was beneath Junius' dignity, however, to engage in a merely literary discussion; and so Philo Junius came to the rescue, explaining that his principal was "always more usefully employed than in the trifling refinements of verbal criticism."[47] He was in fact employed between 21 September and 15 November in a new attack on the administration, whom he accused of condoning the actions of some Horse Guards officers who had rescued Major-General William Gansell from legal arrest. In bringing forward this "fresh Matter," he risked diverting attention from the "great cause" of the Middlesex election to what might be judged a trivial incident; but he sought to avert that danger by explicitly linking the two:

> When the constitution is openly invaded, when the first original right of the people, from which all laws derive their authority, is directly attacked, inferior grievances naturally lose their force, and are suffered to pass by without punishment or observation.... Yet surely it is not a less crime, nor less fatal in its consequences, to encourage a flagrant breach of the law by a military force, than to make use of the forms of parliament to destroy the constitution.[48]

The incident itself is related in the present tense, and with ostentatious brevity: "He attempts it. A bustle ensues. The bailiffs claim their prisoner."[49] The indignant questions defining the government's response are similarly concise: "Has it been censured? No. Has it been in any shape inquired into? No. ... What punishment has *he* suffered? Literally none."[50] After this shocked assertion of some carefully-chosen facts, the tone and sentence-structure gather confidence as Junius relates the episode to his image of a ministry which threatens both legal and political rights. In reply to this letter, Modestus argued with some justice that a minor event had been "wrought up into a charge against government";[51] but Junius retaliated by inventing a new persona with the disarming pseudonym Moderatus. In a quietly-worded letter to the *Public Advertiser*, Moderatus explains that he has been prompted to enquire into the Gansell affair by his opinion of Junius, "who, whatever may be his faults, is certainly not a weak man." Taking no account of Junius' "ornamented stile," he has undertaken a careful investigation of the facts, and has "found every circumstance stated by Junius to be literally true." Since the ministry appears on this occasion "to have taken a very improper advantage of the good-nature of the public," Moderatus judiciously concludes that the public is "obliged to *Junius* for the care he has taken to inquire into the facts, and for the just commentary with which he has given them to the world."[52]

This ingenious and well-sustained piece of role-playing shows the histrionic versatility with which the creator of Junius deployed his various personae. In his initial letter, however, Junius had affirmed that any defender of the ministry would find him "ready to maintain the truth of [his] narrative";[53] and his response when Modestus reminded him of that promise was so perfunctory that Modestus was able to proclaim himself victorious. In the collected edition Junius sought to reverse that verdict by attributing Moderatus' letter to Philo Junius, the "innocent fraud" whom he had "always intended" to acknowledge; but this device threw some doubt upon his claim that this "subordinate character" was "never guilty of the indecorum of praising his principal."[54]

Writing to Woodfall on 8 November, Junius professed himself reluctant to push the Horse Guards affair further because of his "fear of ruining that poor devil Gansel, & those other Blockheads."[55] In the same letter he acknowledged the receipt of some papers from A.B.C., whom editors have identified as Samuel Vaughan; and on 27 November Vaughan was prosecuted before Lord Mansfield for trying to purchase from Grafton the reversion of an office in Jamaica. The short letter to Grafton which Junius published on 19 November declared this prosecution to be a device for enhancing Grafton's reputation so that he could accept future bribes "with security." In support of this interpretation it accused the Prime Minister of selling a patent to Robert Hine in order to discharge the election expenses incurred by Colonel John Burgoyne as ministerial candidate for Preston. This accusation provided the basis for a series of angry rhetorical questions:

> Do you dare to prosecute such a creature as Vaughan, while you are basely setting up the Royal Patronage to auction? Do you dare to complain of an attack upon your own honour, while you are selling the favours of the crown, to raise a fund for corrupting the morals of the people? And, do you think it possible such enormities should escape without impeachment?[56]

This was scarcely the best way of defending Vaughan, who could quite reasonably claim that he was well-qualified for the post and had sought it by the customary route. Junius' principal object, however, was to discredit Grafton; and on 12 December, having had no response to his initial letter, he restated his charges at greater length, and suggested that Grafton's crimes would make a fitting subject for Mansfield's judicial eloquence. This letter did bring replies from ministerial writers, one of whom was later rewarded with the chair of Modern History at Cambridge; but Junius moved on to richer pastures, promising Woodfall "a capital & I hope a final Piece."[57]

Junius' hatred of George III, implicit from the first in his chosen pseudonym, had long been apparent in his bitter allusions to "our gracious sovereign"; but until now he had used Grafton as a stalking-horse, pretending to accept the constitutional convention which attributed all the King's public actions to the advice of his ministers. The main body of the long letter which he published on 19 December, however, was an address to the King; and the vehemence of that address not only horrified Walpole but also forced Burke to admit that it made his blood run cold.

The sensation it caused enabled the *Public Advertiser* to sell more copies than ever before; and it brought Junius' campaign to a climax just before the start of the parliamentary session. The introductory paragraph attributes the address to an "honest man" who has been permitted to advise his sovereign at a moment of crisis; and this device, besides admitting a sardonic comment on the improbability of such an event, permits Junius to develop a new manner and a new persona without relinquishing the authority of his established role. Respectfully but without flattery, Junius' spokesman laments the "pernicious lessons" the King received in his youth, recalls the "animated attachment" shown by the people at his accession, deplores the "ill-judged compliment" he paid to the Scots in declaring himself a Briton rather than an Englishman, and condemns the "precipitate spirit of concession" by which "England was sold to France" in the Treaty of Paris. Though he is willing to attribute these errors to "the prejudices and passions of others," he finds the "immediate cause" of the people's "present discontent" in the King's "personal resentment" against a man who has attacked his Favourite; and he argues that the illegal and unconstitutional methods by which Wilkes has been persecuted have so vitiated the Commons that the people's rights can be re-established only through a dissolution.

Digressing to consider what support the King might expect if he resisted "the united wishes of the whole people," the speaker recalls how Ireland has been "plundered and oppressed," and how the sympathies of the American colonists have been alienated by the King's "decisive" and "personal" hostility. Remembering how Charles I was betrayed by the "deliberate treachery of a Scotch parliament," he argues that it would be unrealistic to expect loyalty from the Scots; and he warns the King that the Guards are no more representative of the army's "marching regiments" than the "Praetorian Bands" in Rome were representative of the frontier legions. Having thus conjured up images of revolution from both modern and ancient history, he reverts to the constitutional issue and considers the various ways in which the King might attempt to meet his people's wishes. Since neither the Lords nor the judiciary can reverse the Commons' decision, he argues, the only possible appeal is to the people: "They alone are injured; and since there is no superior power, to which the cause can be referred, they alone ought to determine."[58] The behaviour of the Commons is represented as a threat not only to the electors but also to the Crown; and the King is called upon to act "an honourable part" by pardoning Wilkes, dissolving Parliament, and freeing himself from the ruinous influence of the Favourite. The dangers he will face if he ignores this advice are made explicit in a final reference to the fate of the Stuarts: "The Prince, who imitates their conduct, should be warned by their example: and while he plumes himself upon the security of his title to the crown, should remember that, as it was acquired by one revolution, it may be lost by another."[59]

The unnamed speaker of this address has a *vox populi* authority reminiscent of Skelton's Colin Clout, and enjoys some of the advantages of a

Wycherleyan plain dealer; but his value as a persona stems less from his
apparent honesty than from his un-Junian innocence, which encourages
us to form harsher judgments than those he expresses. The quasi-fictional
context of the address does not preclude specific reference to places and
people; but it legitimises a generalising rhetoric which allows Junius to
avoid both legal technicalities and the issues on which the opposition is
divided. Political leaders are scarcely mentioned, the advice of ministers
being judged collectively and the notion of an alternative government barely
contemplated. Even the Favourite is simply referred to in passing; and
Wilkes, the only other politician named, is discussed merely to show that
he is of no significance as an individual. The elimination of contemporary
detail enables Junius to envisage revolution not in Wilkite terms which might
alarm and antagonise his readers but rather through historical images
imbued with high-constitutional principle. Tacitean irony is used only at
the expense of the Scots, from whom Junius expected no support; and the
argument's regicidal undercurrents are subsumed in a Ciceronian expansive-
ness congruent with the speaker's professed respect for the addressee.
Though less entertaining than the attacks on Grafton, the letter is a skilful
exercise in the manipulation of audience repsonse; and in the attack on the
Scots, which has been judiciously analysed by David McCracken,[60] it
achieves an ironic density which invites comparison with Swift.

When Parliament re-convened on 9 January 1770, the opposition leaders
were eager to mount a concerted attack on a tottering administration. In
the Lords Chatham moved an amendment to the address, charging the
ministry with "depriving the electors of Middlesex of their free choice of
a representative"; and although the amendment was defeated, Lord
Camden declared from the woolsack that he had never approved of the
expulsion of Wilkes. A similar amendment was moved in the Commons
by Rockingham's friend William Dowdeswell; and although that too was
defeated it was supported by Granby, who said that he now regretted his
earlier vote on the issue. The crisis brought about by these ministerial
defections was aggravated on 10 January when Charles Yorke, having
accepted the Great Seal after an agony of divided loyalties, died in circumstances suggestive of suicide. This tragedy prompted Grafton, who had long
been at odds with his ministerial colleagues, to submit his resignation on
22 January; and although the King staved off the threatened dissolution
by sending for North, few observers expected the new Prime Minister to
survive for long. Junius responded to these events on 14 February with a
new letter to Grafton, which he declared he would have published sooner
but for the advice of men "more moderate" than himself. It is a lively
exercise in the old Junian manner, unscrupulously witty in its polemical
re-interpretation of the record; and its multiplicity of tone conveys moral
outrage at the death of Yorke, ironic pathos at the plight of Grafton's
deserted master, cynical amusement at the complaints of Grafton's
avaricious dependents, indignation at the contrasting fates of Vaughan and
Burgoyne, and irreversible contempt for Grafton himself. The final
paragraph introduces North, "the firm minister of to-day," whom Junius

represents as a mere front-man for "the domestics of the Duke of Bedford." Satirising the Bedfords' claim that constant resignations are increasing "the real strength of the ministry," Junius affirms that their faces tell a different story:

> When the members drop off, the main body cannot be insensible of its approaching dissolution. Even the violence of their proceedings is a signal of despair. Like broken tenants, who have had warning to quit the premises, they curse their landlord, destroy the fixtures, throw every thing into confusion, and care not what mischief they do to the estate.[61]

In reality, the new administration had by this time survived the most powerful attacks that the united opposition could muster. North was to remain in office for the next twelve years; and the letters of Junius, like the speeches of Chatham, were contributing not to an imminent political triumph but to a slow modification of public attitudes whose practical significance would not be clarified till the next century.

The address to the King and the resignation of Grafton were the climax and midpoint of Junius' career. Having achieved such fame and come so close to victory, he was reluctant to acknowledge defeat; and for the next two years he continued to investigate new opportunities, new strategies, and even new ideas. He invented personae named Domitian and Phalaris, who mounted a series of attacks on the North administration; and when Grafton rejoined the ministry as Lord Privy Seal, he fell upon his old victim with undiminished gusto. He took a keen interest in the politics of the City, engaging in public controversy with John Horne and private correspondence with Wilkes; and during the Falklands crisis he crossed bludgeons with Samuel Johnson. When the printers of his letters were prosecuted before Mansfield, he argued for the right of juries in libel trials to pronounce on matters of law as well as fact; and he gave his support to those who were accused of breaching privilege by publishing accounts of parliamentary debates. The campaign against Mansfield, with which he became increasingly obsessed, proved a complete fiasco; but he bestowed considerable skill on the authorised collection of his letters, composing an eloquent preface about the liberty of the press. Dedicating that volume "to the English Nation," he asserted his claim as a political theorist: "When Kings and Ministers are forgotten, when the force and direction of personal satyr is no longer understood, this book will, I believe, be found to contain principles, worthy to be transmitted to posterity."[62]

When Francis' friend Christopher D'Oyley was succeeded in the War Office by Anthony Chamier, a new persona named Veteran was created to ridicule Chamier and denounce his master Lord Barrington; and Woodfall was warned that Veteran must on no account be connected with Junius. As late as May 1772, Junius was complaining as Scotus about Barrington's discourtesy towards the Scots; but thereafter he seems to have given up his career as a writer for the newspapers. On 19 January 1773, responding to signals from Woodfall in the *Public Advertiser*, he explained his unwillingness to renew the struggle: "I meant the Cause & the public. both are given up. I feel for the honour of this Country, when I see that there are not ten men in it, who will unite & stand together upon any one question. But it is all alike, vile & contemptible."[63] With this convincing or at least plausible expression of disgust, Junius vanished "in celestial smoke"; and in October 1774 Francis arrived in India, where he was to quarrel magnificently with Hastings. According to W. E. H. Lecky, Francis' appointment to the Bengal Council was a reward for Junius' abandonment of polemical writing; but Lecky's account, like most discussions of this author, is itself something of a polemical exercise.[64]

DAVID W. LINDSAY

NOTES

1. *Correspondence of William Pitt, Earl of Chatham*, III (London: John Murray, 1839), 21.
2. *The Writings and Speeches of Edmund Burke*, II (Oxford: Clarendon Press, 1981), 450.
3. Quoted in John Brooke, *The Chatham Administration 1766–1768*, (London: Macmillan, 1956), p. 334.
4. *The Letters of Junius*, edited by John Cannon, (Oxford: Clarendon Press, 1978; cited hereafter as Cannon), pp. 443–4.
5. Cannon, p. 456.
6. Cannon, p. 25.
7. Cannon, p. 27.
8. Cannon, pp. 31–2.
9. Cannon, p. 32.
10. Cannon, p. 33.
11. Cannon, p. 38.
12. Cannon, p. 48.
13. Cannon, p. 51.
14. Cannon, p. 52.
15. Cannon, p. 53.
16. Cannon, p. 55.
17. Cannon, pp. 57–8.
18. Cannon, p. 59.
19. Cannon, p. 62.
20. Cannon, p. 63.
21. Cannon, p. 64.
22. Cannon, p. 66.
23. Cannon, p. 67.
24. Cannon, p. 349.
25. *Correspondence of William Pitt, Earl of Chatham*, III, 349.
26. Cannon, pp. 73–4.
27. Cannon, pp. 75–6.
28. Cannon, p. 78.
29. Cannon, p. 79.
30. Cannon, p. 77.
31. *Gentleman's Magazine*, 1769, 295.
32. Thomas Gray, "Ode on the Installation of the Duke of Grafton, Chancellor of the University," lines 5 and 70.
33. Horace Walpole, *Memoirs of the Reign of King George the Third*, III (London: Lawrence and Bullen, 1894), 248.
34. *The Letters of Horace Walpole*, V (Edinburgh: John Grant, 1906), 175 and 177.
35. Cannon, p. 82.
36. Cannon, pp. 87–8.
37. Cannon, p. 90.
38. Cannon, p. 351.
39. *Gentleman's Magazine*, 1769, 306–11, 355–6 and 404–6.
40. Cannon, p. 352. Cannon assigns this letter to 2 August, but a date after Junius' major letter of 8 August seems more likely.
41. Cannon, pp. 457 and 354.
42. Cannon, p. 129.
43. Cannon, p. 457.
44. Horace Walpole, *Memoirs*, III, 251–2.
45. Cannon, p. 116.
46. Cannon, p. 138.
47. Cannon, p. 139.
48. Cannon, p. 143.
49. Cannon, p. 144.
50. Cannon, p. 145.
51. Cannon, p. 148.
52. Cannon, pp. 148–51.
53. Cannon, p. 147.
54. Cannon, p. 13.
55. Cannon, pp. 356–7.
56. Cannon, p. 154.
57. Cannon, p. 359.
58. Cannon, p. 170.
59. Cannon, p. 173.
60. David McCracken, *Junius and Philip Francis*, (Boston: Twayne, 1979), 125–6.
61. Cannon, p. 182.
62. Cannon, p. 7.
63. Cannon, p. 393.
64. W. E. H. Lecky, *A History of England in the Eighteenth Century*, III (London: Longman, 1885), 233–55.